Road Trippin'

Riding and Rebuilding through Resilience

A MEMOIR

Remember,
You are Resilient!

REAL RESILIENCE
PRISON WIFE LIFE

CRYSTAL WYATT

Published by Real Resilience PWL

Cover Design By: Opeyemi Ikuborije
Interior Formatting By: HMDpublishing

Manufactured in the United States of America

ISBN #: 978-0-578-74600-5
Library of Congress Control Number: 2020913772

Follow Crystal Wyatt
Instagram: @realresilience_prisonwifelife
Website: www.realresiliencepwl.com

DEDICATION

To Philadelphia, you beautiful temperamental Scorpio. The intentionality in which you raise up your inhabitants is utterly remarkable. There is no other city-town in these United States that can host two worlds, the incarcerated and the non-incarcerated, as passionately as you.

You are the birthplace of America and Criminal Justice Reform.

You hold the space for me to be both captive and free.

This story is for you!

Philadelphia, Pennsylvania; Incorporated October 25, 1701

"The Black female is assaulted in her tender years by all those common forces of nature at the same time that she is caught in the tripartite crossfire of masculine prejudice, white illogical hate and Black lack of power.

The fact that the adult American Negro female emerges a formidable character is often met with amazement, distaste and even belligerence. It is seldom accepted as an inevitable outcome of the struggle won by survivors and deserves respect if not enthusiastic acceptance."

— *Maya Angelou, I Know Why the Caged Bird Sings (1969)*

TABLE OF CONTENTS

-Kelly Drive: The light at the End of the Tunnel-

PROLOGUE

D riving down the Pennsylvania turnpike, head pulsating from another pre-trip sleepless night. Eyes burning from 10 hours of continuous driving. Ears ringing from the wind seeping through the slightly cracked drivers' side window. I wanted to die. Or at least, I felt like I was going to die. Real death! Not that "oh come on with this trip already, I just want to get in my bed and rest," kind of death, but that "I think I'm about to have a stroke behind this wheel and die," kind of death!

Like many other anxiety-filled road trip days, as death felt like it was approaching, the 11 chatty ladies in my care, returning from the State Correctional Institution Somerset, were oblivious to the thoughts going through my mind. As I sang softly along to Natalie Cole's *Peaceful Living*, belting out the speakers of my 15-passenger seat Chevy Express, I knew they had no clue that I was physically, emotionally and mentally falling apart. Joking-ly, I engaged in their light conversation about how R&B singer Toni Braxton could ever be interested in Birdman, CEO of Cash Money Records, laughingly admitting to them that she and I go way back and it's like she stole my man because he was my secret crush.

But the reality of this trip was that I could care less about Toni and Birdman. I was trying desperately to stay alive long enough to get everyone safely back to our drop off spot in Phil-adelphia at Broad and Hunting Park. I needed to get home to my bed to thoughtfully plan my great escape from being an active prison transportation provider.

With more than 1000 women annually traveling on my van multiple times a month to visit an incarcerated loved one, I was worn out. I was suffering from compassion fatigue and desperately in need of healing. I also knew that I was not alone, as many of the women who traveled with me often expressed the need for some form of healing too. This prison life isn't for the weak or faint of heart and in that moment, on the turnpike, I was calling on all the warrior women who preceded me in life to guide me through this insanely uncomfortable trip and to transport me to that sweet spot of renewal.

I called on my mama, Ms. Yvonne, who never backed down from any obstacle to push me through the obstacles of making it down that highway. I called on the spirits of Grandma Mildred and Grandmom Marie, my mama's mama and my fathers' mother, who once relentlessly loved and were married to incarcerated men in the 1950's, just to keep me steadfast on my mission of returning my precious cargo safely back home to their families. I even called on Harriet.

It was because of Harriet Tubman and her dedication to the underground railroad that I was doing this work in a new modern way—with a van, a GPS system and some soul music--to assist those of us oppressed and afflicted by incarceration in our pursuit toward freedom. I was calling on these Spirit guides to give me a sign as to what to do next with my life, because driving to prisons across Pennsylvania, over 30 hours every weekend, through every season, simply was not it anymore. I was exhausted and in need of immediate relief!

At mile-marker 242, coming up to the York-Baltimore exit, I slightly mouthed the words under the sound of *Think of You*, by Ledisi, "ancestors, what am I supposed to do." Almost instantly, the spirit of those 4 divine beings whispered into my soul "if you need to heal, and you want other women to heal, then stop trippin' and tell your story, Crystal." I knew what story their spirits were referring to and as soon as my consciousness acknowledged it, my eyes started to water as I said to myself, "yes, elders, it's time to tell the Ride and Rebuild story!"

You see, in the conversation of criminal justice reform, "we" women supporters who "ride" for the incarcerated are often removed, forgotten, and almost never considered in the narrative. Rarely are grandmothers, mothers, daughters, sisters, nieces, girlfriends or wives asked, "what led up to the moment you found yourself facing this trauma of supporting an incarcerated loved one?" and more importantly "how did you make it through, emotionally, physically and financially?"

Road Trippin': Riding and Rebuilding through Resilience is my personal truth to honor all the women who has ever loved within the narrative of incarceration. If you've paid bail, found a lawyer, went to court, lost your breath at sentencing, visited a prison, paid for commissary, waited on parole, agreed to a home plan and barely survived the bid, your resilience is unparalleled and you know the truth. Prison life is hard and for many of us, incarceration is a public health crisis rooted in trauma. We know that without a safe space to share our experiences and pain, healing at the personal, familial, and even community level will never occur.

Admittedly, I am sick of prison life. I am sick of the pain caused by crime. I am sick of the pain caused by punishment. I am sick of families being destroyed by excessive sentencing. I am sick of over-criminalization and I am sick of women bearing the burden of incarceration by affiliation. I am sick, sick, sick and as these words leave my mind, extend through my fingers, tapping on to these computer keys, I know that this book is the safe space I've chosen to create for my healing to begin.

Let's Go!

PART I

TRIPPIN' THROUGH CHANGE

-Uncle Vernon and Lil Crystal on 56th Street-

56th Street

I was 13 the first time the Pennsylvania criminal justice system personally tapped me on my shoulder. I remember it clearly. I was living what I considered to be the absolute good life and didn't have a care in the world, other than dealing with my new period, pimples, eczema and being bald-headed. You know, regular Black girl teenage stuff. Meanwhile, a great hustle man, my Uncle Vernon, had rightfully claimed his position as the patriarch of our family by providing luxuries to his sister, my mother Ms. Yvonne, and her two daughters. My uncle was a white-collar criminal and did pretty well for himself and anyone he employed or considered family, which were many.

With his financial support, he had moved my mother, sister and I from Southwest Philly to Delran New Jersey, and from the 3rd to 8th grade I learned how to swim, climb trees, play tennis, shoot pool and skim rocks across creek water. My new school, with architecture unlike the gothic buildings of the Philadelphia public school system, was one level and had sprawling green grass everywhere.

In that magical place, I learned to paint in art classes on easels, with oils and watercolors. I learned to play music with real instruments, thread a sewing machine, make wood projects and type like a highly skilled secretary, all before the seventh grade. I was also a regular on the intramural floor hockey team, and because of my small frame, could do round-offs and cartwheels in any open or tight space. I even learned how to ski.

For five years we lived this great life in Delran. I did well in school and at one point had a white best friend whose family was very nice to me. I was very much aware of race in New Jersey, especially since I had been the only Black person in my 3rd grade classroom, and then only one of two all throughout the rest of elementary and junior high school. There were Black kids who lived in our apartment complex, but those were also the only Black kids there seemed to be in all of Delran. If they weren't in your age group, then there was a high probability that you'd be in a classroom alone.

So, I had no issues making white friends. It only became an issue, when my mother was in one of her moods and the sound of my voice and behavior got on her nerves and she'd tersely tell me, I was "acting too fucking white". It was at those times, I was grateful for having my uncle as the first Black settler of Delran, who made provisions for many of our Philly friends and family to move there. I was able to go to school and hang with several of my Philly cousins and access some of their urban grit to keep me balanced during those times when my blackness became too watered down.

But then everything changed. At 13, my uncle got indicted on federal charges, which meant my mother no longer had access to the extra income his lifestyle afforded us and we lost everything. After living in a home with sliding glass doors, a fully equipped kitchen with a garbage disposal, and bathroom with a shower attached to the tub where everything worked, we were evicted and had to migrate to North Philly to 9th and Lehigh.

In the home on 9th Street we were welcomed by leaky ceilings, tattered linoleum floors, flying cockroaches and rooms with water stained and chipped old wallpaper. If that wasn't bad enough, our new toilet was so old it needed the bowl to be filled with sink water just for the piss and shit to go down. There was no shower and because of the rust around the drain, we could not sit in or use the tub to properly bathe ourselves. The entire house smelled of damp wood and felt sad. I was mortified and sick that the grownups had let this happen. I had come from swimming pools, recreational centers on the premises, pool tables at my disposal, tennis courts free at all times, to community centers with broken playground equipment.

Life was so unsettling during that time and to make matters worse, we moved during the school year. My mother, who was hell bent on making sure I graduated Junior High School from Delran, made me take the bus from North Philly to Center City to catch another bus to New Jersey for the remainder of the school year. Imagine a 13-year-old crossing state lines every day just for an education. Now imagine her being afraid and fearless all at the same time, simply because she didn't know what else to be. After all, the grownups were in charge, so I did as I was told until I graduated.

Since the house on 9th Street was not a style I was accustomed to, I tried to block out the blight by focusing on the people in the neighborhood. I realized there were many Puerto Ricans who lived there. They were friendly, but some were racist. I quickly learned that racism existed between people of color when I had a crush on a boy named Pedro. I met him on Lehigh Avenue the night the Sixers won the 1983 Championship.

Unaware of Philadelphia politics at the time, I didn't realize it was such a big deal that the then Mayor, Frank Rizzo, had told the cops to ease up on the natives as we celebrated in the streets. I considered myself a native, since just over the Betsy Ross Bridge my family and I had spent many nights in New Jersey cheering for our real "home" team. As a transplant Sixers fan, I rightfully deserved to celebrate. I was not disappointed.

The night was enchanting. A DJ had set up his equipment and as we danced the night away, Pedro introduced himself to me and became my dance partner. He was so very handsome with his blue eyes and blond short coarse hair and for the next several days after the Championship, he would meet me on Germantown Avenue to talk. We even went to see a movie together at *The Avenue* once, where I let him rub my leg through the entire picture show.

The only problem with Pedro was that when I asked if I could come visit him on his block, he told me no because his dad hated niggers. Pedro and I stopped meeting on Germantown Avenue after that. Although I was 13, I had just read *The Color Purple* and knew exactly what oppression looked like and I didn't need Pedro's father's unwarranted disdain for my race to wear me down in love.

Besides, I was dealing with other issues in North Philly, especially since every new person I met, told me I "talked white, and thought I knew everything." I couldn't help that I enunciated all of my words or asked questions other students didn't think of fast enough. I had learned in Delran that with all those white kids in my class, if I wanted to be heard I had to think fast, act quick, and ask good questions.

But at Stetson Junior High at B and Allegheny, I learned from teachers and students that "talking white" and asking uneasily answerable questions was prohibited. So, I simply did my best to stop talking and observe more. I observed that the classrooms were dark and uninviting, the lunchroom was in a basement, the teachers were rude, and the students loved to fight. I hated every day that I had to go into that building and I hated every afternoon when I had to return to that house on 9th Street.

The only light in that awful predicament was that my Uncle Vernon, who was heavily in the midst of fighting his federal case, would come to our new raggedy home with his 10-speed bike loaded in the back of his conversion van. He'd take my sister, I and any other kid who was allowed, bike riding through North Philly. It was always late in the evening and because he was well respected and my mother adored him, no one questioned that Black man riding through the neighborhood with young children in tow. He did his best to bring normalcy to our world and because of that, he's still one of my favorite people.

Fortunately for my uncle, he was given leniency on his case and was only sentenced to house arrest for his crimes. I remember sitting in that Federal Court Room on 6th and Market listening intently as the judge gave my uncle his sentence. The wave of relief that swept over my mothers' face was one to remember.

My uncle, however, was confused at the sentencing and as we stood in the lobby outside the courtroom, I explained that he would not be going away but instead be confined to the home on house arrest. "I'm glad you were paying attention," is what he said to me, and in that moment, I made a note to always pay attention. It seemed to be a highly respected gift that I would need to harness.

Each day we spent on 9th Street, I thought about New Jersey in its fullness. Although Delran was the bright spot in my childhood, it was also tainted with the exodus of my father to California, the exposure to my mothers' bi-sexual sometimes and full-lesbian most times lifestyle, as well as her sweet affection toward drugs and alcohol. My uncle was a constant in my life, but not having my actual father around created a void that often-times was hard to fill. Even though he would visit at least once a year, I missed his presence in my day-to-day life. I knew if he had been around, the hardship of dealing with my mothers' turbulent lesbian lifestyle would have eased a bit. You see, having a gay mother in that era was frowned upon and it seemed everyone was interested in what the "gay lady" had going on in her house and depending on the day, could be a lot.

For every good moment there was a bad one in Delran. It was in those early years that I learned how to love despite the pain that was being afflicted upon me, because there was never any doubt how much I loved my family even as a little girl. I'm sure my uncle and mother were doing the very best to take care of their family, but having a family member arrested, losing stable housing, being exposed to alcohol, drugs and sometimes household violence, the seed of what I would later learn as adverse childhood experiences, had been sown into the fiber of my neuro-system, and the impact would be great.

Luckily for me, we only spent one year in the house on 9th Street. My uncle moved us back to Southwest Philly to his duplex on 56th and Chester Avenue, and I again had to commute for over an hour to a school I needed to graduate from. Unlike Delran, Philadelphia's junior high schools ended in the 9th grade, so I commuted from Southwest Philly to North Philly every day for a redundant cap and gown ceremony.

I won't lie. I loved 56th Street. It didn't have half the amenities as Delran, but it reduced my uncle's frustration of not being able to fix what he helped break by having our lives uprooted with his federal criminal case. He was a provider by nature, and having us in a home he owned was his way of saying, "thanks for riding the storm with me." I also loved that 56th Street was in the neighborhood we had moved from, so everything was familiar—the people, the stores, and even the political unrest.

56th Street was much different from our old block, Cecil Street, that we lived on before migrating to Delran. For one it was a two-way street, and it was very wide. You could see the trolley stop from our house two doors from the corner, and I loved that I could spot my mom exiting everyday coming home from work. I also loved our neighbors.

Everyone was friendly and four doors down from our house was one of the homes of the Black liberation group MOVE. They had been under federal scrutiny since the alleged 1978 murder of a Philadelphia police officer. Although they were deemed a threat to society by law enforcement and political leaders, the "members" happened to be thoughtful neighbors, sharing herbs and holistic healing remedies with us "regular" neighbors. Because I had such small feet, my mother would encourage me to send my lightly worn shoes down to their house for the children, in exchange for their gifts of wisdom.

Aside from MOVE Members cursing out the police on a bullhorn every summer Saturday morning after block clean up, and having federal agents posted on the corner of our block with their watchful eye on the MOVE house inhabitants, 56th Street was an easy block to live on. It was interesting being back in the old neighborhood. Although I was only 8 when we left, having attended Kindergarten through 2nd grade at Mitchell Elementary, the neighborhood felt like home.

I loved walking the streets of Southwest Philly. The houses were nice and some of them even had a father in them. I had old friends, made new friends, and was close to completing my first year of high school at Edward Bok Area Vocational Technical high when my MOVE neighbors, including the children, went to exercise their right to freedom on the small block of Osage Avenue in West Philly.

Unlike the large two-way easy flowing traffic of 56th Street, Osage Avenue was a small one-way street and the neighbors abhorred their MOVE neighbors and rallied the city to have them removed off their block. The outcome was tragic and many of my MOVE neighbors who went to rally with their comrades, did not return from the unrest, including the children. They had either died in the city-incited fire or were arrested for the mayhem.

Life on 56th Street was never the same after the MOVE bombing on May 13, 1985, and as soon as we were starting to get our bearings as a city and a community, two short years later crack cocaine came and slowly stole the soul of my neighborhood. My mother, who learned how to free-base cocaine in Delran, found her way toward this highly addictive drug and picked up a bad crack habit. It was an extremely difficult and fascinating experience for me.

While my neighborhood was under siege with the influx of violence and organized crime, my home would have the lingering stench of cooked cocaine in the air, lesbian brawls, and more often than not, furniture and household items being sold in the middle of the night. I could not believe how fast this drug took over the lives of everyone I knew. There was no escaping the epidemic, so I acquiesced. I hung out with drug dealers, learned to bag up cocaine, and developed a love affair with marijuana to cope with the crisis.

In her addiction, my mother, a textile factory worker, made sure she went to work every day, even though she cursed everybody out at the job and could not keep her focus. She also made sure I went to school every day, even though I could not keep my focus and barely passed. Living in a home with that level of addiction coupled with the violence of her lesbian love affair was unbearable. My mother would often make promises that she would quit getting high, and two days later, I'd find her fighting hard to keep her mouth from twitching as she explained to me that "she'd only had a little bit." I loved her so much that each time she told me that lie, I believed her.

I hated seeing my mother in that condition. Up until that point, Ms. Yvonne could do no wrong in my eyes. She was my personal savior—having handled me with care the day she explained her sexuality to me, telling me that it didn't matter who she loved, she would never love anyone more than me and my sister. She was also the funniest woman I knew—being able to entertain an entire room simply by being in it and man was she ever the coolest mom of all my friends—taking us to rap concerts when no other parent wanted to be bothered with that "rap nonsense". She was also my protector—rumbling in the street alongside my sister and I on quite a few occasions.

But watching her weight wither away and the skin around her cheekbones sink into her face, and the black eyes she'd sometimes get from scoring crack in the wrong neighborhood from the wrong drug dealer on the wrong day, made me dig into the reservoir of my own self-will and somehow manage to finish high school and land a job at a local card shop. Not only did I make money, I also increased my vocabulary by stocking cards and spending days reading them. I thanked the heavens for that job daily because there was no college for me and it gave me the ability to keep learning, even if it wasn't in a traditional classroom. Besides, I didn't care about attending college; I was too busy trying to survive the crack epidemic and keep my mother alive.

One day my mother, heavy in her addiction, was telling me for the 1000th time that she was going to stop getting high after one more hit, but was sick, needed it, and didn't have any money. I had just come from a friends' house who was a drug dealer. He was bagging up cooked coke and I was helping. I asked him for a couple bags to see if I could sell it and he obliged.

As I sat and listened to my mother, who was in the throes of withdrawal promise the impossible, I thought about those couple of bags in my purse. Normally, if she asked for money, I would just give it to her knowing full well what she was using it for. But this time, I told her about the bags of crack in my purse. She begged me for them. As I mentioned, there was no escaping the epidemic, so again, I acquiesced and gave her the drugs. I felt immense guilt and because I'm a firm believer in Karma. It took my mother two more years to beat that addiction, and in those two years my life fell completely apart.

Haroon, Sweet, and Me

Although life was a shit-show in my home, I had a lot of respect from the young men in my neighborhood. With crack seeping its sickness into the core of who we were, many young women in the neighborhood had to figure out ways to survive as one by one, parents were becoming addicted and shirking their parental responsibilities. These young women had to entertain men they would have never given the time of day to. But me, I didn't have to fuck for money because I had that cool job at the card shop that offered me the finer things in life, in more ways than one. So, I had the luxury of picking and choosing who I dealt with. I can't say I chose wisely, but the options were always there.

One of those choices was a young brother named Haroon. I met him when he was 13 and I was 15 years old, when all we cared about was getting wet in the water plug at midnight and freaking on somebody afterwards in the remaining moonlight hours. When I think about it, I've loved him way before the thought of actually fucking ever entered my mind.

In my eyes, Haroon was a divine sight to behold. He was dipped in dark chocolate, built like a young boxer, had the brightest smile and the best lips in the city. He was fine. He was also a pool shark, slick talker, spoiled by his parents and so "fly" because of it. He went to private school, knew the subway system like a pro commuter, and how to drive unlicensed through all the streets of Philadelphia. His home was by far the best in the neighborhood. He had a den in his house, which was the smallest of the 3 bedrooms, a deck with sliding glass doors and a surveillance camera focused on the front porch, all in a row home in Southwest Philly. Up until that point, he was the sweetest thing I had ever known, and it was nice knowing that he had a crush on me.

Haroon lived off 55th street, around the corner from me and he rarely came on 56th Street. But, when I visited 55th Street, which was the hub of our neighborhood, he'd be around, and I'd notice how cute and funny he was. Then one day I happened to be in the neighborhood pizza shop on Chester Avenue when he was getting off the trolley coming from school, and noticed him looking all scholarly in his uniform. Something in my pelvis stirred and it was at that point I made the decision to make it a habit of being at the right place at the right time, just to get a glimpse of him.

After that, I'd be posted up in Chester Pizza timing his descent from the 13 Trolley perfectly. He wasn't hard to spot since he was the only kid in the whole neighborhood that wore a uniform to school. I'd see his dimpled smile from my angle at the pizza store and my entire heart would melt. Although I would never admit that I was in that pizza shop waiting for him, when we'd make eye contact across that busy Avenue and he'd smile, that was good enough for me.

We'd be cordial and sweet to one another, ending up in the pool hall, Big Dollar, shooting a couple of our respective games. Although I dabbled with a pool table while living in Delran, I perfected my game during my summers visiting my father in California. My dad's close friend owned a regulated table and all the kids would challenge each other to games. But in the Big Dollar, Haroon and I never played with each other, but would be at our tables keeping a watchful eye on the other. He was in the sport for the gamble of it, I was in it for the fun of it, and I was good. It was in that pool hall that I would tell myself, one day he's going to tell me he loves me.

I know it wasn't right, but I wanted to claim that young boy. So, when he finally got the nerve to say a few words expressing that he liked me, I entertained the crush. I would go to his crib from time to time, watch movies with him, and let him rub his hand up and down my thigh when our heat became too much. Since we were both virgins, the soft touches were good enough for me.

In private, he would tell me that our song was *"Wait for Love"*, by Luther Vandross. In public I'd sometimes ignore him, or if the mood was right, would let him know, in front of his homies, that he was my sweet baby. I wasn't the easiest person to crush on. You see, although I wanted him, I wasn't sure what I'd do with him once he was mine. I knew my indecisiveness drove him crazy at times, but he was my crush and that's the burden of crushing; it's unpredictable.

From the start he knew I was unsure about my love for him, so he was cautious. He didn't want to seem like a young boy being strung along and played by his "old head". He wanted us to be equals, so he would, at times, engage me from a distance. He would never admit how he truly felt about me, and as he grew older acted as if other girls could steal him from me and for the sake of becoming a man, treated me like shit sometimes. As a young girl on my way to womanhood, I loved him and didn't know any better, so I treated him the same petty ass way.

Thursday, Saturday, and Sunday the whole neighborhood would all go to Elmwood Skating Rink to hang out and show off whatever fashion was in at the time. Not only was Haroon a pool shark, he was also a remarkable skater. He would tackle that rink like he was in a roller disco. I could skate, but my skills paled in comparison to his. It didn't bother me though, because I really didn't want to sweat out all my curls and end up looking like shit at the end of the night, because everyone knew the "let-out" was where all the deals and dates were made.

It never failed. Haroon would end up in some girls face and I'd end up in some dudes' face, both of us quietly observing one another exchanging words with someone other than each other—ruining any chance of hooking up afterward. We are both Scorpios and our jealous streak sometimes prohibited us from being rational with the other. So instead of walking away from the pointless girl or guy, we'd out stand one another and would even watch each other leave with the insignificant person. We were absolutely sickening.

This back and forth game went on between us for a while. I guess we just didn't really know how to be together. One minute we'd be sitting back watching flicks, the next we'd be arguing in the street, showing everyone in the hood that our bond could be tampered with. It was a downright pain in the ass to be in love with Haroon, but I kept trying anyway.

He did, however, have a best friend that distracted me from the aggravation of loving him. His name was Sweet, and he was the exact opposite of Haroon. He was light skinned, slim built and was a church boy. Despite their perceived differences, they were both handsome young men and they were inseparable. Unfortunately, Sweet and I did not get along. He hated when I would come around and would even go so far as to say so. The more he hated that I was around, the more I fell in love with both of them. Yes, I knew it was wicked. But when they say birds of a feather flock together, they never mention that because of this fact, it would be just as easy to fall in love with all the birds instead of just one. So, without much reservation, I did just that.

Sweet knew I loved him just as much as I loved Haroon. Not more, but just as much. Deep in my spirit, it was uncomfortable knowing that I was attracted to both of them, but there was absolutely nothing I could do about it. The heart wants what it wants, and I also think Sweet felt something for me too. I would catch him watching me when he thought I wasn't looking, and his eyes always told the truth. That he had a thing for me too! They also told me that he didn't know why he felt it, but it wasn't right, and he would do anything in his power to deny it. And he did just that!

I was what you would consider "hood fly." I mean I had my awkward moments in high school rebounding from my uncle's indictment and my mothers' newfound crack addiction. But with my card shop job, I managed. Instead of having 30 pairs of Sergio Valente jeans to last me through the month, I had 7 to get me through the week. I was able to purchase those chunky ass British Knights shoes and was the first girl in the hood to rock Air Jordans, Stan Smiths, and Izod. I was petite, bow legged, had a fat booty, and enough chicks in the neighborhood resented me because of my "stank" walk, courtesy of Ms. Yvonne—because apparently, I was told we walked alike. I also was not a punk, which was especially important. Long gone was the "white talking" girl who moved back from Delran. I had a slick mouth, quick hands, and my own money in my pocket. Therefore, I managed my hood fly status perfectly.

But one day, Sweet decided to test my status. I wish I could un-remember this experience, but I can't. I was chilling on his block with a mutual friend who lived about 5 doors down from Sweet. It was nothing for everyone to chill on his friend's porch into the wee hours of the morning looking at the stars and talking about life. Needing that kind of energy, I was posted up on his friends' porch, but hoping to catch a glimpse of Sweet in the process.

Apparently, this was not a good day for Sweet. He was on some other shit and he was hell bent on taking it out on me. Now as I mentioned, I was "hood fly," so every day I walked out my unstable home, I looked as if I'd just stepped off the set of a photo shoot for the latest urban streetwear.

On this particular day, I was wearing an all-white Adidas polo shirt with green trim around the sleeve and collar, white Adidas shorts with three green stripes down the side, and a pair of white and green Stan Smith Adidas. I was chillin' so hard on that porch in my all white get-up that I forgot how bad the wrath of Sweet could be toward me. Normally, it was all mean words. But on this day, he leveled up.

As the small group of us were talking and joking on the porch, Sweet came out of his house drinking a glass of Cherry KoolAid. He spotted me on his friend's porch, came down the block and asked me what I was doing on "his" block. I thought he was playing so I said, "get the fuck out my face, this ain't your block." I must mention that before, during and after my "talking white" days I have had a filthy mouth since the age of two when I learned to formulate sentences. The curse words were a gift from my mother, who was fluent in the second language of "fuck this and fuck that."

Well apparently, Sweet was not in the mood for my filthy mouth or my presence on "his block." So, he gave me until the count of 20 to get off his block or he would pour his Cherry Kool-Aid on my all white ensemble. I knew he had to either be delirious or seriously joking, because no one had ever threatened me or an outfit I was wearing.

As I started to question his sanity level, he started counting, "20, 19, 18, (skipping numbers) 15 oh you're still sitting?" Sweet said. "Stop fucking playing," I said as he walked closer to me holding the cup at an angle. "14, 13, (still skipping) 9, oh I see you want to go home and change your clothes, hunh?" he replied. In complete exasperation I exclaimed, "Motherfucker, you are bugging, you better not pour that fucking KoolAid on me!"

This handsome jackass is standing over me as he continues his count, "8, 7, 6, 5 get the Fuck of my block," he yelled in my face. I said, "Muthafucka keep counting because if a drop of that KoolAid touches me, I'ma fuck you up!" Methodically, he said "1", and dripped cherry Kool-aid down the front of my shirt.

Needless to say, I left the block. But not without a string of curse words and a bunch of "Crystal watch your mouth my mother is in the house" from his friend. Sweet just laughed and ran up the street. Of course, I didn't go on the block for a while. Not because of Sweet, but because his friend should have put him off his porch when he first started threatening to throw that Kool-Aid on me. I learned a valuable lesson that day, birds of a feather not only flock together, but they also let one another run amuck as well.

Although Sweet disrespected me that day, it still did not diminish my love for him. Call it dysfunction, but I simply could not let go of the idea of loving him. So, I would periodically and anonymously send him carefully selected "thinking of you" cards from my job, with the hope of one day being able to share my feelings for him. Again, wicked I know. But, while I was lusting after Sweet. Haroon was slowly becoming an adult and a lady's man. He had a motorcycle accident at 15, damn near killing himself and then a baby at 16, damn near killing me. I could not fathom that my Haroon was about to be a father. He was having a baby with a girl who was even older than me. I was devastated. It felt like we were just grinding in his den and now I find out this guy is literally fucking. In my mind, he was supposed to lose his virginity to me and nobody else.

When Haroon got that woman pregnant, I knew I needed a drastic change, so I left the Southwest dudes alone. I was done. Not to mention, I'd had my fair share of them anyway. It was relatively easy to engage them on some late-night shit. But when the old heads organized by three letters decided to gather up all the young boys and put them to work in the crack game, it threw a wrench in my late-night shenanigans, because guys from different blocks started working and hanging together. So, I had to take my attention and affection elsewhere and out the hood. I guess it's safe to say that Haroon's new baby saved me from being called the neighborhood whore.

It wasn't hard to find some new dude in a new neighborhood to "fall in love" with. The early "coke" game had everyone coming out of their hoods, flashing their jewels, wears and rides, and flocking to the hang out that was jumping the most, no matter which hood it was in. I was meeting dudes downtown at the After Midnight, still at Elmwood Skating Rink in Southwest Philly, IHOP on Walnut Street in Center City, High Rollers on Market in West Philly, Seltzers on Locust Street downtown and even Carmen's Skating Rink in North Philly. Me and my girlfriends were everywhere, and it was really good to not be running through Southwest for a while.

Here I was 19, fresh outta high school, had a good retail sales job, clothes were tight and I was living carefree, well except for my mothers' crack addiction. That was still a headache. I would come home from a night of partying after working at the card shop all day to find my mother still out roaming the neighborhood with her lesbian lover trying to score crack.

I tried to deny that she was a full-fledged addict because she went to work every day, still dressed relatively nice, and never lost her sense of humor. I tried that until she started selling our bedroom furniture and dropped almost 50lbs in a matter of months. Even with all of that, I still had hoped my mother would beat her addiction, but knew I had to get away from it.

We had since moved from my uncles' duplex into a bungalow off Elmwood Avenue across from the Bartram Village housing projects with one of her lovers. But with her habit and their domestic violence following us there, I fled her house on

Elmwood Avenue and moved into my Uncle Vernon's duplex back on 56. Street, but in his efficiency apartment on the 2. floor. She soon followed me with promises of getting herself together. So, I overcompensated, took risks, and became the mother for a while.

The card shop that I had been working for decided to open a sneaker shop in the Concourse where the subway trains departed to the west, north, and south of Philadelphia and out toward the suburbs. I was a star employee at the card shop, so they asked me and my manager to run the sneaker shop. Since I was no stranger to the illegal side of life, I would dip in the merchandise and the cash register from time to time, just to keep our house afloat.

At 19 I was finding myself becoming tired with life having so many adult responsibilities. The neighborhood was getting increasingly worse, with homicide rates rising faster than temperatures in a heat wave, and so many young men getting arrested and receiving lengthy prison sentences. Girls were becoming unwed mothers, more parents were becoming addicted, and we the youth were living out our very own William Golding's version of *Lord of the Flies*, trying to find our footing on a foundation of quicksand.

Unfortunately, I was only able to navigate my home, neighborhood, and mother's crack crisis for about 6 months before I became so overwhelmed that I had to jump ship. I decided to move in with my father in San Jose, California. He had repeatedly told me that if I ever wanted to live with him, his door was open. But since I felt like he had abandoned me, I resented him for it and never wanted to take him up on the offer. But with this crisis, I needed to leave. Everyone knew I was leaving, but not why. I told everyone I just needed to get out of the city and wanted to go study real estate and sell houses in California. That tale was truer than not, I really wanted to be a realtor.

For the first time in my life, Sweet was nice to me. After the Kool-Aid incident it took us a while to become cordial again, but since 55th street was our anchor it was hard to hold grudges amongst us. So we would sometimes find ourselves in spaces where we had to speak to one another. When he learned that I was moving to California, he told me he was glad that I was leaving because there wasn't shit for me here in Philadelphia. With his blessing, I kissed my crackhead mother goodbye and set off to become rich in the Land of Sunshine.

In case you are wondering about Haroon, I'll tell you. I wasn't speaking to Haroon because of that pregnancy. He was the other reason I was leaving. I hated that he had a baby and it wasn't mine. I hated that he had sex with somebody, and it wasn't me. I hated that he had gotten that close to somebody else, and I had vowed to never speak to his ass again.

Little Crystal

When I got to California, I was happy as a lark for the first 7 days. On day eight, my dad started preaching to me—he was a devout Jehovah's Witness. Day nine, he was pushing his JW agenda on me heavily. On Day 10 he was ridiculing all things Philadelphia. Including saying that I was addicted to the "street life" of the city and would even sing the Randy Crawford song loudly in my face—he could be pretty petty at times, even for an adult devout Jehovah's Witness.

Finally, on Day 11 he started bashing my mother for being a crack addict. By Day 20 I was preparing for my return home. It wasn't the preaching, the Witness faith, or his disgust for Philadelphia, it was him bashing my mother for not being able to beat her addiction that made me pack my shit. Her state of being kept eating at me. So much so that I would sit for hours thinking to myself, how could I just leave her like that? She'd done so much for me, she's my friend, I love her, and I needed to go save her life. So, I went back. Quietly.

I didn't want anyone to make a fuss about my return. Especially since I hadn't accomplished the goal of becoming a real estate guru. But my girlfriends, Pocah—who I'd met at Stetson Junior High, Mecca, Kaiah and Leslie—who became my close friends from the neighborhood, were happy about me coming home. Mostly everyone was excited to see me and said I could do that real estate shit in Philly, if I wanted to, anyway. I agreed and was comforted by the outpouring of love. That was until I ran into Sweet.

I was standing in front of Mecca's house on Warrington Avenue when he drove down her block. He had our good friend Corey in the car with him. He pulled over and Corey got out and walked over to give me a hug. I expected nothing less from Corey. After all, he was a BOK Alumni and we were the first in the hood to rock monogrammed Sixers jackets. So, we were tight. But Sweet, I wasn't so sure what his reaction would be at seeing me back in the hood. I didn't have to wait long to figure it out. He never looked at me. He kept his eyes focused on the passing traffic ahead.

I let it slide, but a few nights later I made it my business to walk down "his block" in hopes of catching a glimpse of him. It was about 9pm in the evening and I was listening to my Walkman. Luther Vandross, *"Anyone who Had a Heart"* was playing. Ironically, as I approached his house, he was walking out his front door. By the time I made it in front of his house he was standing on the bottom step. I wasn't sure if he was going to say anything, so I turned my music down low enough to hear if he decided and to my surprise, he said "Hey."

I slid my headphones back and said, "What's up?" He said real solemnly, "Why'd you come back?" I wanted to tell him the truth, that my mother was strung out on crack, I had some unresolved issues with Haroon, and my unexplainable feelings for him brought me back. But instead, I looked into his handsome face and simply said, "Because I had too." He then asked, "What was it like?" and we both sat down on his steps and talked about

California for hours. Throughout the conversation, he kept interjecting by saying, "you should have stayed" and I would simply reply, "it wasn't an option." Ironically, I never told him that it was me who sent him those greeting cards. After that night, Sweet and I developed a respectful friendship, even hanging out on "his block" from time to time.

One year later at the end of the summer, when the only thing on my mind was figuring out which color high-top Reeboks to wear for the day, the world decided to flip itself upside down. Four young men from our neighborhood were gunned down leaving a movie theater in University City. Two of them were Haroon and Sweet.

My girlfriend Kaiah and I were finishing up a visit in the "bottom" of West Philly and were headed to the elevated train station at 40th and Market when we heard the gunshots. For a split second we paused, but weren't phased; we always heard gunshots in our neighborhood that were either superseded or preceded by the phrase "get down or lay down." But we weren't close enough to hear any words. After the shots subsided, we heard the police sirens and knew that the shots had come from further down 40th Street, closer to Walnut. In a matter of seconds, I made the worst decision of my life. I asked her if we should go down and see what happened. She said yes, and we walked toward the scene.

As we approached the McDonalds, we could see a crowd forming around two guys sitting upright in the middle of the street and firefighters working to revive a third young man on the sidewalk. He had been shot in the neck. I recognized him from our neighborhood. As we rounded the car to see the two guys in the street, my heart dropped. One of them was Haroon, the other his cousin. Visibly shot, he looked at me and said, "Crystal go down the way and tell them we got hit." Kaiah and I immediately ran to the corner and saw a friend passing by. We flagged him down and told him to take us to 55th Street because Haroon had been shot. He didn't ask any questions, just told us to get in and sped off.

When we reached 55th Street, it appeared that the news had already reached the block because as I approached Sweet's block, the mother of the young man who was being revived in front of McDonalds was screaming on her porch about her son. Almost instantaneously I heard Sweet's mother say, "what about Sweet?" My heart dropped. I hadn't seen Sweet out there. I later learned that he was with Haroon, had also been shot, but managed to run across the street toward the Burger King where he collapsed and was taken to the hospital. I was devastated, yet hopeful. At least he had made it to the hospital.

For hours we waited and waited for the outcome of both Sweet and Haroon, who were in surgery for their wounds. As time ticked by, the neighborhood became restless with everyone pointing fingers at everyone else, trying to figure out how "two good boys—Sweet and his neighbor" who were headed to college the following week, could get shot. By 3am we learned that his neighbor had died at the scene, and that my beautiful Sweet had died at the hospital.

It was the first time I had ever experienced the absolute, soul crushing, breath-taking, heartbreaking, mind blowing, pain of death. I simply could not fathom the idea that Sweet's spirit would no longer reside in a body that I could see, touch, smell or hear. How could this have happened to someone with such potential for greatness? How could this happen to someone that I loved?

In the hours after learning of his death I remember not being able to think or even use my words to describe the immediate magnitude his loss had on my life. I didn't know how I would be able to walk through the neighborhood knowing that I would never have access to him again, even if the relationship was strained at times. Unfortunately, I did not need my own words, because the street had decided to make up their own.

As the next day dawned and with less than 4 hours of sleep, for some ungodly reason that I'm assuming was because I was at the scene, I was implicated in that tragedy on 40. Street. The details of who the shooters were are still unclear to me. But I remember the anguish I felt after hearing I was somehow made a part of something so inconceivable, the death of Sweet.

I got the news the next morning as the call came in from my Uncle Vernon, who always kept his ears to the street. Since I now lived in upper west Philadelphia, he told me not to come to the neighborhood until he figured out what was going on. It seemed that pure mayhem had ensued after the news of Sweet's death. Because, on the call he told me that a few hours prior, while the moon was still out, someone had shot up the house of my childhood neighbor who lived across the street from him while she was sitting on the porch and a car that was directly in front of it, with Leslie inside. Neither were hit physically but I know their lives would never be the same after barely escaping death.

My uncle called me almost every hour on the hour to check on me. During that time, Kaiah never left my side and Mecca, who was trying her best to assuage the rumors by being my voice of reason to my accusers, kept calling to tell me what she was hearing on the street and none of it, and I mean none of it, was good. In fact, it was fucking horrific. Allegedly, someone saw me at the movie theater where Haroon and Sweet were supposedly at, someone else saw me making a phone call at a pay phone, and someone else saw me pointing out Haroon and Sweet.

Of course, none of that was true because I wasn't in the area until after hearing the shots. But at that point, no one was interested in the truth, they just wanted someone to blame and I was a likely candidate. Especially since I was dating someone outside of the neighborhood at the time, who was not a fan-favorite of anyone from Southwest Philly.

While the next couple of days went by at a snail's pace, I stayed in the house and kept my eyes glued to the window. I would notice unfamiliar cars parked on my block with guys sitting in them and I swore I could see guns on their laps. It was the most incredulous time of my young adult life. I tried to call Haroon at the hospital, who had survived his wounds, only to be circumvented by his brother with the words "you can't talk to him because we heard you set this up."

My mind was completely blown. I kept thinking to myself, "this is a fucking nightmare that I have got to wake up from." But the nightmare only got worse when I received a phone call from a detective telling me that he wanted to come out and talk to me. Initially, I was somewhat relieved because I thought that if nothing else, the authorities would be able to help clear my name of this horror. I told the detective I was available to speak and asked if he wanted me to come to him or would he come to me. He said, "I'll send a car for you, within the hour."

An hour later, two unmarked police cars pulled up to my house, with two detectives in each. A detective knocked on the door. I was shocked when I opened it to see there were two cars, and nervous because I knew this was serious. As we drove from West Philly to the Round House in Center City, which is the nickname for the circular building that houses the police districts central processing unit, I looked out the window and watched the city pass me by, thinking to myself "what the fuck did I do to deserve this bullshit?" I didn't know what I was walking into and I felt so very alone.

When we reached the police-station they took me up to the homicide division. Walking through the doors of that division, photos of fugitives hung on the wall. Some I recognized and some I did not. Passing by the photos, a chill ran through my body as they escorted me into a private room with a two-way mirror. I sat in a chair next to a desk, and a friendly detective looked at me and said with a slight smile, "What can you tell me about the homicide that occurred on 40th Street, because we are hearing that you set it up!"

I wanted to cry, but I couldn't. There were several emotions that ran through my mind and body all at once—fear, grief, sadness, anger and finally outrage. I looked at the detective and said, "That is a lie." He responded, "Well tell me why anyone would think that you had something to do with it?" I continued, "I can only assume it was because I was in the area after it happened." He responded, "Well what do you know about a shooting that occurred at a nightclub the week before this?" I told him, "Nothing, I wasn't at the nightclub that night." Which was true. For some intuitive reason, I sat that night out, did not go partying, and apparently all hell had broken loose.

Finally, the detective said to me, "Well we want you to tell us where you were the night of the incident on 40th Street, and we want you to write it down." I responded, "Are you asking me to write an official statement of my whereabouts that evening?" He replied, "Yes." I responded, "Give me a pen." I had no reason to not tell this detective what I was doing and who I was with, especially since it did not involve setting up a fucking homicide.

Once I was done with the statement, I thought the meeting would be over. But I was wrong. He then asked me to look at pictures of guys from my neighborhood. I thought it was weird because the victims were from my neighborhood and I'm sure no one in Southwest would have shot or set them up. As he pulled out the book of photos, I suddenly realized the detective wanted to know what I knew about a certain "group" of men from my neighborhood.

As I looked at the pictures, admitting that I had seen a couple of the guys before but didn't know their names, I was convinced that these detectives weren't interested in solving the case of Sweet; they were merely interested in finding out information on a local drug organization that was reigning supreme in Southwest Philly. It was in that moment that I eased back into my seat with the realization that these detectives were pieces of shit, and they were not going to use me and my despair to elicit and receive any information on anyone in my neighborhood. After

I had denied knowing the 25th guy, the detective was bored with me and summoned a car to take me back to my home.

But the emotional turmoil of that whole experience solidified a few things. For starters I could not grieve the loss of Sweet or even Haroon in peace, nor could I trust authority or anyone else for that matter. The devastation of that shooting left everyone in our community in a state of insurmountable despair and distress. Young men who were once only interested in skating on the weekends, were now toting firearms in the name of those who had been lost. Young women, other than me, were being called down to the police station to give statements as well.

The aftermath and grief of Sweet's death would cause a psychological shift in the landscape of our entire neighborhood, but especially in me. I could not rationalize death, especially his death. Up until then, the level of violence in our community had many of us attending high profile funerals. But in those deaths, the lines that led to their demise were more clearly defined. But Sweet's death just didn't make sense. He was one of the good boys. He was a church boy. He was going places. His death was wrong, and nothing could make it or my mind get right.

Subsequently, Sweet's death caused me a series of firsts. It was my first time having to defend my reputation. It was my first time having to give a statement to law enforcement. It was my first time dealing with the possibility of my own death, because word on the street was that there was a "hit out on Little Crystal" for setting up his murder. With all those firsts, it became the second time my Uncle Vernon rescued me. He bought me a flight out of Philadelphia and seven days after Sweet's death, I went into exile.

Living in Exile

I went back to San Jose and I mourned. I mourned my childhood, community, and my old self. I had planned to stay until the smoke cleared, but instead I stayed for four years. In those four years, Haroon was convicted and sentenced to 10-20 years in prison for the shooting at the nightclub the week prior to Sweet's death. But even with his own loss—his freedom and the life of his best friend Sweet—he helped clear my name at the street level, simply by uttering the words "she didn't have shit to do with that."

But the detectives were a different story. A year and a half after the incident as the trial neared, I repeatedly had detectives going to my house in Philadelphia harassing my mother, stating that if they couldn't talk to me, they would arrest her. I finally agreed to allow her to give them my phone number.

When they called, I was rude. I told them to stop going to my mother's house because if they really needed me for the trial then I would have never been able to leave the state. When I realized they were only trying to reach me to see if my statement had changed, I told them, "Of course it hasn't changed. I didn't see shit, I don't know shit, and I wasn't responsible for shit." After that, they stopped contacting me and my mother. But the damage was done.

All trust for my childhood male friends had eroded. I was so incredibly angry that they had implicated me in that level of treason, and I could not forgive them, or myself, for trusting them in the first place. The damage not only showed up as trust issues, I also developed severe anxiety and marijuana had become my only relief. I remember after arriving in Cali', crying for the first 30 days, my hair falling out in patches, losing weight, and because of being exposed to the sound of gunshots, fireworks were a major trigger that resulted in body tremors and tears.

It was a frightening experience the day I learned that fireworks, and other once fun activities, were my trigger. I had been in California for 10 months and found myself feeling somewhat "normal" again. I had gotten a job at a temp agency and was starting to enjoy the slow pace of everything, finally being able to breathe easily and not walk around with my shoulders tense. My hair was starting to come back and although at the time my weight never exceeded 100lbs, the 10 I had lost during that hell week after Sweet's death, came back.

I was really feeling better. I didn't cry as much, and I made sure to track my mood through journaling. Each entry made mention of me dying. I was not suicidal, but I thought that I was going to die all the time and I welcomed it.

Nevertheless, I still tried to enjoy myself when opportunities presented themselves. So, in preparation for the 1991, 4th of July weekend, there were two exciting events happening that weekend that I was eager to attend. For one, John Singleton's *Boyz in the Hood* was premiering on July 2nd and there would be a 4th of July firework celebration at the amusement park, Great America—California's version of New Jersey's Great Adventure. I was ready for all the festivities. I had an outfit for the movie and was planning to wear my new Bo Jackson Nikes to the park.

The second of July started out fantastic because my cousin Bianca, new friend Moonchild, their friends and I were all excited about John Singleton's movie. We went to the theater in a large group. It was almost sold out, but we managed to get our tickets. We sat near the rear of the theater and as I sat with my popcorn and drink in hand, I found myself extremely entertained by the storyline of four friends finding their way through a violent community in Compton, California. I could relate to their experience as it mirrored mine in Philadelphia.

I was enjoying the film and anticipating how it would end. That was until Ricky got shot. It was surreal. Tears started to stream down my face, and I found myself not being able to sustain my breath. It was at that point that I started crying hysterically and had to leave the theater. I never thought Ricky, who was heading to college, would be gunned down in the street. His life ended the same way Sweet's did. Sweet was enrolled in Cheyney University and died a week before his first day.

The anxiety and subsequent tears I experienced in that movie theater carried over to the 4th of July. On that day, feeling somewhat better, I was ready to face the world. Growing up in Philadelphia, participating in the 4th of July celebration was customary to us natives, and I was interested in seeing how the Californians celebrated. The amusement park was located 30 minutes away from our home, if you caught the light rail—San Jose's trolley system. My friends, who were actually my cousins and their friends, all loaded up on the light rail ready to hop on rides and see the fireworks.

Everything was going great until the first boom of the fireworks. It seemed that every nerve in my body became alert at the same time. The sensation mirrored what I felt in that movie theater and the sound mirrored that of gunshots from a high-powered weapon. As soon as I recognized the feeling, I knew what was coming next—tears. But before I could plan my next move, which was to get the hell out of the park, there was boom after boom, after boom after boom. I told my friends that I had to leave. They were perplexed, and I couldn't explain that I was experiencing an oncoming panic attack. Although I've used the term in this book, I had not yet learned the language of trauma, which included panic attacks and post-traumatic stress. So instead I said, "I just gotta go!"

Practically running toward, the exit of the park, I finally hopped back on the light rail, and the further away I rode from the park, and the less booms from the sky I heard, the more my body relaxed, and my brain stopped feeling erratic. Interestingly enough, I never sought therapy while in California. I just self-medicated with marijuana, which helped tremendously, especially since "chronic" had just been introduced to the world, musically and herbally.

Although I battled bouts of depression, anxiety and now, Post Traumatic Stress Disorder, I managed to reap many benefits in California. For one, I left the retail sales business and using the secretarial skills acquired in high school, developed other marketable skills and a strong work ethic.

This good fortune allowed me to be employed by multiple software companies in Silicon Valley and even meet Bill Gates before he monopolized the tech industry. San Jose was exciting and the hub for newness and cultivation. It had just opened its hockey rink for the San Jose Sharks and there were a lot of underground hip hop shows that also took place there.

Once I received word that my name was officially cleared from that horrific offense in Philly, I made a choice to enjoy myself in California. I knew Sweet would not want me to be back in California and not give it my all. So for him, I allowed myself to enjoy the peacefulness and adventures it offered me.

For the first time in my life, I didn't live in a constant state of fight or flight. I sailed on the San Francisco Bay, hiked on Angel Island and dined in Catalina. I hung out with rappers from Oakland, including members of the Souls of Mischief, and because my cousin was obsessed with Tupac, we followed his career around the Bay area.

I'm thankful that my name was cleared because at an HBO recorded concert in San Francisco, I was spotted dancing in the crowd when it aired on the network. At that point I didn't care about anything, because at that concert I got Tupac's autograph and subsequently had a brief affair with Money B from Digital Underground. I wasn't a groupie, but definitely a stargazer.

I was also a sponge for new experiences and new information in California, and gained so much knowledge about the Black Panther Party while spending time in Oakland. I would go to meetings to learn about the legacy of Huey P. Newton, and just being able to walk on the same land as the original party heightened my awareness of corruption in politics and inequity in Black life. To be 21 years old and discovering so much light in a world that had been dimmed by so much violence was rejuvenating. I kept journaling and would write to Sweet in it, sharing all that I was learning, reassuring him that his death had not been otiose—I was growing.

Life was smooth and mellow in California. I took many road trips from San Jose to Los Angeles, with Moonchild and Bianca, to visit an uncle who lived in the Baldwin Hills and take over his beautiful home overlooking Inglewood. He was really one of my fathers' childhood friends from Philadelphia, that had done well for himself and we were able to benefit from the fruits of his labor. We would rent cars or sometimes, Bianca would get her fathers' Mercedes and we'd travel in style. I always made sure that I was the designated driver because I absolutely loved driving those 5 hours from northern Cali to southern Cali through the mountains, smoking chronic while everyone slept.

I also loved driving because as the designated driver, I controlled the music as it, coupled with the Cali chronic, had become my therapy, and there was always good music to play. For the first time since before my uncle's indictment, life seemed normal and being in California was healing to my soul. It also helped me mend my relationship with my father.

He and I had been estranged since the time I had first come to live with and left him. Abandonment memories would often have me despising him for leaving me in Philadelphia to fend for myself and moving his entire other family, which included one wife and four children, across the country to the land of sunshine. I also despised him for how he judged my mother during her addiction. But although it was hard for me to show it at first, I was grateful that he opened his home to me when I had to flee Philadelphia, because he really didn't have to.

We weren't on speaking terms prior to that, but when he learned that my life was in jeopardy he did not hesitate to work with my uncle and my mother to get me to him. I was broken when I arrived and in my depressive state in those first few months in California, he mended the brokenness he and the men in my neighborhood had caused. He hugged me often and emotionally consoled my aches and pains through deep discussions that gave birth to familial reparations.

He also used his faith as a Jehovah Witness to open my eyes to the power of God. Up until that point in my life, I never seriously considered religion. I knew my Uncle Vernon was a Muslim, but I never quite understood the impact Islam had on his life. I had never seen him pray, nor did it keep him away from the life of crime. So, I had no benchmark for what Islam meant to him, other than a brotherhood. But with my father it was quite different. He was extremely active in the Kingdom Hall, and living in his house meant that you would be exposed to the religion through in-home Bible studies, attending meetings, witnessing to non-believers and not celebrating any holidays, not even a birthday.

Since, I just could not understand why death had occurred to Sweet, who was considered "good," I absorbed all that I could about his religion. I needed answers for why the good could die and the seemingly bad could survive. My father, on the many occasions that grief would take over my thinking, would explain his version of God to me. Invariably, we'd end our conversations discussing Armageddon, since the Gulf War was occurring at the time, and everyone thought this war would truly end the world. I was so emotionally lost during that time that I welcomed the end of the world. I just never had the courage to say it out loud.

In those discussions I learned fruitful things about "without life there is no death and without conflict there is no peace," and more importantly, "things happen in God's time not ours." In essence, I would never understand why Sweet had to die. But I made the determination that given the chance, my life would be reflective of his sacrifice. I just didn't know how.

My father would talk with me about any-and-everything that crossed my mind and when I wasn't asking questions, he would just know that I needed something more. As a devout music man, he would minister to my spirit through daily jam sessions. His favorite artists at the time were Anita Baker, Luther Vandross and Johnny Gill. There wasn't a day that went by that those three weren't permeating the air in my daddy's music room and I loved him for it!

He was a good dude and every one of his friends loved and respected him. He was funny and charismatic and well connected. One of his connections linked him to the manager of Bell Biv Devoe. My daddy was his God-father and whenever BBD would come to town, there would be tickets. Although I would have loved a formal meet and greet with BBD, dancing for free at a few of their concerts were good enough for me.

My father was more than just a man with connections to leisure and fun, he was also a bus driver and a damn good one. He would invite me to ride on his route on occasion and I would go. His customer service was impeccable. He had regular riders who would greet him by name—Bobby! If he had been out of work for any extended periods of time, they would also greet him with gifts and affection.

Watching my father in his business relationships as well as his personal relationships (all his friends relied on him for advice in their life), it was there in California that I realized I wanted to serve others. Since I had seen so much violence in my Philadelphia neighborhood, including dead Black bodies on the street, I knew I wanted to work in the social services field on projects to prevent violence. I just didn't know how to tap into that industry in San Jose, as violence was almost non-existent.

So, I stayed in the tech industry, but made promises to Sweet that I would one day create opportunities for women impacted by violence and caught up in the predicaments of the men they love. My spirit knew I wanted to implement this program in Philadelphia, but my mind and body had no plans of returning there. I was still traumatized by my own experience in that town and had not yet healed.

But then, once again, change inevitably came. On one un-seasonably chilly California February night, my father had a heart attack and died at the tender age of 46. It was not difficult to process my fathers' death because he spoke of his death often, especially living with his crippling chronic disease, sickle cell ane-mia, and his many bouts in the hospital due to its complications. But after his death, California lost its appeal and I had a strong desire to move back home. I wanted to test the theory that my name was clear of any scandal, so for the 4th of July in 1993, I made my way back to Philadelphia for a visit.

It seemed to be the perfect return visit. I must disclose that I did sneak back into the city a year and a half after I left to visit my mother in the hospital. She was surprised when I walked into her room, holding balloons and singing the song, *I'll Always Love My Mama* by the Intruders. I knew she would be having a hyster-ectomy and my spirit would not allow me to have her undergo that ordeal alone.

I was dating a guy who was in the Navy at the time. Ironical-ly he was from Philly, but stationed at Moffett Field in Mountain View California. He had a girl's name and because of his military status purchased a discount ticket for me to fly home under his moniker. It allowed me to be discreet in my travels and safe. But this time, in my own fearlessness, I was using my own name.

When I ventured back to Philadelphia the summer after my father died, many knew that I was coming home. I did not want it to be a surprise. I wanted to look at those who had accused me of the horror of Sweet's death in the face with assurance that they were no longer accusing me of treason. There were many brothers from the neighborhood that I ran into by happenstance.

One, the leader of the "get Little Crystal" crew, I happened to see while walking on the famous South Street. He looked sur-prised to see me, but summoned me over to the high-end SUV he was driving. He asked how I was doing and before I could respond, he said to me, "Listen...you know we didn't really think you had anything to do with that. But it was a crazy time, and we just couldn't be sure." I told him, "I understand." And I did.

I understood that on that night our once untouchable community had been touched in the most violent and tragic way, and none of us could wrap our minds around that level of violation. We were all victims of circumstance and only forgiveness of words, thoughts and actions, would allow us to heal. As I walked away from that apology, I felt like I could finally catch my breath again in Philadelphia.

Admittedly, I had the time of my life during that 2-week visit back to Philly. I went to see the fireworks on the Benjamin Franklin Parkway and did not have one tremor or symptom of panic. I ate all the cheesesteaks I could get my mouth around and loaded my suitcase up with Tastykakes, our famous packaged cake snacks, to distribute to my family and friends back in California. I had so much fun, that when I returned to the Land of Sunshine, I made the decision to move back to Philadelphia within the year. I was 24 and I missed my mother terribly, who was finally crack free as a result of my exodus.

I wouldn't wish what I had experienced on anyone. But if it meant that my mother would use the opportunity to dig deep in her reserve and break free from her addiction without rehab and only her will, then I would learn to accept what had happened to me. I was proud of her and having her healthy and well was necessary for my own mental health if I were to thrive back home.

I was ready for the next phase of life to begin. But I knew I would miss the sunshine in California, the road trips, the air, the mountains, the beautiful people, my new friends, my siblings and the peacefulness that I had experienced there. So, instead of flying back I took an Amtrak train home.

I could have afforded a flight, but since I had no idea when I'd ever get back to California, I wanted to take the long way home. Trekking across America, the 3-day long road trip home by rail was therapeutic. For 3,000 miles, I listened to Toni Braxton's debut self-titled album over and over again on my Walkman and made endless promises to myself that, for the sake of Sweet, I would survive in Philadelphia.

PART II

TRIPPIN' THROUGH LOVE

-Non-profit, No Profit, No Peace-

Starts and Stops

Once home, it took me approximately two weeks to find a job in Philadelphia. The only difficult part was learning the "F" keys on the keyboard of a computer. You see, in California, we were way ahead in the technology game and were already using a Windows environment on our desktops as well as a mouse. In Philadelphia, there was no mouse and there had yet to be Windows installed on computers.

Nevertheless, since I had acquired transferable skills from my work in Silicon Valley, and my 3 years of business administration from my vocational high school, it wasn't that difficult landing an executive secretary position. What I didn't expect was to land a position as an executive secretary at a non-profit research firm, Public/Private Ventures, PPV for short, that focused on evaluating youth and community development programs that served "at risk youth." I had hit the jackpot. It was in perfect alignment with my passion to serve and my commitment to Sweet.

The building was located on 20th and Market street in downtown Philly and the office was located on the 9th floor. It was such an exciting place to work and I soaked up every ounce of research skill bestowed upon me by the researchers. I had what employers referred to as "initiative."

I would take on assignments that no other executive secretary had the desire to. I learned research terms like, "methodology, theory, ethnography, qualitative and quantitative data," and would electronically and manually organize data on the research projects, code qualitative data, develop survey instruments, enter data, and assist with grant proposals and research reports. With every new opportunity that presented itself to me, I knew it was my mantra to myself "to pay attention" that made the learning easy, the task not difficult and the outcome desirable for all parties involved.

My classification at the job was considered "support staff," and all the researchers were considered "professional staff." Even though the terms were as separatist as you could get, I loved supporting the research of PPV. I learned so much about philanthropy and was introduced to heavy hitters like the Annie E. Casey Foundation, who was our primary youth development funder, Pew Charitable Trust, whose main office was in our building, the Ford Foundation, which inspired me to buy my first and only Ford vehicle, and the MacArthur Foundation, who secured our funding to research workforce development. With all that I learned and was exposed to at PPV, the sweetest satisfaction came with understanding the importance of volunteering in the community, as most of the projects we evaluated had a heavy volunteer component. I learned that most community-based organizations cannot survive without volunteers and if I'd ever gotten a chance to, I'd volunteer at one.

Because of my tenacity, my role as an executive secretary was short-lived and after one year was promoted to administrative assistant. I had discovered a passion for research that I would have never known existed growing up in Southwest Philly. And while I was learning the research process, I was still keeping my eye on my old neighborhood.

Haroon was still incarcerated and would call me from time-to-time. Although he was the first person that I've ever loved to have gone to jail, I never visited him. I just couldn't imagine walking into a prison and visiting anyone. It wasn't for me. I would write to him, but I wasn't walking my ass into a prison to see him or anyone else. So, I would take his calls and update him on my life. Eventually he stopped calling because I cursed him out about constantly asking me "whatchu got on" each time we talked. It was sickening, and I just didn't get the point of him needing that information.

Even though I was moving about life somewhat seamlessly, I still had trust issues with the men in my old neighborhood, so I wasn't really interested in dating any of them. Besides, I was too focused on finding my niche at the non-profit, that although it came with a lot of responsibility, it also came with perks. Perks that I always took advantage of, like the night I attended a free Sixers game, as a perk of the non-profit. They were honoring the former Sixer point guard Maurice Cheeks' by retiring his jersey.

I was walking through the Spectrum sports arena when I heard a brothers' voice call out "hey shawty." I turned around and this brown-skinned fella walked up to me and said, "Listen, I don't have no game, but can I call you sometime?" He appeared to be a gentleman and I was flattered, so I offered him my phone number.

We talked later that evening and although he was a barber working at the Philadelphia Hair Company, he shared his hopes and dreams of becoming a poet. I was intrigued. I had never dated a poet before, mainly drug dealers and killers, and from that first night up until four weeks later we were inseparable. We would often hang out in his groovy apartment in Germantown and smoke herb, listen to good music and smoke some more. His music collection was intense. I can honestly say anything by Roy Ayers was the soundtrack of our initial love affair.

He enjoyed parks and movies and digging deep into the psyche of the Black man's personal dilemma—navigating America. I enjoyed his company and his talent. As time progressed, he would write me poems and even perform them on open-mic nights. I loved watching him hone his craft.

The only issue we had was his baby mama. She was an absolute nightmare, and rightfully so. He was still sleeping with her and lying to the both of us. There was constant psychological trauma in that relationship, on both our parts because when he would cheat, I became verbally and sometimes physically violent. I would curse him out, and kick him out of the apartment that we eventually came to share. Ironically, this apartment was one block down from where Haroon and Sweet were shot.

I don't know what drew me to that one-bedroom apartment on 41st and Walnut. Sure, the price was amazing, $385 a month and only $100 to move in. But psychologically it was somewhat comforting and equally unsettling being that close to where that trauma occurred. Although I had to walk to the train at 40th and Market each day to get to work, I would make sure not to walk on the side of the street where either of them were shot. I'd take a deep breath, say a prayer for them, and continue on my way.

The poet, who was well aware of my trauma and the sa-cred-ness of that piece of land, still managed to cause me grief in that one-bedroom apartment on 41st and Walnut. One night after a day of hard work at the non-profit, I was fitfully sound asleep in my bed when the phone rang. It was the poet. He claimed to have been at the hospital with his mother who was battling cancer at the time. When I asked if he wanted me to come to the hospital to support him, he quickly told me no and said that he would probably just stay the night there. For some reason, his response just didn't sit well with me.

When we hung up, I made a mental note that if I were to wake up again before the night ended and no call had come through, I would *69 my phone, a technique that has long since been antiquated. Well two hours later at approximately 2am, I awoke having to pee. Upon my return from the bathroom, I made good on my promise to trace the call since no call had come through since we last spoke.

To my surprise, it wasn't Jefferson Hospital on the other end of the phone but the Days Inn on Roosevelt Boulevard in the Northeast section of Philadelphia. I asked the attendant if there was someone with the name of the poet in a room there, he said there wasn't. I hung up, thought for 5 seconds and *69'd again. This time I asked the attendant for the room of the poet's baby mama. Sure enough, in her sleepy voice she answered the phone. I wasted no time asking for the poet, in which she immediately passed him the phone. Before he could utter a word, I was already calling him a motherfucker.

Needless to say, we broke up, got back together, broke up again, got back together and broke up again. Then the unthinkable occurred, I got pregnant. I had been pregnant by him once before during one of our "on again" times. But that pregnancy resulted in a "fetal demise" during the first 8 weeks and I had to undergo a dilation and curettage (D&C) procedure to remove the fetus. So, I had no idea if this egg would stick and because we were "off again," I definitely didn't want to have his baby.

But as the Universe has a tendency to conspire with God to order my steps, it did exactly that with this pregnancy. After my first ultrasound I knew that I was going to be the mother of the poets' child. After that doctor visit, we decided to "work things out." We would move back in together and he'd try his best to stop fucking his baby mom.

During that trying time, I also started to notice shifts in my beloved place of employment, some great and some not so great. They were still giving me opportunities to learn the science of research, but I also learned they weren't as liberal as I had come to believe. It took a brave soul to pull my coat about the hypocrisy in the workplace. Her name was Diane Dobson.

She was the vice president of the technical assistance department. Diane had grace and style. Her skin the color of a sweet chocolate whopper, and hair cut close to her scalp with a gray diamond patch in the front. She was beautiful. But she was a bit stand-offish. For a long time, I didn't think she liked me, but since we didn't work directly with one another, it didn't really bother me. But one day after I had shared my unwed pregnancy with the staff, she pulled me into her office and said, "Marry him! They may say they are liberals, but they only are when it's convenient. They will judge you." She was talking about the "professional staff".

I took her advice and married the poet one month after our son was born. I believe she was right. Four weeks after returning from maternity leave and newly married, the professional staff said they "noticed my initiative" and promoted me to research assistant, with a substantial pay increase, even though I did not have a "formal" degree.

As a research assistant, I was no longer considered support staff. My workload intensified and I received my own interior office. I was now creating focus group scripts, conducting focus groups, and traveling to some of our research sites across the country to implement the research, and sometimes by myself, again without a formal degree. It wasn't that I did not want a degree, or even at some point want to experience college. It was that PPV deliberately did not support me on that path and I became apathetic.

The organization had a professional development fund. Each employee was allocated funds to use for coursework or conferences within the scope of the non-profits work. Since I never shied away from my truth, everyone knew that not only was I the only Black research assistant, I was also the only one without a formal degree. The other research assistants were intrigued by the notion that on projects, I could do better or as equally as well as they, who had spent four years learning the field of research in a university setting.

In a quest to support me in acquiring a degree, they initiated a plan to draft a proposal to the President and CFO of the organization to gift their portion of professional development funds to me, so that I could apply to college without the burden of paying for it. Especially since I was working full time, with a young son and husband at home, and more importantly had the skills already.

Everyone in management knew the proposal was being drafted, it was a small organization and we all "talked." We were even encouraged to submit it. However, two weeks after its submission the President called me to his office to inform me that what we proposed was not in the company's policy and they could not amend the policy just for me. I was gutted.

Since degrees were correlated to compensation, me not having one meant that, I was underpaid. I later learned that the other research assistants made more than me but did less work, especially since I was still doing administrative duties for projects as well. But instead of causing a ruckus, I decided to create leverage for myself and had no problem doing so after being denied support on my educational journey. One of the projects we worked on was the San Francisco Beacons Initiative. This project was essentially an evaluation of an after-school program. The best part about this west coast project was that I got the opportunity to travel back and forth to California at their expense.

My "work producer" had a deep affection for me. I admit I called her my "work producer" because for some reason I had a psychological discomfort toward the word "boss" at PPV. But I did like her, and she loved my initiative and stick-to-it-ness and did her best to prove it to me.

Whenever we had a site visit to San Francisco, she would give me the Friday before the work-week trip or the Monday after the trip off so that I could fly into Los Angeles for the weekend to visit Moonchild, who had since moved there from San Jose. It was wonderful knowing that I would start or end the week hanging out with my dearest friend and with my lungs filled with good Cali-bud.

But even with the extended travel perk of the job, not getting that approval for the proposal to attend higher education devastated me. It was at that point the rosy lens that I had been viewing the non-profit through had become extremely clear. I had already been conducting research on my own in the field for them. I was leaving my child behind to go on site visits. I was a team player, but I also realized I was cheap labor.

When Diane found out they denied the proposal, she again pulled me into her office and said, "Go Anyway!" I eventually enrolled in Temple. However, I didn't complete it because life was still unfolding as a newly married mom, and I was exhausted by all the changes occurring at once.

For starters, during my relationship with the poet, I was heavily involved in the "neo-soul movement". I was attending poetry readings, smoking herb in parks, being a faithful wife and a wonderful mother to a handsome baby boy, walking around with my hair natural, and getting fat. I had found my tribe and it was good for a while. I loved the poet but realized I didn't necessarily like him and felt as if he didn't like me much either. His cheating didn't stop and the life of supporting a starving artist had become unbearable.

To make matters worse, my mother who once liked him, could not stand him anymore or the misery I was enduring. I remember clearly during the final days of our relationship, my mother and I were sitting in her Overbrook basement watching the movie version of *Waiting to Exhale* on VHS. As the credits rolled, I sat back and sighed, "That was a great movie, it was so much like the book." She turned to me and said, "I'll be glad when you fuckin' exhale." In the few months following that movie day, I separated from the poet, moved my son and I in with my mother, permed my hair, lost 23 pounds, and fell in love with a thug.

Faster from 20th Street

I met Faster at his mothers' house on Juniata Street in North Philly. I was actually there for his cousin who, for the sake of this text will call "Slow." I met Slow at a dance club called Studio 37 on Erie Avenue. He lived with Faster. When I walked into that house on that early Spring night and saw Faster sitting on the couch with his chocolate skin, beautifully braided hair, white tank, boxers on and a house arrest anklet atop his bare left foot, I fell in love.

He was more than easy to look at and he had a subtle intellect. I asked about his house arrest anklet. He stated that he had just come home from county jail and that was part of the mandate for his case. I continued to ask him questions, like "how long were you in there?" If he had any children and if so, how did he feel being away from them for so long. I also asked him how he felt giving the system that time out of his life away from his children. He answered all my questions, thoughtfully, as if no one had ever asked him how incarceration impacted his family life.

The three of us talked for a while and Faster was so animated with his body and expressive with his words that I simply could not get enough of being in his company. I was very intrigued. The only problem was Slow, my date, who I had slightly forgotten about until he leaned over and whispered to me "come on let's go upstairs." It was as if my favorite record on the player had skipped. I looked at Slow, who wasn't half as handsome as Faster, and solemnly said "ok." I hated leaving Faster downstairs and I hated being upstairs with Slow.

I sat on the edge of the bed in that middle room, with no door on the hinges, and made the decision that would change the next nine months of my life. I told Slow "I can't do this." He was oblivious. He thought I meant fuck. So, I let him think that. I told him I was uncomfortable with Faster being downstairs and no bedroom door for privacy. But in all actuality I felt like I was cheating on Faster upstairs in that room.

Slow sat in disbelief, but eventually realized I wasn't budging on my decision to "not fuck". The whole exchange lasted approximately 8 minutes. But after I had gotten my point across, I grabbed my purse, gave him a hug and walked back down those steps. When I approached the bottom, Faster gave me a look that said, "I'm coming for you." I smiled, told him it was a pleasure meeting him, and walked my in-love ass out his front door.

Two weeks later, he was off house arrest and was in the middle of Studio 37 dancing like he was in a competition. I loved a dancing man, so I quietly watched him. Faster spotted me and with a smile on his beautiful brown face walked over, leaned in and lightly yelled in my ear, "What's up baby? You know I'm like Allen Iverson, I go for the steal." I was hooked.

From that night forward, I was a disrespectful lunatic toward Slow. I completely cut him off, and when I would call the house for Faster and Slow would answer, I'd hang up. Faster knew it was me calling, and eventually Slow did too. It proved futile for Slow to complain, because nothing and no one could stop the growing love affair between Faster and so we proceeded to fall madly in love. Faster took a lot of slack for stealing his "cousin's girl" from everybody, including his mother. But eventually, she fell in love with me too.

With everyone finally in the know and minding their business, I started to settle into my love affair with Faster. He reminded me of Haroon, in the sense that he was chocolate, handsome, and a protector. However, there was only one real challenge loving him. He was extremely mischievous. He was attracted to criminal activity and even though I knew better, I was attracted to him because of that. After all, the men I'd come to love up to that point all had criminal backgrounds, except the poet, but in my eyes were good people on the inside.

I realized I was attracted to his affinity toward that lifestyle because I understood his perception of his options in life, and I wanted him to win despite the path he chose. He had become a father at 13 and had endured almost all the hardships that I had growing up in a city besieged by the crack epidemic. It had ravished his family, but also provided a means for his family and because of that, he had already been caught up in the system and couldn't figure his way out. So, when he'd share his dreams and disappointments I listened, offered advice, and loved him despite his transgressions.

It was an interesting time for me during the initial phase of falling in love with him. During the day I was a research assistant evaluating programs across the country. During the night I was laid up listening to Lil Wayne's *Tha Block is Hot* album, smoking weed with a criminal. It was as if I had become an ethnographer in my own life. I was also able to easily live this double life since I now lived with my mother and she would graciously allow me to come and go as I pleased while she entertained my son.

Like me, my mother loved everything about Faster. I think it was because he always brought his authentic self whenever he showed up. He was never a pretender, was very inquisitive, and sometimes acted like she was his girlfriend. It didn't bother me because it was nice to have a man around that my mother actually liked.

During this time my mother was heavily involved in the Church, even though she kept getting kicked out of Bible Study for "asking too many questions," but was well versed in Bible scripture. She'd share a word or two with Faster and even invited him to attend with her, which he did. He would often tell me that he loved the way she demonstrated her Christianity. She wasn't judgmental, still cursed and didn't hide the fact that she still enjoyed her vodka.

For nine months, I could not get enough of Faster. There was a five-year age difference between us, with me being the elder, and there was so much he hadn't been exposed to that I felt compelled to be his guide. It was rough at times because he was so uncensored and when we would go into areas of the city that did not resemble his home base of 20th and Susquehanna, he acted like a park ape. There were times when I had to leave him where he was and take a break. But the breaks never lasted long and when we would reconnect, we'd resolve our issues, step by step, blunt by blunt. I was convinced he was my soulmate.

As we approached our ninth month, the inevitable happened. Faster got arrested twice. The first time was for a drug case that did not require him to stay in jail for more than a week. But the second time was the life changer. It was 2am and my phone rang. I knew it was him, because no one else would be calling me at that hour. I thought he was calling to tell me he was on his way after a night of shenanigans. Well, I was half right. He had been involved in shenanigans alright.

Apparently, he was caught firing a gun by an off-duty police officer. He was calling me from 55th and Pine to tell me to come to the precinct to get his money because he was going to the dreadful "Round House" to be processed. I still remember that place very well, and I had absolutely no desire to go back in that building. Therefore, it was imperative that I meet him at the district jail.

I hurried and woke my mother up and told her the predicament Faster had gotten himself in and that I needed her to keep an eye on my boy. She obliged. I got in my car, went to the precinct, and the officer handed me his belongings. The whole transaction lasted 3 minutes. I never got to see Faster that night. In fact, I didn't see Faster for another three weeks. He was not given bail, and was sent to the county jail, where I had to wait for him to be processed out of quarantine. Once I got word that he could have a visit, unlike my reaction to Haroon's incarceration, I could not get to the county jail quick enough to lay eyes and hands on my sweetheart.

It was strange parking in the prison lot. It was strange walking up to the entrance. It was strange taking a number and waiting 2 hours to be called. It was strange, after being called, to be asked to lift my bra, shake my titties and pull my panties away from my waist to check for contraband. It was strange to go through all that shit, just for a 30-minute visit. But what was even stranger was that I, the person who said she would never ever visit anyone in jail, was visiting someone in jail and knew I would be headed back the first chance I got. Although it was psychologically draining, seeing Faster made it all worth it.

But if I am to be completely honest, I hated that prison and I hated that he had gotten himself locked up. But never once in the beginning did I question if I would ride it out. I just hunkered down and did everything he asked me to. He needed me to engage the lawyer for his first offense, so I did. I didn't need to seek counsel for the gun case because "his friend" was handling that. He needed commissary, he needed to reach me on the phone, he needed me to visit and he needed me to keep him sane. I did all of that, but I was losing my mind.

I had never missed a person that I actively loved as much as I missed him. It felt like I was experiencing losing a loved one to death, again. I couldn't sleep, eat or even think without crying before, during or after. I could not process the loss of him in my day-to-day life. I mean we did everything together, and now I was doing everything alone. To make matters even worse, because he was still on probation and had two open cases, he could not be released on bail. So, he had to sit as we endured the outcome of his trial.

I was immersed in every aspect of it. I visited his lawyers. I took off from work to go to his hearings. I visited him twice a week at the county jail and sometimes took my son. I learned every part of the court system so that I could answer any questions he had about his proceedings. I even checked on his mother and took his daughter to visit when she first got her period since he couldn't be there to support her transition into womanhood. While I was being everything to Faster, I was also being everything to PPV and still traveling across the country for work.

There was no way I could even admit to my colleagues that I was facing this challenge. I still performed well at the workplace, writing memos, giving trainings, developing databases and co-facilitating workshops at conferences. I thought I had a handle on things until 3 months after Faster's arrest, my mother had a heart attack.

I knew those years of indulging in her addiction had taken a toll on her heart, but I wasn't prepared for her heart to fail. It was the first time since her addiction that I was faced with the idea of losing her. Although I never let her see my fear, it eroded my sanity from the inside out. I could not bear the thought of losing my mother and my man at the same time. So, I did my best to love her back to health as I continued to love Faster through jail.

Love is a beautiful thing, but if it's occurring in the middle of trauma it's extremely difficult to do. As I was loving my mother through her heart attack, my son through the day-to-day absence of his father, and Faster through his trial, the ugly signs of anxiety and PTSD were starting to rear its head. I was anxious and irritable all the time and cried more often than I was comfortable with. But, I knew I had to be strong for all of them.

The Bid

After about 7 months of trials and county jail visits, Faster was sentenced in years to a 2-4 for the gun case and 1-3 for the drug case to run concurrently. I was elated by the short time and that the trial and sentencing process was over. Now all that was left was for us to just do the "bid". For such a small word, it had the biggest impact on our lives. For starters, he was sent 3 and a half hours away from Philadelphia to Rockview State Correctional Institution in Bellefonte, PA and I had no idea how to get there.

I considered driving my own car, but didn't trust my Ford making that long trip up and back. I finally decided on renting a car. I went to the Enterprise rental car agency on City Line Avenue and rented a 2000 Saab. I always had a thing for Saabs, partially because most drug dealers from my neighborhood had one, and this particular agency specialized in renting high end cars. Besides, if I was going to take a 3.5-hour trip across Pennsylvania by myself, the least I could do was do it in style.

I rented the car the afternoon before the trip, picked up a PA map, came home and studied the route. Yes, these were the days long before GPS capabilities, so a physical map was necessary. After studying the map and highlighting the route—I76 to PA322 to PA29 and then right on Rockview Place—as well as writing the directions on an index card, I prepared myself for bed, anticipating my 5am start.

That morning I made a cup of tea to go and packed snacks for my solo road trip. Once inside the car, I placed the snack bag and map on the leather passenger seat and the index card below the dash in front of the speedometer for a quick view of the route if necessary, even though I had programmed the route in my head already. As I sat behind the wheel of that Saab, engine running, I closed my eyes and asked God for safe traveling mercy. I steadied my mind, pulled out of my parking spot and prepared my body for the long drive.

The first thing I noticed about this trip was how peaceful it felt driving on the turnpike. It was summer, so the trees were in full bloom, money green, and blowing in the wind. The sky was baby blue, and the clouds were in perfect scattered alignment with one another. As the Saab cruised by each mile-marker, I listened to oldies. The Isley Brothers, Whispers, LTD, Minnie Ripperton and Aretha Franklin were the soundtrack to that first ride.

I stopped at a rest stop on the Turnpike to use the bathroom and to grab some real food. After riding solo for some time, the hustle and bustle of the rest stop was welcoming. As I purchased my food, I wondered how many other people were heading to a prison and if any could tell that I was. It didn't really matter if they knew, because I was headed to see the one I loved, and nothing could wipe the smile off my face.

I hopped back in the car, started that smooth engine and proceeded on my prison journey down the turnpike. As I was driving, I couldn't help but notice how much the road reminded me of Route 5 in California, beautiful and serene. We would often take Route 5 from San Jose to LA to avoid the 101 traffic and highway patrol, since we loved smoking our bud in the car. I realized the only difference between this ride and those rides, was that I didn't have any weed and instead of going to party hard, I was on my way inside a state correctional institution. I had no idea what I was in for and it frightened me.

Two hours later, I was making a right onto Rockview Place and according to the map in a quarter mile, I would be approaching the facility. Nothing and I mean nothing prepared me for the sight of that institution. It was ominous and terrifying. The grounds were green and well-manicured, but the building itself resembled that of an insane asylum from a horror movie.

It made me pause as its white haunting exterior took my breath away. I tried to gather myself as I drove up the circular drive, but my heart began to beat at an unrecognizable pace. I did my best to steady it by taking deep breaths and saying out loud to myself, "it's OK Crystal, he's in there so you have to be, you came too far to buckle now."

After finding parking, I grabbed my purse and proceeded up the steps to enter the institution. I had to wait outside for a moment to be buzzed in. As soon as I entered, the guard ushered me through a metal detector to make sure I didn't have, what I am assuming, weapons on me. He then asked to search my purse and told me to sign in and write down the "inmate's" name and Department of Corrections (DOC) number on the sheet. I did as I was told as the guard rifled through my personal belongings. He then gave me a key for a locker to put my purse in, motioned toward the locker, and then told me to have a seat to wait for Faster to be called down. Again, I did as I was told.

Sitting in that small lobby of that prison, I observed everything. I observed the guards' nonchalant behavior, the placement of the bathroom, the size of the chairs, the location of every metal door and slowly noticed my anxiety rising. I felt trapped. There was no immediate way out of there unless I was "buzzed" out, and I was beginning to inwardly lose my cool. As soon as my anxiety started to get the best of me, the guard notified me that it was time for my visit. Faster was ready!

Heart racing, feet unsteady, I rose from my seat and proceeded to yet another metal door, but this one led to the visiting room. Before being buzzed in, I quickly turned to the guard who was looking at a monitor and said, "What do I do once I get in there?" He turned from the monitor and in a pleasant voice said, "Just hand the guard your slip and wait at the desk." Equipped with that information, slip in hand, money in my back pocket, I walked through 2 more metal doors.

Upon entering the visiting room, the guard greeted me with a smile and held his hand out for my visiting slip. It was an easy transaction. As I stood there, my eyes floated around the tight visiting room. I tried my best not to make eye contact with any of the inmates, so instead my eyes settled on their visitors.

There were only women and children in the visiting room. There was a small room in the far corner that was dedicated to the children, vending machines lined up on an opposite wall, and a bathroom to the right of the front desk. I also noticed an outdoor space with picnic tables and playground equipment, and a view of the mountains beyond them. If it had not been for the high fence and barbed wire, the outside space almost resembled serenity.

I waited approximately 5 minutes for Faster to walk into the visiting room. It felt like an eternity. But as soon as our eyes locked onto each other, every mile I drove, every metal door I walked through, and every drop of anxiety was worth it. He looked well and healthy. His smile was bright and there was absolutely no tension on his face. He had pep in his step and offered me the tightest hug a woman would ever need. He even smelled good.

After the hug and a soft kiss on the lips, we found a seat near the window. I asked him "How are you holding up?" He replied, "Better than I expected." I told him about my thoughtful ride across Pennsylvania, and how unexpectedly easy the trip had been. He said, "Crystal, you've always been about that road life. I knew it wouldn't be hard for you." He was right, often in our escapades I was the designated driver and he knew I could maneuver any terrain. For the next three hours we reminisced about our 9 months together on the outside, my workload at the non-profit, my son, Ms. Yvonne, his mother and children and our future.

It was so nice sitting there with Faster in this very undistracted space. It was nice seeing him not being agitated by the hustle and bustle of street life. For the first time in almost a year, we were able to sit and talk and not about, court, cops and crimes, but about hope, dreams and intentions. I was falling deeper in love with this version of Faster.

As our time approached its end, we both settled into a stillness. He placed his arm around the back of my chair, and I leaned my head back onto it. We were quiet for some time. Finally, I said to him, "I don't want to leave you here." He looked down at me and said, "I don't want you to leave me here, either." We both chuckled, as I eased out of that position and prepared to depart.

We walked slowly together to the guards' desk with his hand resting on the small of my back. It felt good there and I tried my best to hold that feeling in my consciousness for as long as I could, as I knew it would be a while before I felt it again. I retrieved my slip from the guard and turned back toward Faster. He hugged me tightly and upon his release said to me, "Ok Ms. Lady, you be safe on that road." We kissed gently, one final time and I exited the visiting room.

Upon leaving the institution I realized I had an energy that wasn't present at my arrival. I felt in the core of me that I *could* do this bid. The upstate prison wasn't nearly as bad as I thought it would be or as hellish as the county prison was. The ride up was pleasant, and the view was beautiful. Although the prison itself was extremely intimidating, I knew that as long as Faster was in there, I had to strengthen my resolve to get through the bid.

"I can do this, I can do this, I can do this" was my mantra every time my eyes became heavy from tiredness on the way home. "I can do this, I can do this, I can do this", was repeated every time I saw a dead animal on the side of the road. "I can do this, I can do this, I can do this", echoed in my mind every time I thought I couldn't.

Call this Number

I kept the car for one additional day and convinced two of my favorite colleagues from the non-profit to take a road trip from Philly to Atlantic City with me. It wasn't hard to convince one since she had already taken the day off, but the other we had to put pressure on her to tell the bosses that she wasn't feeling well and needed to leave early for the day. It worked, and we had an absolute blast. I think we all needed a beach day, especially with working at what I was slowly beginning to begrudgingly, yet affectionately refer to the non-profit as "the plantation."

The non-profit had lost its golden glow when they pulled that degree crap on me, and once you lose your glow with me, there isn't any coming back from that. But it seems I wasn't the only disgruntled employee. Many of us Blacks noticed disparities with a few things between us and the white staffers (professional and support), like who were paid what, and who were given more work than others, and who had to be "at their desk" at all times. The latter, the desk shit, started happening after my promotion when I got my office. It wasn't my fault that I had the best damn decked out office on the floor. And guess what? Many of my colleagues, even the ones I didn't care for, loved being in my office. If I could have burned incense and smoked weed in there, I'm sure many more would have tried to come in.

There wasn't any doubt that I had opportunities my other peers did not have even without that damn degree. So, people were perplexed about half the shit I was able to get away with. Many knew that I had been going back and forth to California to enjoy time before and after site visits. They knew I had been using the company credit card for personal shit, even if I paid for it after the fact—like renting that Saab. They knew I was given a "coveted" laptop to take home and even "work from home" at times. They knew I would sometimes come in late and leave early, or not come in at all. But what they didn't know was that because they had chosen to deny supporting my educational development and continued to underpay me for work senior research associates were doing, I had given myself permission to take my money off the top, in terms of time.

I knew I was financially and even emotionally being taken advantage of and had I not been so damn overwhelmed with Faster and the bid, I would have devised a plan to take them down after this stunt. We had been preparing for another site visit to San Francisco. I had made all the travel arrangements, coordinated meetings with stakeholders, and organized focus groups and interviews with participants. As I mentioned, even as a research assistant, I still maintained some of my administrative assistant responsibilities and was not compensated for it.

Nevertheless, on this particular site visit, I was traveling with one of my favorite researchers. She had a PhD in early childhood development, had published a couple articles in established psychology journals, and I was excited to see her in action. We were going to conduct our research in the Chinatown district. We would be holding focus groups with youth! Right up her alley, right? Well imagine my underpaid surprise when this wench asked me to conduct the focus groups because she "gets nervous around groups."

Now to this day, I'm still not quite sure what the fuck that meant—groups of kids, groups of Asians, or groups of Asian kids. But whatever she meant, did not add up to her degree or publications. I was livid but conducted the interviews and elicited great data from a population I had never worked with before. I didn't show that I was appalled at her horrific work ethic, and I'm sure because of that she went back and told all the higher ups that I was the best research assistant ever. So, of course that meant other researchers wanted to "use" me for their research projects. But despite the ridiculousness at the non-profit, it was a sweet gig that afforded me opportunities and the time to love a man in prison. For that reason alone, I continued to deal with the foolishness.

Faster and I were slowly finding our groove with the once a week 15-minute phone calls, and when he would ask me "whatchu got on" I finally understood the purpose of needing that information and did not hesitate to reveal whatever I was wearing at the time; panties, no panties, or even sweats. I loved our phone calls and also loved to visit. However, after a couple trips, I knew I didn't have the desire nor want to spend the money to keep renting cars to drive up there. I had been sharing my discontent with him because of the time and financial burden renting a car was placing on my body and finances, and he said he'd figure something out.

Finally, on one of our calls, he told me to "call this number" and ask for a woman that drives up to Rockview. He said it was a van service to the prison. I had never heard of a "van service" but was intrigued and relieved. Immediately after we hung up, I did exactly what he suggested and called the number. The van service lady was a pleasant woman over the phone and told me all the steps I'd need to take to ride on her van—which included meeting at 15. and Market at the ClothesPin statue to board the van. I was excited about my upcoming road trip. I would finally get to meet other women in the same predicament as I, not have to drive, and have some company on that long ass ride.

The following early Saturday morning, my mother who was still a fan of Faster, and young son set out at 5am to take me to my pickup location for the 5:30am departure. Sitting in the car with them I kept looking out the window for the van, nervous thinking I had missed it. But then I saw a small group of other women standing near the curb. I got out of our car and approached them.

All extra-friendly, I asked if they were waiting for the van. They chuckled and said, "Yes, she should be here soon." I was excited that I had found my tribe, until I saw a 1993 Chevy Impala pull up, and the ladies pointing toward it were still chuckling while saying, "the van's here." I was flabbergasted. For starters there were 6 of us ladies, and one was about 8 months pregnant.

I wasn't sure how this car could ever be mistaken for a "van". I had grown up riding in my Uncle Vernon's conversion van with a bed and kitchenette in it, so I'm well aware of what a damn van looked like. No, I didn't expect there to be a bed with a kitchenette in hers, but I definitely expected enough seats to fit all 6.5 of us.

Sulking, I walked back to my car, to where my mother had been sitting watching, and complained to her, "This is about to be some bullshit!" She just laughed and said "You wanna go see your man, don't you?" I responded with misplaced anger, "You know I do!" Not missing my anger, she quickly responded, "Well then get your fucking ass in that tight ass car and go!" I rolled my eyes, kissed my son farewell, and walked toward the clown car.

As I predicted, it was the most uncomfortable ride I have ever taken in my entire life. For starters, we were squished inside, it was hot, and she drove like Cruella de Vil as if we were her stolen 6.5 Dalmatians. But what made this trip even more unbearable was that the "nice lady" from the phone had been replaced by her alter-ego, the condescending recovering addict. The kind of recovering addict that had all the key chains to mark their recovery journey. The kind that had found Jesus on the road to recovery. The kind that judged women who would "ever visit a nigga in jail." Her words, not mine. And for 3.5 hours driving upstate we were a captive audience to the lunacy of a Christian in recovery, who was only doing this because her "nephew asked her too!"

When I finally arrived inside that visiting room, Faster could tell by the look on my face that it was a hellish experience. He let me vent and did his best to console me. He even went so far as to say he was going to step to the dude who gave him the number, because he didn't appreciate him putting his woman in that position.

He also said he felt bad because he wanted to talk to me about something important. I told him to save it since I had such a bad experience, I didn't want to deal with anything else uncomfortable. He conceded, and I did my best to relax into my visit. After a while I told Faster I felt better knowing that he had my back, and as I was saying those words it was in that moment a seed had been planted. Directly thereafter I told him, "We ain't sweatin' that shit, I'm going to start my own damn van service."

Old New York

Even the best laid plans come with delays. I went back home with every intention of starting a van service, but everything else happened first. For starters, my mother was getting sick of me living in her house and told me I needed to get out. Not in a mean way, but in a "hurry the fuck up, you've worn out your welcome" way with a smile each time she said, "did you find a place yet?" Part of me, no all of me, knew that the time had come for me and my son to give her back her space. Although I would miss the comfort of being up under her, I knew we had to go. She gave me until August1st of 2001 to find a spot.

I was excited about apartment hunting. I always enjoyed going into a new space and visually placing furniture with the intention of me dwelling there. I looked only in the West Philadelphia and Upper Darby area, a suburb of Philadelphia. It took some time to find a location that suited my esthetic of serenity, but in July 2001 I found the perfect 2nd floor, 2-bedroom apartment in Stonehurst Court Apartments. It was a hop skip and a jump from the 69th Street Transportation Terminal that could take me quickly into the city for work, and a 10-minute drive to my mothers' house when I wanted to invade her space.

I moved in on the date my mother had set for me. I felt very fortunate to have met her deadline and to still be so close to her, since she was the best grandmother a daughter could ever want and need. I definitely needed her to continue to help me with my son, since the poet was still finding his footing as an artist.

It finally felt like life was leveling out a bit, but what wasn't quite leveling out was my work at the plantation. I guess with all the changes in my life, my anxiety presented itself in a new way. I had started to develop an extreme fear of flying and an increased need for weed. I had always felt a bit uncomfortable at take-off but loved the pulse of the airport. As the anxiety increased and I realized I could no longer fly and be productive once I landed, I went to my "work producer" at PPV and devised a new work plan that didn't involve much travel. I became a data specialist. In this role I managed all the quantitative and qualitative data on our research projects. I still traveled, but less frequently and more locally.

Amid moving and visiting Faster whenever I could, I was also deep in the process of designing a database for a project in Harlem that tracked students from elementary school to college along with their after school and extracurricular activities. I was being as resourceful as I humanly could, given the database developer was in Santa Barbara, California, her partner was located in the UK, the project was in New York, and my ass was in Philadelphia. Shit, organizing the conference calls alone was a nightmare.

The project was an octopus. I told my "work producer" who I was starting to despise when she agreed to take on this endeavor, that it was going to take much more than me to bring this massive undertaking into a viable program assessment tool. And since she didn't listen, every time she asked when it would be done, I would tell her "we need an extension."

Her face would turn beet red and she would storm out of my office, stomping her thick-ankled-ass down the hall back to her "not as busy as my ass," office. I had just gotten so tired of making the impossible possible for them and enough was enough. I was utilizing the power of "not right now and wait for it," efficiently.

The only good thing about this Harlem project was that a site-visit was scheduled the first week in October and it coincided with an event I was attending, featuring the poet. We had somehow developed a new-found friendship and were doing our best to co-parent. I had gotten so tired of fighting him about child support that I chose to take him out of the system and let him live.

Yes, it meant that I was paying for private school, uniforms, class trips and food all on my own. But the poet was a barber by trade so at least I didn't have to pay for haircuts. The trade-off was also greater than just haircuts; I also didn't have to sit in a courtroom trying to retrieve blood from a stone. He wasn't working steadily because he had decided, with my consent, to pursue his poetry career full-time. I believed in his work, he's a great poet, he just wasn't a great husband and if I can be honest, I wasn't such a great wife.

Nevertheless, he had been honing his poet craft. One remarkable night he happened to be in the right place at the right time, when music mogul Russell Simmons was shopping around for poets for his new Def Poetry Jam series. The poet had become one of the moguls' favorites, thus securing him a coveted spot in the line-up. They were scheduled to record their HBO debut show the same day I was scheduled to be in New York to meet with the program team in Harlem. I was excited about the timing, because I'd get to sit in on the taping.

I was really looking forward to the Harlem trip because it was just a train ride away from Philadelphia, and I loved the hustle and bustle of New York City. I was also really excited to sit with the staff of the program and share the progress we were making and walk them through a demo of the tool we had created. I was so very prepared. But then three weeks before my trip on a sunny September day, the two towers at the World Trade Center came tumbling down.

I should've known the day was going to be crazy, because it started off with the poet. He had our son overnight and since he'd brought him back in the morning, I invited him to ride with me to drop him off at pre-school. Since our child support war had ended, we were in a civil place on September 11. and had been that way for a few months prior.

After our son was safely in the school, I dropped the poet off at his girlfriends' house and proceeded to the plantation. While I'm driving towards my designated parking site, I'm listening to the radio and simultaneously channel surfing trying to find some music, because for some reason radio stations think you want to hear talk in the mornings as opposed to music.

As I approached 52nd and Haverford, breaking news came over the air waves from the local radio station Power 99, letting me know a plane had just crashed into a building in downtown New York. My stomach dropped as I flashbacked to recent nightmares I'd been having about a plane crashing into the plantation. A bit shell-shocked by my clairvoyance, eerily I listened to the radio personality telling me in horror that "another plane had flown into a second building in downtown New York." I started panicking because that's now 2 planes, and the shit was sounding too fishy.

My heart pounded and my breath was short as I waited for the next words to permeate the air. Finally, someone at the radio station brought a TV into the DJ booth and both announcers were watching and discussing the catastrophe as it was unfolding. I could not believe my ears. They said two commercial planes had flown into the Twin Towers of the World Trade Center and they were on fire. I almost threw up.

A year ago, to the date of the current events, the poet and I were there, at that same exact time, in that location. I was in New York for a conference hosted by the plantation and our accommodations were at the World Trade Center Marriott. The poet was in town interviewing at this barber shop in Harlem. He figured, if he was going to pursue his poetry career, he had to be in the city that never sleeps. He needed a place to stay the night before the interview and I allowed him to stay in my room. So on the morning of the 11. the poet and I were waking up (in different beds of course, we ain't that cool) in the World Trade Center Marriott, oblivious to the fact that one year later almost to that exact time it would be in flames on its way to extinction.

After having flashbacks of the previous year, and diggin' the fact that I had just been with the poet, I went to the nearest pay phone and dialed him up. When he answered, the first thing I said was "Do you believe this shit?" He said, "Fuck no, but I'm on the phone with my mom. Where are you? I'll call you right back." I told him I was at a payphone outside of Cozy's bar on 51st and Haverford, and there wasn't a number on the phone, but never mind that I was going back to pick up our son from school. He suggested I wait to see how this thing was going to manifest because we didn't want to scare our child if we didn't have to. I agreed because I was starting to become delirious, and I needed some direction.

When I hung up, I went inside the bar because I could hear the news being broadcasted on their TV. There were four people already drinking in the bar and it was 9:30 in the morning. Black folks of course, just some poor souls that had been whipped by the world so bad they needed to get juiced before they faced the day. I wished I'd gotten "juiced" before I saw that television screen.

I could not believe my eyes. It looked like the Devil had taken a bite out of New York's skyline. I was mortified. For the first five minutes I couldn't move…until I realized they were showing the same shit over and over again. That's when I decided to go into work and see what was up at the plantation. White folks seem to know all the bad shit that's going to happen before it happens. I think they get memos. I wanted to see how the "liberals" were adjusting to the news, because if they weren't showing any fear then I knew I shouldn't be believing what I was seeing.

I drove my car to 46th Street and parked. It was weird because it was a beautifully quiet, pretty sky-blue kind of day. The only problem was that I didn't hear any birds chirping. So, I really started tripping. When I approached my regular transportation worker, collecting the fares inside his booth, I immediately informed him on what was going down, because all he does is read the paper. I never saw a radio in the booth. He looked at me as if I was kidding. I told him "No Sir, this is some real shit."

When I reached the plantation, only two people were in the conference room watching the news on the portable television (of course they were Black, and from accounting at that). I stopped and watched for a few minutes, then proceeded to my office. It seemed that all the white people I encountered on my way to my office didn't know that a catastrophic event had just occurred in old New York.

They were either sitting in their respective offices working, or in the break room sipping coffee. So, I gently informed them that they needed to get the fuck up and go to the conference room. Apparently, from the time I saw the footage on the bar TV to the time I walked into that office, the news team had come up with a story that involved men from an Arab nation being responsible for the mayhem, and was earnestly referring to them as "terrorists". After I put my pocketbook down on my desk, I went back to the conference room.

The room was packed when I returned and slowly I'm realizing, as before, we're watching the same thing over and over again, repeats of the planes going into the buildings. Aside from being informed that many people were still in the buildings, it seemed the news reports weren't changing. So instead, they repeatedly drilled the chaos into our psyche one plane at a time, over and over again.

As soon as I started to think it was going to be an isolated incident, the footage was interrupted with breaking news of a plane crashing into the Pentagon in Virginia. My knees started to buckle. It felt like in unison, all of us in the conference room started to realize this was going to be the worst day of our lives, as many of us were visibly shaking.

After five minutes of mind racing questions about what the fuck and who the fuck was really responsible for what my eyes had seen, the first building started to crumble to the ground. Everybody in the conference room took a deep collective patriotic gasp and sighed out bewilderment and angst. As I was about to lace up my Nikes and sprint out that plantation, Diane, whose son happened to work for the Daily News, came into the conference room and said we were shutting the office down because the Mayor was closing the city.

I only heard the "D" in down, because I ran out of that conference room, around the whole office until I was panting outside my office door. I grabbed my bag, my keys and was about to be out, when my office phone rang. It was my mom, calling to check on me and to tell me she was on her way home because they had just been evacuated from the office building she was in. Then the call dropped.

Frantically, I tried to call my mother back because she was calling from her cell phone, but the lines were all messed up. It didn't matter because I would be meeting her at her house, after I picked up my son from his school, because I sure as hell wasn't going to my house. I needed to be with my mama.

After picking my son up from school, who was clueless but excited for the early dismissal, I stopped by my moms and told her to hop in the car, we were going to the liquor store. There was no way we were going to get through this day without alcohol. The store was crowded when we arrived, and everyone was talking about the planes and terrorists and the news. It was so overwhelming.

When we arrived back at my mothers' I poured myself a shot of tequila, rolled up a blunt and went to sit on her back steps. I took my shot of tequila, lit the blunt and leaned from my waist, back onto the step landing so that I was facing the sky. After every exhale of that sensational bud, I thanked God that this tragedy had not occurred one year ago to that day or I would surely not be alive.

As I laid on the landing looking up at the blue sky through sunglasses, I thought of Faster being held in captivity while the whole country lost its damn mind. I thought about what the implications of this tragedy would be on the nation and the state of the union. My mind kept vacillating between Faster in prison and those dead people in New York City.

I thought of the people who worked in the shops under the World Trade Center and if they were able to escape. I was reminded of the blue purse I had purchased in that underground mall at the Gap on this day one year ago, and thought about the salesperson who helped me pick it out and wondered if she survived. Lying on my back, looking up at the sky, finishing my blunt, I closed my eyes, thought about how much I needed Faster at that very moment, but couldn't have him and I cried, hard.

PART III

TRIPPIN' THROUGH FREEDOM

-Freedom Smile-

Normalcy

The next three weeks were a blurry nightmare. For starters, I could not get a hold of Faster as the prisons were in turmoil due to what the news and the nation were referring to as a "terrorist attack". Not only was I not able to communicate with Faster, the plantation had decided that it would be in all our best interest to maintain the status quo and send my traumatized ass to New York to meet with the program staff in Harlem.

I fought hard not to go to New York. I even stated the obvious, "Those people are not thinking about a damn database right now; they are still searching for loved ones." My words fell on deaf ears, because my "work producer" looked me in my face and said, "Crystal, I think they just need to get back to some normalcy, and this will help." I wanted to punch her in the throat.

I never once thought to explain that it was me who wasn't thinking about a database right now, because my mental health was suffering. I didn't want to go to New York. I didn't want to take a train into a city that was literally still smoking. I also couldn't understand why I was still traveling when everyone else at PPV had paused their trips to process their fears.

Ironically, because HBO and the producers of the Def Poetry Jam had invested so much time and money into producing the show, they chose not to cancel. The show would go on! It was great because at least I'd get to experience something phenomenal, even though I was being mind-fucked in the process.

Three days later, with my heart pounding in my chest, coasting upward on the escalator to the street level out of New York's Penn Station, there were countless photos taped on the walls and exits of missing people. There were flowers, candles and shrines everywhere. I could feel my heart breaking and bile rising in my throat as I thought about lives lost and my inconsiderate colleague sending me into this abyss of madness.

When I arrived in Harlem for our meeting, I sat with the staff and said to them, "I know this database is the last thing on your mind right now, so if you want to talk, breathe or simply do nothing, that is fine with me." For the next 2 hours, we did just that; talked about fears, anxiety, resilience, hope, then back to fears, anxiety, resilience and hope. The database was never discussed, and it was alright with me. Leaving the staff, I extended my prayers and headed to Times Square for the Def Poetry taping.

If you've ever been to Times Square in New York, you know it is well lit and full of people and life. On that early fall October evening, you could hear a pin drop. It was haunting. I was so grateful for the bustling of the taping of the poetry show or there would have been no light, love or laughter in that vicinity.

I was also grateful that the taping came fully stocked with alcohol as I made sure to keep my cup full of spirits. I thoroughly enjoyed myself and later learned that my face was edited into three shows that would be aired later that season. Apparently, HBO liked my look because this was now the second time in my life that I was aired, and spotted, as an audience member on one of their shows.

After the taping, the cast and a few other artists including the poet, Dave Chappelle and Cedric the Entertainer, and little ole' me, went to an after party. I'm so glad the drinks were flowing at the taping because the after-party was on 24 and Broadway. Eerily, the closer we drove toward it, the darker the skyline became.

With the falling of those towers, there was no light illuminating from the Financial District. What made the trek even more incredulous was that as we drove past fire and police stations, there were photos of missing service men and women.

My heart broke again for everyone, including myself, and those of us who were trying to remain sane amid the insanity that was New York city.

I couldn't sleep at all when we got back to the hotel after the party. I was crashing with the poet and a few other artists, and since I couldn't sleep, I decided to catch an earlier train back home to Philly. Unfortunately, my anxiety was at an all-time high and I found myself freaking out in the train station. In my fear, I perceived that every unattended backpack had a bomb in it and every person who "looked like" a terrorist was a terrorist.

I had gotten myself so worked up that I convinced myself to not take the earlier train, because what if it had a bomb on it and I wasn't even supposed to be on it and it blew up. No one would know I had died. So, I sat in that train station for two extra hours waiting on my original train while my mind shilly shallied between me dying and not dying in Penn Station.

When I arrived back to work on Monday, I held onto any information related to that damn database. I was pissed about having to go there in the first place, and I would release that information when I got good and damn ready. Finally, after about a week, when my "work producer" asked me for the fourth time if I had any updates on the project, I simply told her "we need an extension!"

The Truth will set you Free!

When I think back on that time after "the attacks," I often remember feeling extremely vulnerable. It seemed that America had become the place that hated everyone foreign, but especially anyone from the middle east. As an American I had my own fear, but I didn't understand what it was like for someone from an Arab nation, until I went to a party in New York a few months after my initial post-911 visit.

My friend Yumn, a Muslim sister whose family had migrated from Pakistan to upstate Pennsylvania, was a research assistant at PPV. When we met, she had just graduated from Bryn Mawr College and was there to sharpen her research skills. We didn't work on any projects together, but somehow our personalities meshed, and I'd find myself in her office shooting the breeze and sharing life stories. She'd share how her family narrowly escaped the war in Pakistan with the clothes on their backs, and I'd share how I narrowly escaped the war on drugs in Philadelphia with my sanity migrating to California. War stories are war stories, and because I felt so comfortable sharing the darkest moments of my life with this woman, an unlikely friendship developed.

Since then she had left PPV a few years' prior to pursue a law degree. In her pursuit, she fell in love with an Egyptian man, married him, and they moved to NYC. They were hosting an annual party and although the country was upside down, I was excited to go.

Over the years, her parties were something I looked forward to. Her friends were diverse, and the atmosphere was not only fun but educational. But this party was extremely different from all the others. It was somber as many of her Arab friends recalled counts of racism, anti-patriotism, and terroristic threats in spaces that were once so welcoming like the grocery store, their neighborhood, and even their workplaces.

It was the first time I was able to empathize with being considered "other" in America and it increased my anxiety. The level of fear that permeated the country was suffocating, and I found myself anxious all the time. I cried a lot and I absolutely did not want to be in a relationship with a man that was in jail. I felt trapped. I felt alone and unprotected, and I also wanted to be free. I guess the free part came from the news constantly telling us that our "freedom" was at risk and we needed to go to war.

I wanted to go to war. I wanted to go to war with Faster, for leaving me out here by myself. When we would talk on the phone for those few minutes, I couldn't articulate my fears to him because I knew that there was absolutely nothing he could do about them or for me. So instead of trying to get him to understand, I started to distance myself.

There's something cathartic about living in a state of constant fear. You get to justify every terrible decision you make. And I was beginning to make some very terrible decisions. Have you ever wondered why there are babies being born in war-torn countries? I'll tell you why, because making love brings some sense of relief to an otherwise catastrophic life.

In my terrified loneliness, I justified the need to be touched. I convinced myself that I needed to feel like I was a part of something larger than me and other than fear. I started hanging out more, missing jail calls and not visiting. I didn't feel connected or whole. What made matters even worse in that moment of incompleteness was that Haroon came home from jail. He had served 10 years of the 10-20 bid he had received in '91.

Because he had to spend 3 of them in a halfway house, he had been home for at least 6 months before I saw him. I happened to be hanging out with one of my closest friends, Mecca, when I received the news. We were riding in her car when she nonchalantly turned to me and said, "Oh yeah, did you know that Haroon's home...have you seen him yet?" I was outdone by the cavalier way she revealed this monumental news, especially since she was fully aware that his incarceration was part of the reason I had left Philadelphia ten years' prior.

I told her, 1) No, I did not know he was home, 2) I had not yet seen him and 3) how fucking long did she know he was home before she decided to tell me! She said she had just heard from the street that he was home. I asked her to drive down 55th Street, as it was still the hub of our Southwest Philly neighborhood, and where Haroon's parents still lived. I knew if he would be anywhere and if I were to run into him, it would be on 55. Street.

As we turned onto the bustling block, I stared into every face anticipating seeing his. I didn't have to wait long. Slowly driving toward Belmar Avenue, I spotted him standing in front of the Chinese American food store. Window rolled down, Mecca pulling up to the curb, I said "Hey Haroonnnnnn!" in a sweet sing-song voice into the night air. There they were, the dimples. As he smiled at me, his dimples danced on his cheeks. I got out of the car, walked over to him and said, "Where's the love, give me a hug baby!" He did as I requested and in that instance, the need to be touched dissipated.

We spent the next 30 minutes catching up in front of the store, with the stench of one-week-old Chinese food grease permeating the air. The smell didn't bother us, it had become the customary aroma of our urban community. We just learned to breathe beyond it.

Mecca left and came back, and I had to force myself to stop talking and leave him when she returned for me. He looked like he had been in a time capsule. His skin was flawless, his body toned and healthy, and his mind was sharp. I had to tell myself, "Do not fuck him. You are in a relationship, even if your mind is telling you that you're not right now."

It took everything in my power not to keep running down 55th Street to see him. I mean I had a man right, a job that was crazy, a son that was entering kindergarten, and a country in turmoil, there was no room in my chaotic life for Haroon. I wasn't ready for that level of remembering or even rehashing all that had occurred to cause the 10-year separation. So, I forced myself to pretend that he was still locked up.

That was until I was hanging out one night with some friends and got a huge dose of reality. I was in a bar having a good ole' time, when a childhood friend approached me. It was a friendly approach. She said she hadn't seen me in so long and was so happy to finally run into me. I told her likewise. She next said, "I mean I haven't seen you since you were about to argue with Faster's baby mom, Anissa." For a second it didn't register because Faster, my Faster, had only 2 baby moms and neither one of them were named Anissa. He did, however, have a young girl that he was fucking when we met, named Anissa.

Imagine my surprise when I elicited more information from my friend about Faster's baby mom, Anissa. She was pregnant when he was in the county jail awaiting trial. He was aware of this and was claiming the baby. I was floored. It didn't help that I was also drunk at the time of receiving this news, because the fury and pain and anger and sadness that overwhelmed me in that bar at that moment was embarrassing.

I couldn't wait to get in touch with that motherfucker. Here I was bidding with this man for two years now and there was a baby that I wasn't aware of. I felt betrayed and stupid.

I sent him a letter telling him that I found out about the baby. He wrote me back stating that he had tried to tell me that there was a possibility this baby was his, when I came up to the prison on that horrible ride with the "van service lady," but I told him, I didn't want to talk about anything "uncomfortable". I was even more livid.

I responded in a follow-up letter with, "Motherfucker, that was a conversation you should have forced me to have!" He finally called and kept apologizing and apologizing, but because I was already looking for an exit, I did not accept his apology and for the next 12 months, lived the care-free single life. I continued to party hard and yes, I fucked Haroon, and it was good. But none of those experiences were enough to clear the clutter in my head that had accumulated with Faster and prison life.

Going Back To Cali

Being free from the constraints of a relationship that involved a prisoner slowly allowed me to see all that I had been missing, like the poet living his best life. He had done well on the Def Poetry

HBO series and remained a favorite of the rap mogul. It led to him being offered a coveted spot in the Broadway rendition of the HBO series. However, before going to Broadway, there needed to be a test run in San Francisco.

Imagine my delight when the San Francisco line-up coincided with our son's 5th birthday. I planned the trip to celebrate the father and the son, but deep down in my soul it was an opportunity for me to leave the east coast for a moment to allow that Cali-living to sink into my spirit and clear my conscience. I needed the sun, the wind, the mountains, the bud and the smiles—Californians always smiled—against my skin, in my lungs and in my view. I needed a damn break.

I decided to fly into San Francisco, spend 3 days there, rent a car and drive the 5 hours to Los Angeles to visit Moonchild, who had just had her first daughter. I had it all mapped out. I would enjoy the fruits of the poets' labor, and then smoke bud down Route 5 to hang out with my homie. Yes, I planned to smoke with my son in the backseat, why not?

This would be my first flight since 9/11 and I had to admit, I was petrified. But there's something about traveling with your child. You have no room for fear. It was as if I was in "I wish a motherfucker would" mode during our entire time in the airport and on the airplane. I do, however, believe having that demeanor exacerbated the experience of traveling out of Philadelphia International Airport because it was chaotic.

The security checkpoint was extremely long, and we had to take off damn near everything—from shoes to jewelry—and my kid did not understand why or wanted to release his Spiderman backpack to be searched at the checkpoint! It was annoying, but after the extensive search, admittedly, I felt safer. The flight was easy and relaxing. I was able to watch a movie and having my son snuggled up beside me eased any tension that was caused by the thoughts of terrorists. I was his protector and we were going to be just fine.

Landing safely in San Francisco, the first thing I noticed was the decreased sense of emergency in the airport. There was no extra security. No dogs, air marshals, and no frantic behavior. People were smiling and moving about as if 9/11 had happened in a country far, far away from the United States and not just 3000 miles away on the East Coast.

Immediately, I eased into the comfortability of Cali. It felt good to not feel my shoulders raised almost to ear-level from constant stress and media reminders of "code orange and code red." Californians in that airport gave me hope about my stay. Deep in my spirit, I knew this was the trip I needed to take to re-center myself. But California has always done that for me, and I knew this time would be no different. It was my every intention to live as freely as humanly possible, given the climate of the rest of the country.

We, my son and I, picked up the rental car and headed to the extended stay apartment where the poet and the rest of the cast were housed. My son was extremely excited to see his father, and I was glad to be relieved of my solo parenting duties even if it was just for a few days. Arriving at the apartment, I was not surprised at the luxury of the accommodations. It was a rather large apartment and had a street view. But beyond the street was the view of mountains to the east and water with the penitentiary, Alcatraz, to the west. I forgot how much I loved San Francisco and in that moment felt like I was in heaven.

Heaven also came in the form of edibles! The poet had a batch of assorted pastries containing a medicinal amount of marijuana in each. There were brownies, carrot cakes, tarts and cookies. I had never had edibles before, and I was eager to try.

That evening the cast had to go to the theater for rehearsal. My son and I were left alone in the apartment. Due to the long flight, and 3-hour time difference, my son was conked out. I on the other hand was salivating over which edible I'd try first. Having been told that the brownie was a classic, I set my eye, hand

and mouth on that one. It did not disappoint. It was absolutely delicious and I didn't even taste the weed. I also didn't notice any significant difference in my behavior or attitude. I just felt extremely relaxed.

An hour later the cast returned. They were all heading to another cast-mates room for a rehearsal wrap party, as the show was scheduled to start the following day. Of course, I was invited. I had met a few from the taping in New York and despite our lows, the poet always talked about his "ex-wife" rather fondly, so they were interested in getting to know me better. But I made one crucial mistake. I hadn't eaten anything other than the brownie, and the munchies were kicking in. With no other food in the poets' apartment other than edibles, I took the rest of the brownie to the wrap-party as my snack.

The next day, I didn't remember shit from the wrap party, was still high, and I hated it. It felt like every time I swallowed, I got high all over again. It was horrible and forced me to make the declaration to never eat edibles again. It was not for me. However, I took a few along on my road-trip from San Francisco to Los Angeles and shared them with Moonchild and her brother.

My son and I had a great time in Los Angeles. We went to Santa Monica pier, walked on the beach and let the water tickle our feet. We went to Universal Studios and enjoyed City Walk. I was happy to be in the company of my friend. She just made life seem possible even though she was experiencing her own hardship—her mother was battling cancer and was currently in the hospital with another setback.

Although I was there to escape my own life, there was no way I could be in Los Angeles and not visit her mother; she was one of my favorite people and always had words of encouragement for me. She even taught me how to make sweet potato pie when I lived in California. Seeing her in the fight of her life was difficult, but she never lost her smile during our visit and for that it gave me hope to tackle any obstacle that I was facing with

Faster, the plantation and my anxiety due to 9/11—which after 9 months was still an issue for me.

Leaving LA to drive back to San Francisco to catch our return flight, Moonchild showed me how to smuggle my weed back on the plane. You see with all that extra-security shit I could no longer just bring weed back in an easy breezy way. She told me to take a maxi-pad, cut the inside, push a bit of padding to the side and place the weed in the pad. After that, put on a pair of panties, then place the pad with the weed in it into another pair of panties and put those on. "It'll be snug, but you'll get your weed back to Philly," she said.

I did as I was told and when I arrived at the airport, I was nervous as shit, especially since I had my son with me. But low and behold, the San Francisco airport could care less about my panties filled with weed. They ushered me and my son on our way and for the entire flight, I felt like I had the best secret ever.

When we arrived back in Philadelphia, I had this over-whelming feeling to quit the plantation. I wanted to be free of all things that reminded me of "being taken advantage of" but I just wasn't sure how. My mother always said, "Don't quit a job unless you have another one" and I didn't have another one, so I had to figure that part out first.

Informal Support

While trying to figure out an exit strategy from the plantation, I was still plugging away at completing the database, and also managing the data of new projects. One project piqued my interest, but not in a good way. It was a Ready4Work initiative focused on helping returning offenders find employment. This project had all the bells and whistles of creating support and opportunities for offenders, but it lacked two key ingredients—empathy and cultural competency.

Sure, all do-gooders think they know the plight of an offender, but if you haven't walked in an offenders' shoes or loved an offender, you don't know anything about helping an offender. I was invited to many of the initial planning meetings, not because they thought I had knowledge of the population, but because I knew how to collect data, and with all PPV projects there was data to be collected. But attending these meetings infuriated me to no-end.

I felt ridiculous sitting there listening to "liberals" talk about what's best for an offender, his children and the community. Especially since I had first-hand experience, and by this time, had no qualms about letting people know that I did. But these people never considered asking me what I thought. I tried my best to keep quiet during those meetings, but one afternoon in New York, I had had enough.

The "team" had been invited to a meeting at a foundation in Manhattan to watch a video with ex-offenders who had gone through a re-entry program. "Re-entry" was the buzzword at the time and there were several re-entry programs springing up across the country. This program was considered a success because of the number of offenders who came through their doors and completed it. Upon release from prison, offenders would enter this program, complete a training, and be offered a minimum wage job in hopes to reduce recidivism.

We were in the meeting watching a video of program participants, when my anxiety started to flare up. This wasn't the "my nerves are bad" anxiety, but the "I'm about to yell obscenities and get fired" anxiety. The video focused on four men, who happened to be Latino and Black, each having one horrific story to tell about their childhood of abandonment and abuse that forced them into the life of crime. The offenses were split between selling drugs and robbery. The men kept referring to the program as "an opportunity to change their life for the better," and that they were "so grateful" for the creation of the program because they didn't want to be in the streets doing anything illegal and risk going back to prison.

As I looked around at the liberals, they were all smiling and seemingly giving themselves virtual pats on the back for creating such an amazing program to help the unfortunates. I, on the other hand, was steaming. Here's why: as the video played out, the men shared endless stories about how upon release they had to go to child support court to find out what their arrears were. Many owed the system thousands of dollars. Although these fathers had employment now, a large portion of their minimum wage paychecks were going to arrears on child support to the county for children who received assistance from welfare during their incarceration.

These fathers also mentioned that because they had little money left over from their paychecks, they could barely afford housing or worse, spend money on the children now that they were home. With little to no money it was causing strife in their relationships with the mothers. Mothers were pissed that the fathers could not "do more." They were pissed that even though the father had a job now, it was still not helping the overall household. So, some of the mothers were still forced to take care of the children on their own.

One father stated that he had a good relationship with his kids' mother. She was working, and he couldn't find a job, so they devised a plan that he would provide the childcare needed for the family while she worked to cut costs. Unfortunately, his Parole Officer told him that he had to find a job to pay back the welfare the mother had received while he was away. He got in the program and lost his family. The mother could not afford working and paying for childcare, so she moved her children to Florida because there was a job available and family there who would watch the children while she worked.

When we got to that portion of the video, the liberals either had their eyes cast down or some were doodling. I was near tears. Because after all the despair in the video, when asked by the interviewer if they thought the program was helpful, all the program participants responded "yes!" I was in a state of shock. For the life of me, I could not understand how the possibility of losing your family would make a program worth participating in. The video ended, and the liberals had a nerve to clap as if it was an academy award winning film. I sat stunned and briefly speechless.

During the questions and answering portion of the meeting I could no longer hold my tongue. I asked one simple question "What about informal support?" The liberals had no idea what I meant so they asked, "What do you mean by informal support, Crystal?" I said, "Well, one of the outcomes you're tracking to measure the program's success is whether or not these fathers pay child support, but are you tracking the other ways these fathers are supporting their child(ren)?"

Again, one of them replied "What do you mean other ways?" I stated, "Well one of the fathers was providing childcare for his family, but was forced to abandon his family in order to work and pay back welfare which subsequently led to him losing his family. Why wasn't the informal support he was giving to his family sufficient enough to satisfy his PO and any old debt owed to the system? Why isn't old debt forgiven once a father is showing that he is present in his children's life? Why isn't old debt forgiven when it's noted that he was incarcerated when the mother was given assistance? Do you think it's better for him to neglect the children he's currently supporting informally, in order to pay back a debt to a system that my tax dollars have already paid for?"

The liberals could not answer any of my questions. So instead, they stated statistics. They started telling me and the room how many men had completed the program. Not cutting them any slack, I asked about recidivism. "How many men have gone back to jail?" I was told they didn't quite have all the numbers yet. I smirked and internally thought to myself, probably half.

I knew in my heart of hearts that there was no way a man who was used to providing for his family could adjust to a minimum wage job that child support or welfare was cutting into without considering other money-making options. I also knew that given the burden prison has on women during their partners' incarceration, these women were not giving a fuck about where the money was coming from, they just needed time and a place to rest their weary feet. So, if it wasn't cash then yes, daddy, watch these damn kids! But the system and this program was saying, that's just not enough.

I was so frustrated after leaving that meeting that I knew it would be the last one I attended for a while. When I returned to our office in Philadelphia, I didn't have the appetite for any philanthropy work. I just didn't believe in it anymore and it was all PPV's fault.

It had been 8 years and I could not help but think about all the pain that I experienced in that place. For it to have been such a small staff, there was a lot of death there. Death due to cancer, a colleague perished after a heart transplant, another at childbirth, and one death was a murder suicide. In all that loss, I had also lost my desire to hear the accolades of all the data that I was able to collect.

If I had a grade for every time a researcher said to me in the field, "Crystal, we would have never been able to elicit that data if you hadn't been here," I would have surely left that plantation a graduate with a degree. But I didn't. I was tired of studying populations that looked like me, mirrored my dysfunction, yet reaped no benefit from the research being conducted other than, being over-surveillanced and reported on to funders and policy makers who only cared about proving their theories correct—that the disadvantaged were still disadvantaged.

With all that frustration vibrating inside me, I started coming to work late and leaving early. I'd smoke weed before I came to work or during my lunch break, then get back to the office and go home early. I was at my wits end and my last-ditch effort to salvage my sanity proved beneficial to my spirit.

My colleague was the former Mayor of Philadelphia. He had been the first Black Mayor of the city. Although he was considered a dignitary in the city, he still had a passion for social service work and partnered with the plantation on furthering his agenda to establish a mentoring program for children of the incarcerated. I really liked the former Mayor. Each time I'd see him and ask how he was doing he would respond "I'm excellent!" I loved how he responded as if the tragedy involving the MOVE members never occurred on his watch. He definitely showed me perseverance despite circumstances.

One early evening toward the end of the workday, I stopped by his office and asked if I could have a word with him. He invited me in to have a seat. Sitting, I immediately said, "Dr. Goode, I am struggling here." I told him how I felt used and abused by all my work responsibilities and poor pay. I told him about the degree bullshit, of course without curse words, and how I was losing my desire to work in the non-profit sector. I told him how I thought that the liberals were racist and that I was sick of being the token Black person going out on site visits collecting data from people that only looked like me, and who's trials resembled all of mine growing up in the "hood." I told him that if I didn't quit that job soon, I'd lose my damn mind.

He listened intently and as I finished, he told me, "Crystal, this is what we are going to do. For the next 5 days we are going to pray together at 6am. I will be where I am, and you will be where you are, but we will pray at that time together each day. I know that when our prayer time is over, you will have the answer you need to make the best decision for you."

For 5 days I did exactly what the former Mayor suggested, and each day I felt a renewed sense of support. It felt good to know that someone was praying for my mental health and overall emotional well-being. When our prayer week was over, I knew the next step to take.

I went to my primary care doctor and got a note stating that I was stressed and needed to take some time off. I was out of work for two weeks. In those two weeks my favorite coworkers were reporting out on what was going on at the job. They told me that there were 5 people doing my job, and they could not believe how I had done all that work by myself. I could care less. I knew that I would not be working there much longer.

Kelly Drive

When you break a limb, you immediately go to a hospital for treatment. But when you feel like your mind is breaking, many of us are reluctant to seek treatment. I found myself going stir crazy and knew that if I didn't seek mental health treatment, I would surely lose every bit of the mind I had worked so hard to keep sane. Before I left the plantation for my two-week hiatus, I made an appointment with a therapist located in downtown Philly.

I arrived early for my appointment, as there was a ton of paperwork to fill out. The therapist was a middle-age white woman with many degrees on her wall. Her office smelled of lavender, and was neat and inviting. I was nervous and excited all at the same time. Although this would be my first time telling a clinical stranger that I was feeling nuts, I was eager to see what recommendations she could give that may help me figure out if I should stay or leave the plantation.

After filling out the paperwork, she took it and started to read over my responses right there, right in front of me. I knew this was protocol, but there were answers to questions that I wasn't prepared for her to see until she at least talked to me for a few minutes. Questions like, "Have you ever thought of hurting yourself or others?"

She read my responses, looked up and smiled at me. I smiled back. She said, "Crystal, what brings you here today?" For the next hour I told her about my mothers' crack addiction, the homicide that took Sweet and changed my life, California, the poet, motherhood, Faster and finally that fucking plantation and how taken advantage of I felt and that I was losing my damn mind.

She convinced me that I wasn't losing my mind, but that I had every right to feel what I was feeling because some very bad things have happened in my life that were beyond my control. She said that when bad things happen to a person that is beyond their control, they feel either compelled to control everything or have no desire to control anything. She said I fell into the category of trying to control everything "and that my dear" was not my responsibility. My only responsibility was to accept personal accountability for what I put into and take out of the world, not what others put into or take out.

I found that extremely hard to accept because I felt like others should be held accountable for their actions as well. She assured me that I was correct, and they should be, but I could not control whether that happened or not. She said, "The moment you realize you are only responsible for your part of taking care of the world, the world will start to take care of you, as long as your intentions are in the right place. And, Crystal, your intentions are in the right place." I then asked her, "Well, what about the job?" She responded, "You'll figure it out!"

For the next three days I went to the water to "figure it out." There's a place in Philadelphia called Kelly Drive. It is absolutely spirit settling. I discovered the place by happenstance. I was traveling to work one morning in heavy traffic and decided to detour onto an alternative road that would lead me into the center of the city. On this road, there was the Schuylkill river on the right, with a bike and walk path and lush green grass. On the left were exits toward Fairmount park.

My eyes were fixated on the river as there were rowers scattered throughout. I could not believe that this gem was in the heart of the city, a city that I had experienced so much pain in, a city still besieged with violence, drugs and crime, and I had never seen it nor knew it even existed. I made a mental note from that day forward that I would get down there as often as possible because the allure of the Drive was pulling at my spirit and the Scorpio water sign in me. With this work/life balance crisis unfolding, I knew the water and the Drive was exactly what I needed and would serve me well.

The first day I arrived at the water, after meeting with the therapist, it was 24 degrees outside. It was freezing and the wind coming off the water made the temperature feel as if it was in the teens. I had on sweatpants with long Johns underneath, a long sleeve tee-shirt with a hooded sweatshirt over it, a bomber vest and a pair of Nikes. I also had on a skull cap to protect my forehead and ears from the elements. I started my walk from Lloyd Hall and continued on the path toward the Girard Avenue bridge, which was about one-mile one-way.

As I walked, I thought about my life up until that point. I thought of all that I'd accomplished without a degree. I thought about the prisoner who, although I hadn't communicated with in months, I still loved. I thought about how miserable I was at the plantation and how it was important for me to leave in order to save my life. I thought about all the research I had conducted across the country, the surveys I created, the interviews, the traveling, the airports, the participants and the lives that were barely changing. I even thought about the poet, who was now married again to a woman who I actually liked and was a great support during this time of work-life turmoil. Finally, I thought of my mother who was really concerned about my mental health and told me that even though I didn't have another job, I needed to figure out a way to leave that job because she could see that it was driving me crazy.

When I completed my walk that first day, I still didn't have a plan, but I felt less stressed. On the second day, I started out at Lloyd Hall again, but this time I walked a mile further to the Strawberry Mansion bridge and then turned back around. This longer walk gave me more time to receive and release thoughts. It also gave me an opportunity to see more of the Drive that I had missed by stopping only a mile and a half up at the Girard Avenue bridge the day prior. Taking in the water and the few people on the trail, I knew I was getting close to a revelation that was deep inside me.

On the third day, with temperatures in the upper 40's, I was in the middle of another prayer, asking God to reveal which course of action I should take and to order my steps, when the walk birthed my plan. I was returning from the farthest point I had traveled in those three days combined, Falls Bridge, when my spirit said, "You have all the tools you need to create your own reparations proposal!" As I continued to walk back toward Lloyd Hall, the content of the proposal became clearer and clearer.

I told myself that I'd create a win/win situation. You see, the plantation was known for paying people to leave. Normally these payoffs came in the form of layoffs when projects ended, and grant funds dried up. But even without the layoffs they were known to get rid of people who no longer served their agenda. In the 8 years that I had been employed there, I had always served their agenda and was never threatened with a layoff, even though I prayed for it each time it happened.

As I walked by the water, I knew that I had to develop a proposal that at the core of it, had my best interest at heart. I would ask for a title change since I was doing the work of 5 different people. I would ask for a salary increase since I was doing the work of 5 different people and my finances could use the boost. Finally, I would ask for more staff, again, since I was doing the work of 5 different people.

In my reparations proposal, I would also include job and salary comparisons as well as my performance reviews over the past 3 years to prove my case. I knew that if they didn't agree to all that was included in the proposal they would figure out a way to let me go, especially since I was already out on "stress leave" and eventually would be a liability at some point in the near future. To me, this was the best win/win scenario for all of us. Either give me what I want and I stay or pay me to leave. After figuring it out, I told God if this works, I will give everything I learned at that damn job away for free. I would volunteer somewhere to show the Creator that I was grateful!

I went back home and for the next two days I wrote my proposal. I was scheduled to return to work the following Monday, and knew that I'd have to get the proposal in by Wednesday of the current week so that the "liberals" would have time to review it before I went back. In my mind, I would have an immediate response to this masterpiece of a proposal.

That Wednesday after 6pm, when all the staff had gone home for the day, I went into the office and placed a copy of the reparations proposal on the Presidents' desk, his secretary's chair, the desk of the VP of Research, the CFO and my "work producer." I was nervous as hell but satisfied with myself for taking this bold step toward my freedom. After I left the office, I went to my mothers' house to brag about what I had done, and she was proud.

It took the plantation two weeks to respond to my proposal and during those two weeks, I was a complete asshole in that workplace. I wasn't updating anyone on assignments. I would attend meetings and literally stand the entire time, even though there were plenty of seats in the room. I was entertaining heavily in my office and always had Jill Scott blasting out of it. My "work producer" was absolutely sick of me and when she stormed out of my office after one more "we need an extension" on a project conversation, I knew shit was about to hit the fan.

Five minutes later the CFO came to my office. She wanted to chat with me about my behavior with my colleagues. I told her, as she stood in my doorway, "I find it interesting that you want to talk to me about that but not about the proposal I left on your desk two weeks ago." Her face turned crimson as she responded, "Oh, oh, I'm sorry, we are still working out the logistics on that, someone will be getting back to you shortly." I said to her, "Well until that happens, there's nothing further to discuss!" Fifteen minutes later, the president was calling my office line. He asked me if I was available to meet the next day, a Wednesday, to discuss the proposal. I told him, absolutely. We chose 11am as the meeting time.

The following day, I came dressed as a professional. Normally, I'd dressed casually, since it was essentially a laid-back work environment. But this day, I wanted him to know I meant business. I knew the meeting was going to be intense, since he was a Yale lawyer by trade. I knew he'd get me in his office and try to lawyer-me-up, so I mentally prepared for him.

There would be no small talk on my part, because I had to follow his crafty ass word for word to see where my future was heading. Don't get me wrong, he wasn't such a bad guy; he had been a great institutional leader over the past five years. But, he was also the person who denied my proposal to pursue a college education, so I definitely had mixed feelings about him.

Right before my meeting, my office phone rang. It was my mother. She asked if I had had the meeting yet and I told her that I would be heading there in 15 minutes. Her only words to me were "go get dey asses!" A smile spread across my face as I hung up with her, knowing that whatever the outcome was, I had her blessing to leave.

The presidents' office was pretty extravagant with a private bathroom. It wasn't my first time in there. Since he had one of the only two couches in an office, during my pregnancy I would sleep on it from time to time. Nevertheless, this meeting was happening regardless of how good he had been to me during my pregnancy.

As I sat across from him, he started the meeting by asking how my two-weeks out of the office had been for my mental health. I told him, "Fantastic, it helped me clear my head in order to see all that I had been doing at the job and how overwhelming my responsibilities were, which is why I wrote the proposal." He said "Yes, the proposal. Crystal it was really well written and organized." I told him, "Yes, I learned a lot here." Making a dig toward the fact that he did not support me going to college. His response, "I can see."

He then rambled on about how I was asking for a lot of "stuff" in the proposal, all of which were within reason; however, it would never happen in the timeframe that I would probably like. I continued to listen, waiting for the pitch. He continued with, "Perhaps you're interested in pursuing other goals outside of PPV." I didn't blink, so he continued, "If there is other work that you are interested in, outside of PPV, perhaps we can help you with that endeavor, I mean we would make sure you left here with compensation, to pursue those other goals…" Finally, I said "I would like that!"

He had been rambling so much that he wasn't sure what I was agreeing to. So, he said "What would you like?" With a slight smile on my lips I said, "I'd like to pursue other goals, outside of PPV, with compensation of course." His face lit up! He was about to be free of the problem child. He started promising me everything including the kitchen sink.

I would receive reparations in severance pay for each year that I'd been there, and they offered to pay for my health insurance for the next 6 months. I would also be able to collect unemployment immediately after my last day of work. I agreed to the terms, and he asked me when I'd like my last day to be. I told Mr. President "This Friday, and I will come back in two weeks to clean out my office." He agreed, shook my hand and told me it had been a pleasure working with me. Two days later, after signing an agreement that I would not sue the organization for mental distress, I left PPV with a hefty five-figure check and my freedom.

Emancipation

For the first couple weeks I was in shock that my reparations proposal had worked. I would wake up every morning thinking I had to go to work, but then a few seconds later realize that that part of my life was over, and I'd smile. I was so incredibly happy with my life. I had financial freedom and endless possibilities. I attempted to start a magazine with my former colleagues and friends, but that became overwhelming almost immediately, so I gave it up. I was not interested in living a stressed life, and anything that resembled stress was not welcome in it.

I was in love with everything about living. I was going to the Drive every day, sometimes in the morning alone or in the evening with my son just to walk and take in the river breeze. In the morning I'd get there early, park at the Girard Avenue bridge and take my trusty hula hoop out of my car, and hula hoop for 15 minutes before I walked. I know I looked crazy because no other 33-year-old was out there, hula-hooping. But I didn't give a damn, I was free.

Living in my freedom I realized I had to stop smoking weed and drinking. Shortly after being emancipated from the plantation, I was on my way to visit my cousin's church and experienced a panic attack. Fortunately, I wasn't driving, but was about to leave my house when an overwhelming sensation started to course through my body. It felt like my heart was about to pound out of my chest, my head became dizzy, and the room started to spin.

I sat on the couch and started praying. I kept asking God to still my heart and my mind. Since my first panic attack at the amusement park almost 12 years' prior, I had learned a lot about panic attacks. I knew that you had to take control of your breathing in order to regulate your heart. Between prayers, that's exactly what I did, breathed deeply. I closed my eyes and kept asking God to steady me. After about 6 minutes the panic attack was over, and I was exhausted. However, I still managed to make it to church, but on that day decided to give up my "crutches" until my anxiety realized that I was free of stress and that my mind could relax.

Being drug free for the first time without stress attached to it, was the remedy for clarity. My life felt much better and after three years of sitting on a virtual shelf collecting dust, the idea of starting a van service re-entered my mind. The vision became clearer with each passing day.

I would go on the Drive and envision the service. I saw the van, the families and the road. It seemed that every time I would be thinking about the van service a Philadelphia Sheriff's van would pass by either on its way or coming from the Criminal Justice Center transporting brothers to and from court. I saw it as a sign that now was the time to create what had been lying dormant inside of me for far too long. It was time for me to hunker down, write my business plan, and start my prison van service.

During the day I would write and during the evenings I'd go to my mothers' house to eat and chill until she put me and my son out. Like I said, life was good. It was so good that I was starting to miss Faster again. His mother had reached out to me a few months prior to tell me he was headed home, and shortly after that, he had also reached out to me.

Although in my mind I had resolved the whole baby issue, I still ignored his correspondence. But my spirit told me it was time to reconnect with him. So, I wrote him a letter and told him that I wanted to visit. He responded almost immediately and shared he had hoped I'd write to him soon, because he missed me and would love for me to visit. That news felt good to my soul.

No longer interested in taking a "van service", I rented a car and drove to Rockview to visit Faster a week after hearing from him. The visit went as expected. He was excited to see me, and it showed in his hug. We sat and talked about the baby shit for a second, because at that point the impact of him having a baby had resolved itself.

He'd have to take a blood test when he hit the streets to see if the child was his and since his release date wasn't scheduled until later that year, there was no use in me getting worked up over it in that visiting room. We then talked extensively about the van service. He said he had been thinking about it the entire time he was up there and couldn't wait to come home to partner with me on it. I told him about my emancipation from the plantation and he was hyped about how I did it.

I then told him that I was noticing a change in my mother. She just didn't seem to have that passion for life that she'd previously had. I knew her life had changed drastically in the past 3 years; the factory she had worked in for 28 years closed as the owners had decided to export their work to Mexico. She had a fruitful experience there, especially after her addiction.

She had become a union delegate and traveled a lot representing textile workers across the country. Her salary had been great, and she was highly respected for not only the work she produced, but the support she gave to her coworkers through the union. When the job ended, she went back to school and received her GED.

She graduated summa cum laude and my Uncle Vernon, my son, his daughter and I were all in attendance at her graduation. She now worked at a Black-owned parking ticket processing company in downtown Philadelphia that she enjoyed. But something was changing with her and I just couldn't put my finger on it.

I told him that since I couldn't figure out what it was, I had been up her ass relentlessly trying to. I spent all the time that she would allow me to, with her. We would go to the movies, lunch, get manicures and pedicures, and often spend time on the Drive together. I loved soaking up her energy. She could make me laugh even when life was nuts.

Although she was funny as ever, she had stopped doing some of the things that she used to do, like going to church. Every time I would invite her to go with me on a Sunday, she would say shit like, "I heard all that stuff before, I'ma sit this one out." I was perplexed but I knew that there was no way to get her to do something she wasn't interested in, so I left it alone.

As our visit came to an end, I told Faster that he and I were good. There would be no more bad blood between us, and I promise to keep the lines of communication open. I would keep him informed on the van service and that it felt great to have my friend back. We hugged on the departure and I headed back down route 322 excited about starting the service.

PART IV

TRIPPIN' THROUGH HEARTACHE

-Ms. Yvonne circa 1970-

Ms. Yvonne

A month after my visit with Faster, my mother had another heart attack. She was at work and wasn't feeling well, so she took a cab to the University of Pennsylvania Hospital. She called me as she was headed there. I was sitting in a local bookstore working on my business plan and at the sound of her breathless voice, gathered my things and drove over to the hospital. She had been admitted immediately and placed in a room.

When I arrived, I expected to see a hellish scene, but my mother was in her bed running her mouth. I was so relieved to see her talking and requesting things. Her face lit up when she saw me, and I knew she would be alright. I stayed with her that evening as long as I could and when visiting hours were over, I promised to return in the morning after I got my son off to school.

The next morning as I approached her room, I heard her arguing with the nurse. When I walked in the room, she was stating that she didn't want to spend another day in that damn hospital. She felt much better and was ready to leave.

The nurse had been telling her that she needed to have a procedure to check to see if there were any more blockages in her arteries. Apparently, her cholesterol was extremely high and her blood pressure wasn't coming down. I listened intently with concern as my mother, making side glances at me, finally agreed to the procedure and was wheeled out of the room.

An hour later, she was being wheeled back in. She was a bit groggy but lucent. I asked how she was feeling, and she expressed her discontent with all the poking and prodding. I just lent her my ear, because I had no idea what she was going through physically or emotionally. I just knew that it was getting on her nerves and I wanted to do whatever I could to help. There wasn't anything I could do but sit and wait for the results of the test.

I let my mother doze off while I watched her sleep and stole glances at the television. She had always been a feisty number. Always overcoming the unthinkable. Never knowing her father, the only girl of 3 boys, she'd had a rough road to navigate.

Her mother Mildred had died when my mother was 19, from a heart attack, in her sleep. A year prior to that, her oldest brother, Nate, at the tender age of 18 had killed himself playing Russian Roulette. In the midst of dealing with that trauma, she had to escape an abusive marriage, birthed her first daughter who died one month later from yellow jaundice, on her very own birthday.

So, my mother had been through a whole lot before I was conceived and seeing her resting in that hospital bed, I felt sad for her. Sad that she'd always had to be the father and the mother to me. Sad that she couldn't just enjoy being a woman, taken care of the way women should. I was sad that she had to work so hard, at everything. I was sad that she was sick, and I knew that her health was a direct result of all the pain she'd had to carry with her for the past 56 years of her life and I couldn't shake that sadness. I allowed my mother to sleep and after a couple hours I nudged her awake to let her know I was leaving to pick my son up from school. She groggily stated, "ok" and I departed.

When I arrived the next morning, she was at it again, ripping a new one into the nurse. I learned they wanted to run another set of tests that could have resulted in putting a stint in one of her arteries. She was adamant about not having "one more got-damn procedure."

As I listened, it became obvious that my mother had another heart attack during the night. It was slight, but it showed on the EKG and the doctors were worried about her. But the more they tried to convince her to have the procedure the more she fought and said she just wanted to "go the fuck home!"

Finally, they gave in and discharged her with a few recommendations: no smoking, no dairy, no stress and plenty of rest. They also told her that if she felt congested or any signs of a cold at any point, to immediately come back to the hospital. As my mother and I prepared for her release, I told myself that it was her choice to leave or stay, literally and figuratively, and I'd have to accept whatever she chose.

She remained out of work for the entire month of June and we had a ball. It felt so good being able to go to matinees' and lunches with her. Although she was healing quite nicely, she had not stopped smoking those funky ass cigarettes and I also noticed that she had even started to include vodka in her diet again. I tried not to "mind her business" because one thing Ms. Yvonne hated was somebody in her damn business, even if it was me. So instead, I just kept my eye on her, and my mouth shut.

Besides, I was in love again with Faster, and my heart was so full of possibilities that I knew with a lot of prayer, my mother would be just fine. I, on the other hand, needed to complete my prison transportation business plan so that I could get my show on the road. Faster was coming home that September and I wanted everything in place upon his arrival so that we could live happily ever after.

I spent most of my days at the local chain bookstore putting the pieces of the business plan together. The writing process was liberating. It was helping me put my journey with Faster into perspective. I was discovering so much about myself while writing that plan. I discovered that for starters, I knew what the hell I was talking about.

I understood the ins and outs of the Philadelphia and Pennsylvania prison system, and I knew that this business would be a viable resource to not only families but communities as a whole.

I felt that with family visits, I would surely have the capacity to reduce recidivism. I also knew that if I was going to create this service, I would need to create something for children impacted by incarceration.

I had been sitting on an idea for quite some time that involved the former Mayor's mentoring program. His program provided faith-based (active churchgoers) mentors for children whose parent(s) were incarcerated. It was a great idea, but I couldn't help but think of those children who weren't able to be placed with a mentor. Who was providing them with support? I then started to devise a plan to serve those children. Those children would be mentored by their own father, inside the institution. I sat with that thought for a while and finally developed a concept paper on this new-found initiative. I then called the former Mayors' secretary to get on his schedule to meet with him about the idea in hopes that he would consider it as an adaptation to his already successful program.

I was on a roll! Not only did I initiate that meeting with the former Mayor scheduled for the third week of July, but also remembering the promise I made to God about giving away my talents for free if he released me from the plantation, I contacted an arts-based non-profit, the Art Sanctuary, about volunteering. I had learned about their work while at PPV. Diane had been a financial sponsor of their programs and spoke highly of the work they were doing in the community, and I knew they would be the first on my list to volunteer with.

I was formal about my method of contacting them. I called first to see if they needed volunteers. The young lady who oversaw all volunteers, stated that "we can always use volunteers." I told her my background in research and knowledge of community-based programs, and she asked me to send them my information. I wrote a cover-letter and mailed it in with my resume. I knew the odds were good that they would use me because, why not?

Between scheduling meetings, going to the Drive to keep my head cleared, exercising, keeping an eye on my mother and trying to volunteer, I was heavily engrossed in writing the business plan. I was conducting research on other van services in the area. There were approximately two that were legal, and one was run by a non-profit organization with a 100-year history of fighting for the human rights of inmates and their families. I was intrigued by their model and made a mental note to use them as a resource at some point.

Also, since I had only traveled to the upstate prisons of Camphill and Rockview to visit Faster, I researched the other institutions in the state for distance and population. I was interested in finding out how many inmates in those institutions were from the Philadelphia area so that I'd know which ones to add to my transportation list. In conducting that portion of research, I connected with the Pennsylvania Department of Corrections Research and Statistics Department. They were extremely helpful, partly because I had informed them on why I needed the data and they were excited that I wanted to start this business. Their reasoning was simple, "those guys need family support!"

I was happily plugging away at the business plan and enjoying my lazy days, when two months after her heart attack and on one hot summer day in July, Ms. Yvonne died in her sleep.

Without her Breath!

-An excerpt from a Journal Entry: August 2003-

God moved my Rock. He removed my mother from my life and my heart is broken. She died on July 23, 2003 and I haven't been able to think straight since. I'm trying though because I know it's His will. I've been in a fog, simply trying to see my hands in front of my face and for the life of me I just can't. The tears keep my vision blurred.

You see, I don't cry because God did his work. I cry because I now know more than ever that God is real. He's marvelous, a miracle worker, a provider, and a generous loving God. He gave me 33 years of instruction under the leadership of Ms. Yvonne and I will forever be blessed for having her as my teacher.

He took her in her sleep, just like he did with her mother. People like to say he comes like a thief in the night, but I don't consider him a thief if he's taking what's already his. He also allowed me to be the last person she talked to before she went to Him.

It's funny too because I didn't talk to her at all the day before, but she called me at about 9:30pm on Tuesday the 22nd to have me check on something for her in the morning and to see how my meeting with Dr. Goode went. I told her it was cancelled and that it was God's Will because he probably wasn't prepared to hear what I had to say that day anyway. She agreed, and said, "Don't worry about it, when the time is right you'll be able to get that youth program developed".

We talked shit about this war between America and everybody else, and how the media were publicizing the killing of Suddam Hussein's kids. We both agreed that the end of the world was closing in on us, so we'd better live it up! She said she'd quit smoking cigarettes for real this time, but she was congested, coughing and wheezing and was tired. I asked her if she was cool, and she said, "Um hum, that's just what happens *when you quit smoking." She told me she'd call me in the morning from work to find out the outcome of my investigation (I was checking on some money for her) because she was tired and was going to bed. It's strange because even though she was talking about being congested, coughing and wheezing, she was still funny as hell and full of energy that night on the phone.*

So, at 9am on the 23rd I made the call and found out the news, which wasn't good. I was upset that I was going to have to report it back to her, but I called her on her cell phone several times and got no answer. I waited all day to hear from her; I even called my aunt, who she worked with to see if she had been at work that day. My aunt said she didn't see her that day, but it didn't mean she hadn't been there. Finally, at 7:15pm, I didn't feel easy having not reached her all day. I gathered up my boy and told him we were going to Grandma's house. He was cool with that because we'd been hanging out so much together these past 6 months that it was second nature to get up and go over there.

I had that feeling though. I had that feeling that my mother was not alive anymore. You just know! You feel it, then you try to quickly push it out of your head because you know it's considered the unthinkable. But somewhere deep inside of me, as I drove over to her house I knew. Just that past Sunday evening, she, my son and I went to Kelly Drive to do some walking and as we drove back to her house, I told her ... "Mommy I'm living in the year of Jesus right now, God is preparing me for something...I don't know what it is, but he's preparing me for something, He took the taste of weed and liquor out of my mouth and he's getting my focus back...I just know he's preparing me for something big." And she responded "um hum, maybe He is" real slow like she had that feeling too.

We were that close you know. Ms. Yvonne and I. Close enough to feel the end together. So, as I traveled the short distance from my house to her house on the 23rd , I asked God, "Is this it God, is this what you've been preparing me for?" When I drove on the block, the uneasiness was thick in my central nervous system, and I could hardly get out of the car. Luckily the children were out playing on the block, and my son jumped out the car and started playing. I walked up to the house, quickly. The door was locked, which was unusual; it's summertime and every time she came home, she'd leave her front door open. My hands were shaking, as I slipped the key in the lock. As soon as I pushed the door open, I knew my mother was gone.

Her door keys were the first thing I saw lying on the dining room table and her pocketbook was upright in the chair. As I surveyed the room, I saw her cell phone and teeth (she wore dentures) lying neatly on the living room table. I called her name and waited a second for a response. That's when I just said to myself, "Crystal your mother is in this house, you gotta go upstairs." So, I ran up the steps calling out "Mom-may". As soon as I got to the top landing, I saw her.

She was lying across her bed, in her nightgown, on her side, head resting on her pillow, with the fan pointed towards her face. I walked in the room, stood in front of her, called her name again, praying she was asleep. She didn't respond. I then touched her arm. She was ice cold and moist. I stepped back and leaned against her dresser and looked at her stomach to see if she was breathing. She wasn't. That's when I said out loud, "My motherfucking mother is dead in this house." No, it wasn't a spiritual thing to say but that's how she and I talked, we said the real shit, and the real shit was that I could not take care of her with my son on that block.

So, I walked out of her bedroom, ran down the stairs, closed the front door behind me, locked it, sat for a second on her front steps, called my Uncle Vernon and told him she was gone. I could hear the shock in his voice—his only sister and favorite person in the entire world was gone. I then called the poet and told him I was bringing our son to his house because my mother was gone. He was shocked and also wasn't in town, but his new wife was there, so he told me to take him straight to his house. I then walked up the street to get my child. I told him I needed to make a run and he had to go to his dad's. He was complaining the whole time, asking why he couldn't stay with Grandma while I made my run. I simply told him that he couldn't and let's go.

I dropped him off with his new stepmom and drove back to my mother's house. As I traveled back, I kept telling myself, maybe she was asleep, maybe she was asleep, she might have still been asleep. Then I said, "No Crystal, this is the real shit, get it together... " So I steadied my mind and drove back on the block, parked the car and went into the house.

As soon as I walked back into her home, I grabbed the phone and called 911. After that I ran in the basement to get a blanket to put over my mother because she had a habit of sleeping in the smallest nightie with no panties on. I didn't want the paramedics coming in and the first thing they saw when they got to the top of the steps was her big naked ass. She was a classy broad and I wanted to keep her that way. I didn't cover her up like she was gone, I just covered her up from the waist down because she looked so peaceful lying there like that, and I didn't want it to be a morbid scene.

The fire department and paramedics came almost as soon as I called. The station was right around the corner, but I was still shocked at their swift arrival. When they walked in, I sat on the couch. They asked me where my mother was, and I told them she was upstairs in her bedroom. They quietly walked up the steps. After about 5 minutes, one officer walked down and asked me if there had been any signs of forced entry, I smiled and said "No officer. Are you asking me that because she's naked from the waist down?" He nodded and then said "Yes, but it's also protocol."

I told him I understood and said, "She always slept like that." He then asked me if she had been under a doctors' supervision. I stated, "yes she had" and explained that she had recently had her second heart attack. The paramedics then came down as I was stating that and asked for the doctors' information. I gave it to him. He then told me that, because she was under doctors' supervision, there was no sign of forced entry and it appeared that she died of natural causes, there would be no need to take her to the city morgue, which again was protocol that I had never heard of. Instead, they would contact the doctor and have the doctor sign the death certificate over the phone, which would then allow me to immediately call a mortuary to have them take my mother away.

They stayed for a while gathering the information and contacting the doctor, while I sat on the couch trying to gather my thoughts. I could not believe that my mother was upstairs without her breath. I could not believe how peaceful she looked. I could not believe that she was gone. I could not believe that I was without a mother. But for some reason, I could not cry.

Instead I called my girlfriend Pocah, she came with her daughter LaLa, my Uncle Vernon showed up with his daughter, my other uncle who I hadn't seen in 20 years came, my two aunts and my cousin on my fathers' side, as well as my good friends Mecca and Jewel also came. Those who could stomach seeing death went up and sat with my mother while I contacted the funeral home to have her removed from the house.

It was weird because the strength God provided for me that day was incredible. I had no problem going up and down the stairs and sitting with my mother, and finally crying over her, talking to her and making promises to her that I knew I could keep. I told her that I would take care of my son regardless of the support from his father. I would start that van service. I would take care of the home she worked hard to purchase. I would continue to walk in her light because I loved her. I truly felt that her spirit was still in that room, and she was listening to me as she laid there, motionless and without her breath.

I'm not ashamed to say this. I was in love with my mother. The kind of love that you hold for the most-high. I saw those God-like qualities in my mother. I saw the plight of Jesus in my mother. The struggles, the triumphs, the victories, the glory, the faith, the grace, the mercy, the endurance, the pain, and the fulfillment of prophecy. My mother was the epitome of all things good and bad and I loved every part of her from the resemblance of our hands, as I looked at them while she laid in state in her bedroom, to our same sense of style and the swagger in our hips. God allowed my mother to give me all the good shit of her, the brains, the wit, the attitude, the charisma and the strength. Because had I not seen my mother overcome so many obstacles, I would not have been able to handle seeing her laying there without her breath.

It was hard, and it still is. I think about her constantly. I was able to grant her wishes of cremation, along with having the most joyous memorial service in the land. Because my mother was not a fussy type, I knew this service had to be done right. There would be no sad music and it would be held in the evening so that no one had to miss a day's work. It was a celebration of her life and there would be nothing less than hugs and love served at the ceremony.

Although it turned out exactly as intended, I must admit I almost did not make it to the service. I had finally gotten dressed and made it to the car. I placed my hands on the steering wheel at 2 and 10'oclock but could not move. I closed my eyes and said to myself "I can't do this." As soon as I said "this" my eyes fluttered open, I turned toward the passenger seat and saw the beautiful blue velvet urn case and said to myself "shit, I have to go, I have the got-damn urn!" It was at that point that I actually laughed as I pulled out my parking space and headed to the church.

As I drove, I thought about all the help I had that week leading up to the service. My sister who I had been estranged from, came back into my life and took my son for me. It was good having her back in my life, but it was so difficult to tell my son that his Grandma was gone. The poet and I decided that we would do it together. As we walked up my sister's porch steps, my son was coming out of the house with his scooter.

When he saw the two of us approaching, the look of worry that came over his face was undeniable. He knew something was wrong, especially since the two of us were together, as we had not been in a good place recently. As my son looked frantically into both of our faces, I slowly and as compassionately as I could, told him that Grandma had gone to heaven. My soon to be six-year-old knowing child dropped his scooter, fell into his fathers' arms and cried out "Why?" We could only tell him the truth. Her heart had stopped working and it was time for her to go to God. I honestly did not know that he would take it so hard, but then I had to remember she was his favorite person and he was hers and this hurt.

Aside from my sisters' support, there was so much more. My Uncle Vernon paid for the cremation because the insurance would take time, my aunt handled the money thing I was checking on for my mom, and my cousin cooked all the food for the repass that was held at Mecca's mom's house. My friends called all that week to check on me and gratefully they have not stopped caring for me in this sad state.

The one interesting thing that happened at the service was the former Mayor attending. I was a bit shocked that he came and was even more shocked that since he was now an ordained pastor, he was invited to sit in the pulpit with the presiding pastors of the church. What really floored me was that he got up and said a few words on my behalf. It was thoughtful of him especially since he didn't really know my mother. I mean he saw her a few times when she visited me at the plantation but that was about it. Nevertheless, it was the thought that counted.

God conducted the whole thing and I'm still marveling at his grace, mercy and blessings. The hardest part of the week was writing my mothers' obituary. It wasn't that I couldn't for-mulate the words, it's just that I knew putting those words on paper and then having them printed meant that she was really truly gone and there was a small part of me that didn't want to accept it. I felt like I still needed her to guide me and writ-ing that obituary meant I would have to release that need and guide myself. I had to grow completely up. No more counting on Ms. Yvonne to steer me in the best direction. No more making mistakes and having her there to clean them up. It would just be me now, Little Crystal with no parents, and I wasn't ready.

But by the time I arrived at that celebration of life service for her, I was ready. It just happened. I remember giving out so many hugs and making sure the deacon did not play one sad ass song. Friends and family spoke on her behalf and there was so much laughter. When it was time for the reading of the obituary, which I had no intention of letting anyone other than myself read those words written for and about my mother, I was more than ready to release her spirit into the universe.

Before I spoke I acknowledged the guests and told them that I kept hearing them say in reference to me "I don't know how she's doing it...I don't know how she's making it." I told them, "If you prayed for me, know that it is working, because I don't know how I'm making it either, but God!" Everyone called the next day and told me how much they enjoyed my mother's service, how she raised me well, and how she would have been proud of me. I was thankful, because it was all God who provided her for me to measure up to.

As I'm writing about my mother, I'm realizing that this is the most difficult thing for me. I've been dealing with extreme bouts of crying and loneliness. I couldn't even see myself writ-ing again. But like I said God is amazing, because he's got me writing now. He knew I wouldn't be able to put my heart into anything until I wrote about my Icon, Ms. Yvonne. She was the truth, and she accomplished the un-accomplishable. I love my mother and miss her terribly. But she and I know that God was preparing me for something big, and it was to deal with this life without her. It's what I can do as long as I keep God where he's been all along, right inside me.

But the sadness creeps up on me when I least expect it too. Yesterday, I was sorting out boxes in her home and found a box of her hats and gloves. Gloves that I had given her, hats that she wouldn't be wearing this winter, and it overwhelmed me. I found her marriage license, divorce papers and the sister I never knew (the one who died a month after she was born) birth certificate. I found her old job photo ID's and scriptures written on 3 x 5's.

And I cried. And as the tears flowed, I told myself, "It's Okay Crystal, you can cry for her because she was yours."

Art Therapy

Three weeks after memorializing my mother, I found myself standing in the middle of my kitchen in my sunny Upper Darby apartment. Just standing there. Doing nothing. Just standing there, wondering what in the world to make of my life. I hadn't written anything in my business plan since the day I found Ms. Yvonne without her breath, and I just couldn't find the strength to think of one new thought. I was too busy spending my days in sadness and memories. Memories of her journey through this life.

I was thinking about the 28 years she had spent working at that factory on 5th and Race to only lose her job because of the company's decision to export its work to Mexico. I thought about how they had given her only $100 for each of those 28 years as severance when she left. I thought of how devalued she felt after receiving that severance. I also thought about her "don't give a fuck" attitude toward her health after being released from that job. I thought about how her quality of life had changed in just three short years. Yes, I blamed that company for using my mother for everything she had to give and then giving her nothing in return. Although she would never work in that field again, we laughed and laughed when we later learned that the business was failing in Mexico, because every time a shipment would be prepared for import back to the U.S., the trucks would get robbed. Served them right!

Deep in that thought, the phone rang. I considered not answering because I did not want to talk. I found myself not wanting to move my mouth or feel the words slide across my tongue to describe "how I was feeling" one more time, as I had been doing since she died. But instead, I picked up and was pleasantly surprised. It was the arts-based non-profit I had contacted months prior asking if I was still interested in volunteering.

The gentleman on the other end of the line was passionate about the work occurring at Art Sanctuary as they were preparing for their annual event, Celebration of Black Writing (CBW). He talked fast, and it seemed as if he would never stop. It was fine by me, at least I didn't have to use my own words, so I listened intently adding the occasional, "wow", "sounds great", and finally "I'm impressed, how can I help?" By the time he had described all the great work they were doing, I knew there was no way I could turn this opportunity down. I also knew that I needed to "do something" or I would be overcome by my sadness.

The gentleman, who described himself as the Program Coordinator, asked me to come in to meet with him and the founder, Lorene Cary. I was excited about the opportunity because I had been a literary fan of Lorene Cary for quite some time. She had penned the memoir *Black Ice* about her experience in a predominantly white boarding school, but also penned one of my favorite novels, *The Price of a Child*, about a slave woman who escaped to freedom while living in Philadelphia. I was excited to not only meet her, but to lend whatever research, community engagement or data collection experience sitting in my virtual toolbox that I could to her organization.

A week later, I was in their small office on Broad and Susque-hanna telling them of the road that led me to sitting in front of them at that very moment. They were intrigued by my resilience to overcome so many obstacles in the workplace and although I was in mourning, still had the desire to serve through volun-teering. I felt their sincerity and was delighted they asked me to help with not only CBW '20, to honor the 20[th]year of this festival founded by bookstore owner Larry Robin of Robin's Books, but also their signature after school program, North Stars.

I was needed in the field and in the office, and was thankful. They asked me how much time I could commit and thinking about not spending any more time with my mother, I said, "As much time as you need." They were thrilled to have me on their team, and I was grateful for the distraction.

I started volunteering almost immediately. It was easy to dive back into a "work life". Especially since the work I was do-ing was being appreciated. Each time I completed a task, the program coordinator would bestow accolades upon me. I won't lie, it fed my ego. I was glad that all the skills I had learned at PPV were benefiting an organization that was operating on a shoe-string budget. I gave everything that I could to make their business day run smoothly, even though when I would go home and tuck my son into bed at night, I would cry myself to sleep. I felt so alone without my mother and it was frightening.

But the time spent at the Sanctuary was gratifying, almost therapeutic and two months after my mother transitioned and two weeks before Faster was officially released from prison, I decided to cut all of my hair off. Cut it off like a boy. Cut it off to shed the pain of losing Ms. Yvonne and the memories of that day. Whatever I could do to not carry that energy with me, I was willing to do and cutting my hair was part of it.

It wasn't the first time I cut all my hair off like a boy either. I had also cut it two weeks after delivering the poets' child. He cut my hair and became my barber for a while. But since his career had taken off and we were no longer attached in that way, I knew he could no longer serve me. So, I shared with the program coordinator that I needed a barber and he escorted me to his barbershop, which was directly across from the Sanctuary on Broad Street.

The barbershop was an interesting place. It was owned and operated by all African American Muslim men, who did not normally cut women hair. But because the program coordinator was well respected in the community, they altered their policy to allow me to have my hair cut there. I looked forward to my bi-weekly haircut.

My barber would wash my hair with the hands of a healer. He would cut my hair with such precision that I felt sharp every time he finished, even though I was unraveling on the inside. Although I was still experiencing extreme bouts of sadness, it seemed like my appointments always coincided with the afternoon Islamic prayer, Asr or the sunset Islamic prayer Maghrib, and witnessing the brothers stop everything to pray, made my sadness dissipate.

However, outside of the barbershop and the Art Sanctuary, my grief was manifesting in other ways. I've always had the skin allergy, eczema. As a child it would attack any and every crease on my body, my inner elbow, behind my knees and my neck. Not only would it attack those areas it would attack my scalp and cause my hair to fall out.

I was used to having this skin condition as a child, but as the years passed, I had outgrown the outbreaks. But with the sadness, tears and the despair, the eczema came back with a vengeance. Ironically, it only attacked my hands. There were puss bumps that itched all over my fingers. Although I kept going to the doctors to find a remedy for the outbreaks, as the weeks wore on it got increasingly worse and I had to wear soft cotton white gloves to keep any dust from getting on them and aggravating the eczema.

I knew my hands were an outward representation of what was occurring within me. I also knew that I would not heal if I continued to stay in that sad place. Realizing I hadn't been to the Drive since the day my mother and I were last there, threedays before her transition, I decided to go there to pray.

It did not feel weird being there. In fact, I felt an over-whelming sense of calm. Looking at that water, my prayer start-ed with thanksgiving, transitioned into hysterical crying and seg-ued into thanksgiving again. I was thanking God for bringing me through the loss of Ms. Yvonne and keeping me somewhat sane. The prayer revealed three things, 1) I needed to stop crying, 2) I would be fine in the absence of my mother and 3) in order to prepare for Faster's arrival, who was as heartbroken as I was over the death of her, I needed to be level headed so that we could seamlessly adjust to one another and start the van service together.

After going to the Drive to clear my head, my hands slowly started to heal, and I was able to dig deeply back into my vol-unteerism at the Sanctuary. Going to their office every day was fulfilling. The staff were great and predominantly Black, which was something I had never experienced before, and all the volun-teers were wonderful. It was obvious to me that they were there because they believed in the mission of the Art Sanctuary and it showed in the support they gave at various events.

My favorite part about volunteering there was sitting in on meetings with Lorene Cary. She was brilliant, smart, funny and fair. She was a caring woman and her staff did not have one bad word to say about her. The work was not difficult but there was a lot of it, and I felt valued for the gifts that I was able to bring to assist in furthering their agenda.

I welcomed the distraction of going in the community and gathering information to make their event and after school pro-gram successful. My work at PPV was proving extremely fruitful at the Art Sanctuary. I was assisting with cleaning and redeveloping their volunteer database, calling parents to encourage them to allow their children to participate in their awesome after-school program, and I was making arrangements for literary artists to attend the Celebration of Black Writing.

This work was feeding my soul. I was no longer working with pretentious "liberals" pretending to conduct research, but I was at the grass roots level getting the work done. I was now on the front line and there was no looking back for me. As the months wore on, the Art Sanctuary became a refuge for the mental clarity I needed to experience Faster being back on the street and in my life.

Home Plan

I had been doing a lot to prepare for Faster's arrival. For starters, and even in my grief, I moved out of my apartment and into my mothers' home. But in the process of that, I had to practically gut the house because if I was going to be able to sleep peacefully in there, it could not have any resemblance to the day she left.

It had been a difficult process, from hiring and firing contractors to sorting through her belongings. But, I had gotten it done and I was proud of myself. The house was ready to have a new life and new relationships in it and I needed love.

Faster was released at the end of September. His mother and I took the drive to Rockview to pick him up. The drive was exciting, partially because I was grateful that it would be my last time up that mountain to enter prison grounds to visit someone I loved. My baby was about to be free. When he walked out of the jail it was as if the sun had risen behind him and there was nothing more for us to do but build a beautiful life together.

Prior to his release, his Parole Officer came to my house to inspect it and to make sure there were no firearms on the premises before his home plan could be approved. As an ex-offender, he could not live in a home with firearms. All was clear, and the plan had been approved but first he needed to go to a halfway house until he had employment. I didn't like those rules, but after a while I understood why it was necessary.

He had to report to the halfway house 3 hours after reaching the city, so as soon as we got to Philly, we stopped and visited his favorite aunt and a few other relatives. Everyone was happy that Faster was home, and each had the same words as we departed. "Don't get caught back up, Faster." I remember thinking to myself, "Not on my watch!"

At the halfway house, Coleman Hall, family members had to take classes that would assist with the re-entry of ex-offenders back into the home. I was interested in attending the classes because I wanted to do everything in my power to keep Faster on the straight and narrow. So, I showed up weekly to play my part in learning "the system of ex-offenders."

The classes taught us how to assess signs of depression, negative behaviors, and anything that would lead to recidivism. I was too hyped; I felt like I had all the tools to keep my man out of the penitentiary. That was until I found out that Faster had a cell phone in the Halfway House. I was pissed, and we argued in whispers for hours on a visit inside the halfway house over a box of Kentucky fried chicken.

This brother was trying to convince me that since other men had phones, it wasn't a big deal that he had one too. Even though, having a cell phone in the halfway house was a direct violation and could prevent him from being released. He argued me down that he wasn't going to get caught with it, that he was a grown ass man, and he wasn't going to be treated like a criminal anymore. He was done with people telling him what to do. It was at that point that I knew Faster wasn't ready to be home.

For about six weeks, he proved me wrong though and acted like he was ready to be a productive citizen in the Commonwealth of Pennsylvania. He managed to not get caught with the phone, found a job, and was able to be released from the halfway house to my home in November, right before Thanksgiving and right before his good friends' annual birthday bash. I had chosen not to attend the birthday bash because I was interested in seeing how Faster, newly released from jail and the halfway house, was going to go to this hot ass party and make it to work in the morning.

He was scheduled to be at his job at 6am the morning after the party. He came in from the party at 4am. He was drunk and high. I was so disappointed. I asked him, knowing full well what the answer would be, "Are you going to work?" He drunkenly responded that he was going to figure it out.

For the next 10 minutes, he tried to convince me that he had "this." I was sick of the performance and finally said, "Well you need to figure this shit out because you have to be there in 2 hours." Finally, Faster picked up the phone, called his new job, and told them he could not come to work because his grandmother had died. I was disgusted for several reasons.

First and foremost, his grandmother was alive and well. Second, he had only been working at the job for 4 weeks. And finally, he didn't value our relationship enough to not get that fucked up that he couldn't maintain the responsibility of keeping a job—because he got fired the very next day.

We had talked consistently about the steps he needed to take to make sure our relationship worked, and the most important thing in that conversation was keeping a fucking job so that he wouldn't revert back to the street life. Faster didn't have the same issues as those brothers from the re-entry program in New York. He didn't have child support issues. There was no one demanding time and money from him, not even me. I just didn't want him to go back to jail.

Even though Faster cost himself that job, I still wanted him to win. While he was incarcerated, he had gotten a certificate in masonry. After losing his job, I asked him what he had planned to do with that certification. He stated he just couldn't find a job in that field. So, I would supply him with newspapers to help with his search, but for some reason he couldn't yield any results. Finally, I got the Yellow Pages and went to the section of "concrete companies" and started calling companies in the area.

I was extremely transparent, stating that I was calling for a loved one who had been recently released from prison, was certified and needed a fresh start. I spoke to three who said they weren't hiring at the time, but the fourth company told me to have Faster come down and meet with them. Ecstatic, I gave Faster the information, hoping he'd see that I was a team player willing to go above and beyond my duty as his woman to help him grow. But much to my chagrin, Faster never followed up on the lead. He was too busy fighting his own demons.

I knew there would be temptations. After all, he had not followed one suggestion or creed instituted by the halfway house, like staying away from the old neighborhood. He had been going back and forth to the old neighborhood like it should be part of his daily routine. He also was smoking weed heavily and using other illicit drugs. He was "borrowing my car" and driving without a license. He was being a hot damn mess and when he asked me to marry him; although I had never doubted that I would, I just couldn't see myself being his wife. I also couldn't even grieve for Ms. Yvonne properly dealing with Faster and his altered Home Plan, and I was starting to resent him.

He was berating me too, with the marriage shit. Kept asking me when it was going to happen, and I just couldn't give him an answer even though we had gone down to the courthouse, applied for and received the license. We even had rings. But something was stopping me from going through with it. Then one day I went to the Art Sanctuary to commit to my daily volunteerism responsibilities when I tapped on Lorene Cary's door. I don't know what made me go to her office that day, but let's just say I was spirit-led.

As I knocked on her door, she looked up from her computer and said, "Hey, Crystal, come in!" I walked in, stood by her desk and said, "I'm getting married…" She looked deeply into my eyes and as she pulled a chair up lightly laughing, said to me, "Sit down dear…do we need to have an intervention?" At first, we both laughed, but as I started to reveal the history of Faster and I, along with my emotional health after losing Ms. Yvonne, I realized I absolutely needed a got-damn intervention and I absolutely, was not going to marry Faster.

Not only had I decided to not marry him, I had decided to put him out of my fucking house. I could no longer deal with the high shit, the lying, the hanging out all night, the no job, the using the car, and all of the irresponsibility. I needed a break from being responsible for him. I only wanted to worry about my son and myself. Faster and I had stopped talking about the van service after he got fired and quite honestly, I didn't want him as a business partner.

When I broke the news to him that we were over, his pride would not allow him to see where we had gone wrong and his part in it. Instead, he left my home accusing me of giving up on us. As we exchanged heated words about who was right and who was wrong, I suddenly realized that if Faster couldn't help me heal in the absence of my mother, then no one could and that I'd better get used to living this life fully and truly alone. I allowed Faster to leave because if I was going to have to navigate life as an orphan, then I'd rather do it by myself than with a man-child by my side. We were done!

But I made one mistake a few months before Faster came home. I told Haroon that my man was on his way from the Bing, and I was getting married and could no longer sleep with him. Something we had been doing off and on since he'd been home from jail and Faster was inside. A couple weeks after I released Faster, I went hunting for Haroon. I found him in our old neighborhood. He was still looking as handsome as ever, standing in front of the bar, politicking with the usual suspects.

I pulled up and told him to hop in my car. He did. I started the conversation with "I miss you." He replied that he had missed me too. I said, "Well you'll be happy to know that I'm not getting married." His jaw dropped in shock. I expected that, but what I didn't expect was his next words, "Crystal, I'm sorry to hear that but, um I'm married now!" I lost my shit.

I asked that legacy love, "Why the fuck did you go and get married?" He responded with lunacy and said, "When you told me you were getting married, I knew that you wouldn't fuck me again, unless I was married too. So, I leveled the playing field." I was flabbergasted.

I wanted to slap the absolute ridiculous shit out of him. But instead I said, "Oh well, you'll have to get a divorce then!" He told me he would not get a divorce, nor could we sleep together again, because I was not Muslim nor his second wife. Pissed off and heartbroken, I left him on 55th Street, hating all men and deciding to just be celibate.

PART V

TRIPPIN' THROUGH BLACKNESS

-Kwanzaa at Penn-

Black Culture

With no love distractions in my life, I decided to throw myself headfirst into my acts of volunteerism, so back to the Sanctuary I went. There was one young woman I'd met there that completely contributed to my life taking on a new course after the break-up with Faster and being dumped by Haroon. She was a student at the University of Pennsylvania, working toward her masters' degree in the School of Social Work.

She was also an African American Yoruba princess and a quilt maker. She had chosen the Art Sanctuary as the site to conduct research for her masters' thesis. She was smart at all things intellectual, but did not know a lick about the research process. I took a strong liking to this young sister and helped her develop her surveys in a way that would elicit the most robust data for her to complete her program requirements for graduation, and she was grateful.

One day she came into the office filled with excitement telling me that there was an opportunity to support the Black Cultural Center at the University of Pennsylvania. I told her that I wasn't looking for full-time work and that I also did not have a degree. But that did not diminish her enthusiasm.

For an entire week she kept approaching me with the "Crystal, just meet with the women there, you'll love them." Or the "Crystal, I told them about you, and they are so excited to meet you." Finally, I told her, "Ok, ok, ok, I will meet with them just to see what they're talking about." She could not have arranged that meeting fast enough.

On a winter day in early 2004, I decided to meet with the women at Makuu Black Cultural Center. When I arrived at the Arch Building located on Locust Walk in the heart of Penn's campus, I was impressed with the 100-year-old building and the serenity of the grounds. The Center, which were three small offices used separately for the director, office manager, and program coordinator where students were congregating, were all decorated with African or African American Art. There were paintings, ceramics and masks everywhere, and most importantly there was a subscription to Essence Magazine available to be read by all visitors. The vibe was definitely right for my style, since I had a penchant for wearing dashikis.

The office manager, who was a silver haired elderly Black woman, greeted me by saying, "This is going to be a meeting with popcorn!" I was delighted because popcorn was my favorite snack. As we waited for the Director to return from a meeting to conduct our "meeting," I watched the office manager interact with students and I immediately determined that if I decided to work with these people, she would be my favorite person. She was so caring, generous and funny, and the students adored her.

The Director showed up, and in her light Caribbean accent, apologized for being late. I told her not to worry, the office manager had taken great care of me. She immediately bestowed accolades upon the office manager, and in that moment, I knew that I would like both women, again, if I decided to work with them. You see, although I was there for what I finally realized was an interview, I still wasn't interested in working full-time, for anybody, and especially at a University.

But I knew if I wanted to work there, the job would be mine. I had learned through my work at PPV how to interview effectively. No matter the position, or who the interviewer was, I'd always go in with the mindset of "convince me that this is the best place for me to spend my time." Whenever I'd go into an interview with that approach, it seemed that my nerves were non-existent, and I had control over the entire interview process. It would be no different in that room with those Black women.

There were so many thoughts going through my mind while I waited for the interview to start. The main thought was figuring out what God was trying to do with my life at that moment. It would be a cruel joke, to have me go from PPV with all those pretentious degree holders, to the belly of the beast where most of those degrees were achieved. As I waited, I knew those two Black queens really had their work cut out convincing me to give up my unemployment, sanity and free time.

But the longer I sat with those two women and learned about their goals and vision for the Black Cultural Center, that was only one-year-old, I became more and more intrigued with supporting their efforts to be as good, if not better, than the other Cultural centers on Penn's campus that had longer histories. For example, there was the Latino Cultural Center, Pan Asian/Pacific Islander Cultural Center, the Multi-Culture Cultural Center and even the LGBT Cultural Center, with a university presence ranging from 2 to 20 years. Needless to say, I was excited to help these Black folks make their mark on the University.

I was offered a position as the program coordinator at that very meeting. I told the women that I would process it and let them know as soon as possible. I left the University and really truly soul searched if this was the right move for me. I had so many hang-ups about higher education in a city that didn't really advocate for its own publicly educated students to enter the many prestigious institutions that we were known for like Temple, Drexel and Penn, and I wasn't sure if I wanted to subscribe to the doctrine that "Higher Ed is the only way to live the American dream." I mean after-all, I was able to conduct research with the best of them, I could organize great events, and I knew how to hold my own in a room full of intellectuals and do all of that with only a high school diploma. I questioned whether or not I wanted to subject myself to the pretentiousness and elitism of higher education at an ivy league institution.

When I went back to the Art Sanctuary a few days after that meeting, the young Yoruba quilt-making princess was there telling me how the women at the Black Cultural Center, "loved me" and hoped I'd accept their offer. There was no way I could not accept. Like I said, I was intrigued by their mission and the workspace seemed to be a good fit for my spirit. I called later that day and accepted their offer that would pay me $10k less than I made when I left PPV with the hope that my hard work would eventually be reflected in my pay at some point. I even told myself that I would take classes at Penn, since it was "free!"

I started working at the Black Cultural Center three weeks after the Celebration of Black Writing 2004 concluded. The entire Art Sanctuary experience was therapeutic. Lorene Cary purchased silver Tiffany's bookmarks with the encryption CBW'04 for the office volunteers. I had never received anything from Tiffany's before and was grateful for the gift.

Also, in showing my gratitude to the Yoruba princess for introducing me to the Black Cultural Center, I commissioned her to make me a quilt that included pieces of fabric from my favorite dress, two of my mothers' favorite jackets (a dark chocolate leather one from the 70's and sweater with African masks) and my son's first sweat suit. It took her a month to make the quilt. But when I received it, I knew that her hands were gifted, and those fabrics would forever bond my past, present and future with love.

Black culture has always been part of my deoxyribonucleic acid, but only as it related to African Americans, the slavery struggle, and hood shit. I know had it not been for working at the Center I would have continued to think that Black people only consisted of African Americans and a few Jamaicans. It's true. I had never been exposed to so many variations of Blackness. I had no clue that there was an entire Diaspora of us out there all impacted by slavery, waiting to be reconnected with one another.

At Penn, there were students from everywhere in America and all parts of Africa and the Caribbean. I also learned that these students had their own group that they proudly belonged to on campus. There was the Black Student Union, The Caribbean Students Group, The Haitian Student Group and outside of those groups were the performing arts groups, the scholar groups, fraternities and sororities.

What I loved most about the Black student groups at Penn was that they were organized by the seven principles of Kwanzaa, the Nguzo Saba. Now I was familiar with the tenets because my adorable now six-year-old was enrolled in a charter school in West Philly that implemented the Nguzo Saba in their core practices and curriculum. Every morning my son would start his day in an Umoja (unity) circle and end it as a class sharing what principle they had practiced that day. I absolutely loved my sons' school and could not help but think during that time, of the irony that he and I were living in such a paradigm of alignment on our Black culture journey.

At the Center, the student groups were guided under the umbrella of the Umoja board and according to their organization, were grouped under the remaining principles of Kwanzaa. For example, the sororities and fraternities fell under the principle of Kujichagulia—Self Determination, and the performance arts groups fell under the principle Kuumba—Creativity, and the professionally associated groups were under Ujamaa—Cooperative Economics. It was my responsibility to make sure these students managed their group activities and their classes.

The most interesting aspect of working with the students was helping them navigate Penn and Philadelphia. Many of these students were the first in their family to have ever gone to college, and being away from home at this ivy league institution was intimidating and at times was difficult for them. The work was hard and so was the burden of being the "first" in their family to not only attend college, but an institution with a solid reputation like Penn.

There were many tears in my office, but there were so many joyous moments as well. Students were thriving and graduating with honors. I'll admit, it was hard for me sometimes working with the students because not having my own college experience

I found myself blurring boundaries. I cursed a lot, or I'd be invited to an event and stay too long, or give advice based on my own personal experience and not on any Penn law. It was challenging at times trying to figure out when to be an administrator and when to be a friend. But no one died, so that was a good thing.

One day while at the Center I noticed myself growing. It was one of those days where you couldn't do anything but notice yourself growing. A day where you fully realize you are evolving into that next level of the person you've prayed to become. It started with me having to finish the newsletter for the block.

Yes, I had become the Block Captain of Ms. Yvonne's block. It's just another hat I decided to dance in front of the mirror in. I petitioned to be the block captain because in the Spring of 2002, a year before she left, I told her that if I lived on her block, I'd be the Block Captain.

In case you're wondering what a Block Captain is, I'll tell you! Philadelphia has an organizational structure among its residents on city blocks in hopes of keeping neighborhoods clean and safe. The Block Captain is supposed to listen to everyone's complaints and try to find possible solutions. The Block Captain is also responsible for rallying up the neighbors one day out of the summer months to clean the block.

So, I finished the newsletter, made copies and stapled all of them to be distributed to my neighbors sometime in the next couple days by my son and his friends, because they were my little assistants. As I completed that task and was about to pay some bills (yes all at work) I decided to divert from the task at hand to put on a cd I'd received in the intramural mail at the University. After ripping it out the cd case, I realized it wasn't a cd, but a dvd instead. It was titled Black Ivy and was a product of the University. Curiosity got the best of me, so I put it in the computer and hit play.

I was unprepared for what I saw. It was a film documenting the lives of four Black women at the University. Each woman was from a different socio-economic background ranging from almost poor to doing well. Two were born in America and the others were not, but they all had issues with being Black in a predominantly white, affluent ivy league institution. The women were past and current students. There were two Black professors included in the documentary as well, one male and one female. Both giving their expert advice on the Black experience in America and Penn.

The documentary was 45 minutes long and I was stuck. Watching those women and thinking about the women I know and have grown up with, I've come to realize the struggle is the same for Black women across the board. Whether we're in the mood to admit it or not, we are all trying to adjust to the same thing, being considered a minority, even though we know we deserve the majority of everything. We're all tired of carrying the weight of being considered less than, having to try harder than everybody else because of some trauma that happened before our time. Simply put, we're all trying to shake that slavery shit.

I watched that documentary and thought about the common struggle. We all have some form of generational sickness in our family, like diabetes or high blood pressure from the garbage slavery forced our ancestors to eat and we still can't seem to let go of it, no matter how bad it is for our health. We all have some form of dependency or addiction, from something the slave master denied or gave to our ancestors, and because we haven't learned to heal from the trauma we often succumb to the temptations.

That slavery plan has done its work. The mastermind behind that scheme was a pure genius. It has left us traumatized and somewhat unable to make sense of our own needs or methods toward healing. What's equally worse is what slavery has done to white people. It either allows them to bask in their supremacy and inflict either institutional or personal pain on people of color, or quietly makes them pay for the sins of their father by forcing them to smear their white guilt across people, places and things with an unwanted painter's brush.

Deep in thought, the documentary topic switched to relationships, and how these women would fare in the market. So, I tuned back in. The women shared how difficult it was to find someone they were compatible with and having the same goals in mind like working toward a college degree or already having one. The female professor on the dvd proclaimed they'd either need to lower their standards or be alone.

She also mentioned that by lowering their standards she wasn't saying "go out and find a convict or drug dealer," but a menial labored working Black man. I said to myself, "Wow, no drug dealers or convicted felons, these chicks don't stand a chance of finding a relationship in Philadelphia if they cut out that demographic." But then I dug myself. Although the professor was being elitist, perhaps she genuinely believed that these women could not possibly love a man with a criminal record. But even without a degree, having my own experience with Faster, I knew that to be false. It was a hard love, but one I did not regret experiencing.

After watching the documentary, I decided to give a little more to the job and ceased with the shenanigans of my Block Captain work, even though I was officially done. The sisters needed me! Any Black female student that walked in my office from that point forward, I shared a bit more of my personal story with them, including loving a criminal. I finally realized that across the Diasporic spectrum, we women were all we had and if we weren't supporting one another, then who would.

To be fair though, I didn't just interact with the young women at Penn. There were a few young men who left a mark on me. Two were poets, and the other a politically savvy gentle-hearted brother. The one poet was from Nigeria, which I found fascinating because I had never met anyone from Nigeria. He was studying at Wharton School of Business and was brilliant. He eventually wrote a book and acknowledged me for inspiring him to pursue his artistic craft.

The other poet was a young man who was simply gifted. He worked directly in our center and shared with me that the poet I had married was the reason he had really tapped into using his voice to tell his stories. That student would later recite poetry for the first Black President of our country.

But, of all the students, the politically savvy brother was my absolute favorite! He helped shape the Umoja board during his term and was responsible for getting the student groups recognized on the University level. When this young brother showed up to meetings, the administration had no choice but to listen to and support his requests for funding and space equity for our groups to conduct great programming on campus. In fact, him showing up to check on me every day made coming to work worthwhile as relationships continued to actualize and some demised at the Black Cultural Center.

Pilot Study

The Director and I worked well together in the beginning, but as time wore on, she became my nemesis. This is why I had no problem doing Block Captain work or paying bills at the job. I had watched her do so much non-work-related business at the Center that I wished she had the heart to say something to me about what I was doing.

I believe our relationship broke down for several reasons: her smart-ass mouth and her jealousy at how the students loved being around me. But the two major issues that caused me to start to despise her was that as a Caribbean woman, who was extremely opinionated, she did not have a problem talking negatively about the plight of African Americans or someone's weight. Both conversations were triggering, but the weight comments about staff or students were extremely difficult especially because I had managed to gain the "freshman 15" each year that I worked there and the Director was extremely fit.

But what was worse than the weight conversations were the conversations about African Americans. I found myself stating over and over again, that it was easy for a Black person of Caribbean or African descent, who had not experienced the history of slavery in America to have an opinion of how African Americans have dealt with that trauma. I would share that, "Yes, your family may have moved here to escape persecution or famine and left your oppressor, but for us African Americans, slavery happened here. We haven't left and are reminded everywhere we turn that our ancestors were raped, murdered and denied freedom on this very land. Sure you can view this land as the land of opportunity but for so many of us with American slavery in our bloodline, we still haven't gotten over that shit." She was a hard nut to crack because although she heard my point, I would still catch her talking shit about lazy African Americans and I would want to put hands on her.

The other difficulty in working with the Director, that I didn't want to admit, was that she was a classist. Now up until this point in my career, I had only dealt with white people who I felt, in their own "liberal" way, looked down upon Blacks or minorities in general, using them for research purposes only and with pity. I had never met a Black person who looked down on other Black people, at least not in this condescending way. She would always figure out a way to let me know that I would never receive the pay I wanted because I didn't have a degree, and would religiously inform me of the "elitist ways" of Penn.

She would even go so far as to say that the students would not respect me if they knew I didn't have a degree. It was also why I made sure to inform them that I didn't have one, and when I did that, they would share with me one hundred and one reasons why they thought I didn't need one. Especially since they benefited from my "lived experience" with program planning support and even as I mentioned navigating Philadelphia, as many were not from the region.

For the life of me, I spent many days wondering why the fuck she had hired me. She was the first to know I didn't have a degree because we discussed it at the interview and she said it wasn't a problem. I know I told myself that I would take classes at Penn and I did. I took one.

But when I wanted to take more classes, the Director found an issue with it since she was taking classes to get her Doctorate and well "somebody had to run the office." Not only did she take classes and obtain her degree, she was pregnant during my interview, which I wasn't aware of, had that baby, and subsequently had another baby while I worked there.

I enjoyed working with the students but the rift between the Director and I was beginning to show up in not so subtle ways and I'm sure the students saw it. She just wasn't a nice person to me and I could no longer pretend to be nice to her as well. So, after selflessly giving my time, talent and treasure, that included helping organize the first 21 student group led Cultural Celebration—Umoja Week, advising students, long nights and many weekends attending events, I had no regrets in deciding to leave the Center.

I had helped the students and the center accomplish more goals than they knew they could. We developed overnight retreats for student leaders, and their programs were being heavily attended by more than just Black students. Students weren't failing their classes and deep in my heart I knew their overall quality of life at the university had been enhanced by me serving them. Once again, knowing that propelled me to leave a space that undervalued me.

But before my departure, I decided it was time to conduct a pilot study on the van service. Although Faster and I were a thing of the past, my spirit had been itching to see if the idea could really work. As much as I tried, I couldn't seem to shake the thought of women struggling to visit a loved one in prison. Especially since I personally knew women who were still loving men who were getting locked up.

I had purchased a minivan while Faster and I were still together and aside from him dogging it out and getting it impounded, I had not done one constructive activity with it. So, I reached out to (follow these next words carefully), the poet's second wife's son's father, who was incarcerated at Graterford State Correctional Institution, about an hour away from Philly. I wanted to see if he would aid me in getting a small group of riders together to test out the service.

I had never met him. I'd only had conversations with the second wife about him because of our shared trauma of once loving a man that was incarcerated. But more importantly, I had seen the type of father he was while incarcerated, having weekly visits and weekly phone calls with his son. He was the epitome of a father. Fathering despite the circumstance of incarceration and I knew he would be the right energy to connect with to get this pilot off the ground.

I went on the Pennsylvania Department of Corrections website and found a handy tool called the inmate locator, entered his name and institution, and found his inmate number and the address of the institution. Once I had his information, I sent him a carefully crafted letter, informing him of who I was and asking for his assistance in spreading the word. He immediately responded back stating that anyone who was a positive influence in his son's life would receive his support; apparently my ex-husbands wife who knew I was reaching out to him had put in a good word for me. True to his promise, my phone started ringing the next week with requests for rides to the prison.

I was only conducting the rides on Saturdays and charging $25 per person. I had decided to conduct a door-to-door service, since I was only using a minivan and the load would be light.

I enjoyed driving through the city on early Saturday mornings when the natives were still asleep, and the streets were empty. I was excited to pick these people up and bring them to the prison to visit their loved one.

But after the third trip and second "wait a minute while I find my ID or bra with no-underwire" I was over the door-to-door service. Especially since it seemed I had spent more time driving around to pick them up than it took for me to get to the prison. Nevertheless, there were several key things that I learned conducting that study.

Most the riders were women. At first, I had expected entire families to ride including fathers or male friends of the person being visited. But then I reflected on my visits with Faster and realized that most visitors in the visiting room were women. After a while it became shocking if a man traveled.

It was important to play good music. I knew I had a musical ear that could set any vibe. After all, I was deemed the designated driver in Cali and kept us belting love songs down Route 5 on our way to LA from San Jose on our bud-filled road trips. Not to mention that every time I went to a bar with my friends, I had the jukebox rocking with slow jams. But what I didn't expect was for these women to ask me repeatedly, "Crystal who's that we're listening too.?" or "Crystal, you play some good music, girl."

Women like to reflect when they leave a visit. I immediately noticed that the women were chatty on our way to the institution but as soon as they left the visit and settled into the music on the ride home, the entire van would be quiet. I would even notice tears streaming down some of their faces as they looked out the window.

Finally, my service was needed. I could not believe how many women told me that they had no way of getting to the prison and was grateful for my service. Some even expressed that they hadn't seen their loved one in months or even years, because of lack of transportation. When I asked why they couldn't get a family member, or one of their loved ones friends to take them, they would give me the knowing side-eye to express that those folks weren't supportive.

Even though I knew my service was helping women, I wasn't quite ready to go into full implementation mode because I definitely didn't have my shit together. I knew I still had to get a business license, the proper vehicle, and insurance before I could hit the road legally. I also knew that my work-life was still an issue and I needed to refocus my energies on surviving the much-needed transition out of the cultural center, and as quickly as possible. So, after about four months of transporting women to visit a loved one, I shut down the bootleg service, with the hope of carving out more time to complete my business plan to get the proper show on the road.

Bad Blood

Unfortunately, after conducting the pilot study for the van service, procrastination had kicked in. I found myself consumed with gaining more weight while navigating other peoples' problems at work. After several bouts of weed-induced deep thinking, I realized that five years after my mothers' death, anxiety and depression had finally set in like no other time before. I was both triggered all the time at the Center but also no longer had that get up and go! I knew I needed to find a new job. But I would find myself coming home after work, feeding my son, rolling a blunt, laying on my couch and falling asleep until the next morning. I knew it was time for a change, and only I could make that change.

But I was struggle-ing. The weight of depression felt like I was wearing a winter coat in the summertime. It was heavy. I missed my mother and I missed her giving me direction in times when I needed to make major changes, like now.

For weeks I sat with this heaviness and finally said to myself, "What would Ms. Yvonne do?" I knew she wouldn't approve of me sitting there directionless, so I willed myself to activate. The first thing I did was contact my physician for a check-up to see what could be done about my mood.

I was apprehensive about her recommendation to try anxiety medication for the first time, but I knew that I needed something to get my mind on track, because the weed was not helping. The medication she prescribed was a low-dose Ativan. It was primarily used for situational anxiety. I started taking it mostly during my premenstrual days, when my mood would change from optimistic to pessimistic and my words had no censor.

With the help of the medication, my mind leveled out and I started checking Penn's websites for jobs and applied for a position as a data collector at an HIV behavioral health center in the School of Medicine. I don't know what compelled me to want to work in HIV research, but I was just happy to have a way out of the current hell I was enduring. I was overworked and overwhelmed and missed working in a research environment.

I wasn't surprised that I was called in for an interview. After all, I had skills. I aced the interview and was offered the job. I immediately accepted and was excited to still be connected to the University, keeping my benefits, especially the yearly three weeks of vacation I had accrued working at the Cultural Center.

Two weeks later, as the Class of 2008 was entering their senior year, I said farewell to the Black Cultural Center. The students were shocked that I was leaving, especially since some of my favorites had not yet graduated. But I knew that if I had stayed, I would have been fired and locked up for kicking the directors' ass, and they knew it too.

At the HIV Center, I was hired to collect data on a couple of their studies. One study I worked on was to evaluate condom use for Black men who have sex with men. It was on that project that I knew I had made one of the worst decisions of my professional life.

Although I learned more about the research process in terms of applying for funds from the National Institutes of Health (NIH), unfortunately I also learned how to look at every Black man I encountered with the side-eyed suspicion that he might be secretly having sex with men without telling me. It also didn't help that one day on a much-needed lunch break, a fine Black man saw me standing outside, tipped his cap, told me how beautiful I was and 10 minutes later I was consenting him to participate in our study. That damn job was hard on my already non-existent sex life because I wasn't interested in fucking anybody.

Since working with participants had become a mind fuck and I needed a break, I had a discussion with the manager of the data collection team about my discontent and increased stress level. The stress was due to the hardship of hearing horror stories of the trauma these participants endured before and after their positive status. The discontent occurred knowing I was ill equipped to give these participants the therapy they needed. She was supportive and suggested I apply for the administrative coordinator position that was opening to assist the Director of the Center who, according to a published article, was one of NIH's top funded researchers in the country.

Not to mention that he was a Black Caribbean man and I'd never worked for a Black man before. I was definitely interested in this new experience. Having only interacted with him in staff meetings, I truly respected his hustle. I had no doubt I would be able to support him and was excited about the opportunity.

Initially it seemed like a good idea. I had done that work before in my early years at PPV so I knew it wouldn't be that much of a challenge and after weighing my pros—more money and cons—being someone's assistant, I decided it would be best to start praying for the blessing of landing the job. When I say I prayed for that new position, I mean I prayed in bed, in the bathroom on the toilet, in traffic and in the church. Suffice it to say, I damn near begged God to bless me with that job.

Two weeks after applying for it, I found out that I got it! I've always said, "God gives me everything I ask for whether good, bad or indifferent!" and the blessing of this new position was going to prove all three. My salary increased by $10k, I got a private office where I could blast my music, which was key because I was obsessed with Adele at the time.

The office had a beautiful view of Market Street, my commute was lovely because the trolley dropped me off right in front of the building, rain or shine I could gaze at the City through 7ft plate glass windows in the 16th floor cafeteria, and all our technology was Mac-based and wonderful. God had been good to me, no question. But I also realized that God is a teacher and with every prayer and blessing exchange, there is a requirement that I sometimes forget about and that requirement is called the Lesson(s).

The lessons I learned from that prayer being blessed, kicked my ass so bad, that in a matter of months I was begging God to remove me from that place. For starters, I had no idea the economy would eat up my $10k plus some income with their so-called "2008 recession!"

I didn't know that I'd be so busy I couldn't enjoy the view from my office, and when I did it was usually when those wretched high school kids were dismissed from school—cursing and fighting up 36 Street toward Market. Nor did I have a clue that I'd work late and wake up late and as a consequence could not take the trolley to work, but instead had to drive, which resulted in receiving so many parking tickets that my car would be booted and towed by Philadelphia Parking Authority, twice. I also learned that the food in the cafeteria was not really that good, so I didn't visit the 16th floor as much and benefit from the view, on the days that I could actually take a lunch. And after a while,

I despised the Mac toys because the email notifications would come through morning, noon and night.

But if that wasn't bad enough, I was told by six out of the total 11 other staff there that the Director was crazy and only remembered you by your last mistake. Since I felt like I wasn't about to make any, I told myself "fuck it, you got this girl, this ain't about nuthin!" Well wouldn't you know they were right! The man had been up my ass since that first mistake of not checking to see if he had been mentioned in a publication, which he had been, and since I didn't inform him before he had been congratulated by another colleague, he somehow thought I was guilty of a transgression.

One minute we were cool, the next I didn't know if he wanted to fire me. In starting that new position, I had to undergo a new probationary period, and with that first mistake under my belt, and then a couple of missed emails, he extended my probation and then when it was time to hire me, he hired me with a warning letter already in my file. What kind of shit was that?

If nothing else, since the PPV and subsequent Black Cultural Center days, I prided myself on my work ethic. There was never any question that I got shit done. I have never had a problem accomplishing any task exceptionally well. But with this dude it seemed like I was sub-par on everything. I knew I could add, subtract, write letters and reports, organize shit (meetings, events, emails), I'm a problem solver, I don't miss deadlines and I have people skills.

But with this guy, everything I just mentioned, he had a problem with. I mean the job required me to do a whole lot of shit that he really needed 3 people for. I've always operated as a 5-in-1 type of woman because it's been my experience that you have to operate at an insane capacity if you're Black. So, at first, I wasn't tripping. But the heat that was on my ass working for him was so ridiculous that I felt like a boxer in a losing match, repeatedly being pummeled up against the ropes.

Unfortunately, each time I was criticized for a task not completed or done to a specification that was never articulated to me until after the fact, I just took it. Like a battered wife, I accepted the criticism for my mistakes. But only because I begged God for this blessing and as I mentioned before, in each prayer and blessing exchanged there is a lesson involved.

So instead of focusing on the bullshit he kept throwing my way, I focused on the lesson. I asked myself, "What is God teaching me here, in this very situation right now, what am I to learn?" Sometimes, the answers didn't come quick enough and I'd get in a funk, feel like a failure, want to cry, kick his ass and quit the job. But when I got through those first 5 minutes of processing his lunacy, I'd ask myself that question and the answer would begin to reveal itself to me.

For one, I learned I have to forgive people for their mistakes because with the tables turned it was hard on the psyche, 2) I learned I could stand to be a bit more organized if I planned on running my own business, 3) I learned new ways to not feel entitled, because of his status, this guy believed he could treat people like shit, and 4) I learned that that job was a spiritual persons' battleground that had many of us co-workers at each other throats, trying not to find ourselves under his wrath. I knew I needed to stay prayed up, if I was going to survive what I was now calling the Bad Blood Center because of all the disharmony.

The Struggle Bus

I was literally on the struggle bus, sinking into a dismal place during this time, from the draining job, my gift of a house falling apart, and drum roll please...allowing Haroon back in my life. He was only there because I had summoned him. Although I was petrified of sex with Black men from working at the Bad Blood Center, I had finally realized that Haroon had become the "break glass in case of emergency" in my love life.

He had gotten a divorce and was able to love on me when-ever I needed him too. So, I took advantage of the opportunity whenever I was feeling loveless. The only issue with him during this time was that he kept pestering me about having a three-some. I must admit although I'm a Scorpio and there's this no-tion that all of us are freaks of the week, there were just some things I wasn't comfortable experiencing. Now had I had one before, yes. Did I enjoy it, yes! But I was not interested in having one with Haroon. He kept exclaiming to me about having been in jail all those years, he had missed the threesome wave and felt like if anyone should give him one it should be me. I tried to tell that man that I was not the one for it, but he was relentless. No, I did not acquiesce, because I just could not see myself willingly sharing Haroon with anyone.

Besides, I also couldn't see myself having a threesome with him or anyone else when I needed repairs done on my home. Be-ing a homeowner is a beautiful thing but is also a headache that I had not anticipated with this inheritance. The repairs weren't necessarily major—drywall repair from a bathtub leak—but I had been waiting on Haroon to do them for a month.

The house had become my sanctuary since Ms. Yvonne's departure, but looking up at that hole in my kitchen ceiling pissed me off every time I went in there. I ultimately got someone else to do the work, but of course they did a shitty job which made me really pissed at Haroon, because I should have just waited on him like he told me to. But he always had so much shit going on with him and neglected to keep me in the loop, and quite frank-ly vice versa. I never saw my fault in our arrangement, instead I'd get frustrated and stop communicating with him altogether, which ended up making everything bad.

It was rough between us during this particular episode. Up until this point in our love affair, he had never cursed me out the way he did on my answering machine this one Spring day. I saved the messages too, so that when all my home repairs were done, I could play it for him while I was telling him to kiss my ass. I know it wouldn't really happen like that, me telling him to kiss my ass. I had made that mistake before when we were teenagers and he punched me so hard in my leg that it gave me a Charley Horse. But I was going to have to figure out a way to get him for cursing me out like he did.

Here's what happened. Six days had passed since we last talked to each other. Now, I'm in the thick of a leaky kitchen ceiling, because my bathtub pipes had rusted and were useless. Haroon had come by to survey the problem and brought two different guys to do the work, and for some reason directly after the assessment, all those brothers, including Haroon, went missing. So, while he and his team were missing, I was making moves to get the work done without him. On the sixth day of his absence he decided to dial my number.

I didn't answer. Instead I texted him, *"wow, 6 days n u decide to ring my fuckin fone, do me a favor and lose my fkn #, u ain't never there when I need you!"* He started calling me back to back and I still wouldn't answer. Instead I waited 15 minutes until I knew he had simmered down or got distracted with something else and texted him: *"Could u please do me a favor and lose my FKN #!"*

He started calling me back to back again and I still wouldn't answer. I just didn't want to hear what he had to say. Well the last time he called he left me a message that could have gotten him locked back up. He had the nerve to start the message with *"Bitch"* and ended it with *"don't make me shoot your fucking house up."* I was livid and refused to call or text his ass again. But with the stress of the job and the stress of the home repairs and the stress of him being missing in action, I went out drinking to get drunk. When I got back in the house, I texted him the longest drunk text ever:

"I want my key back Haroon. I was wrong 2 give u one in the first damn place. U are NEVER there 4 me when I need u. N this shit has been going on 4ever. We don't owe each other shit. Me lovin us is 2 much n

I'm tired. Put my key n the mailbox and walk ur inconsiderate ass away." Then without a care in the world, I drunkenly fell asleep.

The next morning, when I checked my voicemail, he had left a message asking me if I wanted to go to war. When I got into the office, I called him. He didn't pick up, but 5 minutes later he was ringing my phone. Not being able to avoid the confrontation any longer, I answered with my hung-over head resting in my left palm. He started off with "Bitch!" I tried to cut him off but he was on a tirade, hollering about it was my responsibility to call him about the repairs, because the last time we had talked about it, I told him I was waiting on the insurance adjuster and that I would let him know the outcome of the call when I came to pick up some money.

Unfortunately, all of that was true. I never went to pick up the money from him, nor did I call him about the insurance adjuster. He then kept hollering about how I'm always blaming him for shit that isn't his fault and because he was right, and I was wrong, I hung up on him.

He called me right back, and stupid me answered. He was even more upset and hollering even louder. I told him to simmer the fuck down because all that hollering was pointless. Then I told him I had somebody do the work. I could tell he was still festering, but somehow, he managed to simmer down.

I asked him if he could come and paint my hallway. I had been PMS'n and decided to do it myself, knowing I don't know how to paint, and not only did I fuck up the wall, but now I needed new carpet because there was paint everywhere. He said he'd be over to look at the wall that night.

Of course, he didn't show up and on July 23., the actual five-year anniversary of my mothers' death, I cursed him the fuck out for real. This time I explained to him that I was under a lot of stress. I told him, "My son is in California for the first time alone without me (he went to visit my sister) and because of that leaky tub my house is no longer the Sanctuary that I've grown accustomed to, my job is stressing me out and I miss my fucking Mother. I'm feeling disconnected and sometimes Haroon, just sometimes, I want somebody to take care of me!"

He got noticeably quiet. For a second, I thought he had hung up. But finally, he calmly said, "I understand, sometimes when you're going through a lot of shit, you take it out on the person closest to you, and you just needed to take your shit out on me…you're my Bitch, so it's cool, you can take your frustration out on me." When I asked him why he was insisting on calling me Bitches, he said, "that's the way I'm feeling right now" and left it at that. The very next day, the carpenter locked me out of the house, so I had to call Haroon to let me in. Thank God he kept that key!

He came with a hoagie from his brother's store because I told him I was starving. He had paint and compound all over him. As we entered the house and walked toward the kitchen to see the work the carpenter had done, I was immediately embarrassed. Here was the man I've loved since he was a boy, who can fix shit, surveying some shoddy work done by a man I had hired. What made it worse was that he and I were seeing it for the first time together. He just shook his head and said, "Don't worry about it, I'll take care of it."

He left with the promise of a speedy return. I ate my hoagie, went upstairs, smoked some herb, changed my clothes and headed down to the kitchen to clean it, since the carpenter had left it like a pig sty. I was in that kitchen for 3 hours. When I finally made my way back upstairs at 11:30pm, I checked my cell phone and saw that I had four missed calls from him. I called him right back. He asked where I'd been, I told him in the kitchen and he replied, "I'm on my way over".

When he arrived six minutes later, I guess he was in the neighborhood, I was still sitting in my sweaty clothes and needing a shower. He still had compound and paint all over him, but it didn't stop him from stripping down to his balls and ass and lying across my bed. I went to the bathroom in preparation for my shower.

As I was sitting on the closed toilet finishing my smoke, I listened to him as he spoke on the phone with his closest friend. It was interesting because if you just sit and listen to men talk you realize your conversations are identical. Like the women in my life, he and his homie were talking about going to the gym, a new business venture they wanted to start, when they were thinking about doing it, and what they needed to do to make it a reality. He wasn't talking no killer shit, no shady shit, and nothing about baby mama drama. He was just being a man lying his filthy ass across my clean bed.

I started the shower in the dark. I always take my shower with the lights off, bathroom door open, but with only my bedroom light on. I loathe bright lights in a bathroom during toilet or shower time. As I lathered up, I thought about him lying on my bed. I called him to the shower and asked if he had any intention of washing up. He said, "of course." Then he asked if I wanted him to get in with me. I said, "sure." So, he stepped in.

A little bit of magic happened while we shared our shower and afterward, I washed up again and then exited the shower. He stayed in for a while longer and by the time he emerged I was laying across my bed smoking more of my herb and feeling mighty groovy. He dried off and laid across the bed completely naked beside me. I watched him as he slowly dozed off, thinking about the times when he first came home from prison, and we'd hold each other in the quiet darkness of my room and lovingly remember Sweet together. Sharing how our lives had forever been changed because he had once been in it.

I nudged him awake and told him, "I need you." He smiled, pulled me to him, and we made love for real this time. When we were done, I was grateful that he had that key, because when I awoke the next morning he was gone, and I had not been disturbed. He came over a few days later, painted the hallway and touched up the horrible job the other carpenter had done in my kitchen. Then as usual, the calls and text messages slowed down and eventually stopped, and as in previous times before, our lives continued separately.

Zero Tolerance

Meanwhile, things had not gotten any better at the Bad Blood Center. It was traumatizing working in that environment, and I was not doing well. I kept trying to get my shit together, but was failing in other areas of my life. I blamed that job. I blamed it in my head, in my words, and in my behavior.

I stopped paying my bills on time and truly stopped giving a rats-ass about anything that had any level of responsibility attached to it. I was drinking and smoking way too much and didn't have the energy to be nice. I wasn't working on the van service and hated myself for it.

But, instead of doing something about it, I started implementing the same behaviors that I had developed when I wanted out of the Black Cultural Center, coming home from that dreadful job, rolling up a blunt and sleeping on the couch. Ironically, I was still active on the PTA at my son's school, going to church regularly, and hosting Bible study at my home. It was weird that my life had slowly slipped into the dichotomy of serving others and neglecting myself.

I was still mothering, but barely, and to make matters even worse the poet had moved to Newark, NJ to follow his third wife, and I had become an official "single mom." I could not seem to catch a break. It wasn't until the poet had moved out of the city that I realized how much I relied on his support. He had lived 10 minutes from my house and was always available to get our son whenever I needed him for business or pleasure.

Not having access to that kind of support made me resentful, mean and sad. I tried to keep my spirits up by doing the PTA and Church thing and even taking my son, who had become an avid skateboarder, to the skatepark with his friends, since they were all into skateboarding because of him. But when I wasn't "staying busy," I was being really still and not taking care of myself.

My lack of self-care and neglect came to a blistering head one winter day while sitting in my office at the Bad Blood Center. It was around 2pm when my office phone rang. It was a 685 number on my outside line. I knew all official city numbers started with 685, but I had no clue who would be calling me from one.

I answered in my fake cheerful voice, "This is Crystal, how may I help you." The caller stated that he was an officer from the 18th Police District and that he had my 12-year-old son in custody for taking 19 bags of marijuana to school. My heart dropped. Finally, I said, "Not my Son!" The officer on the other end calmly stated "Yes, Ma'am, your son!"

I could not catch my breath as I asked the officer what I should do. He instructed me to come to the precinct and speak with the detectives, they would be able to further assist me. I hung up, grabbed my purse and left.

On my way to the precinct I called the poet, who happened to be in town that day. I could not contain my anger and frustration when he picked up as I belted out that "our son is locked the fuck up." He thought I was joking, and rightfully so. Our son was on the honor roll, our son was a skateboarder, our son wore glasses, our son was sweet, kind and gentle, this could not be our son. Arrested at 12. I told him to meet me at the precinct because that's where I was headed.

I was shocked upon my arrival that the poet had beat me there. What was even more shocking was that the school administrator was also there. He met me at the top of the steps that led to the detectives' unit. I was embarrassed and almost couldn't face the man. We had just been in a PTA meeting one week prior. I was the co-chair of the Fathers' Day brunch and we had even exchanged cell phone numbers.

He greeted me with warmth and kindness and stated that he was just as shocked as I was that my son was caught with drugs in his backpack, and that if I needed any support, he'd be there for me. I apologized for my son's transgression, thanked him and he left. Five minutes later, the poet and I were buzzed back inside the detectives' area and entered a room where my 12-year-old honor roll child was handcuffed to a chair. My heart caved, and I burst into tears. The poet told me to sit this one out and he would handle it. I left the room and did my best to get myself together.

After about 10 minutes, I was able to go back into the room and conduct myself like a mother in a crisis normally does. I became a detective. I asked my son, where did he get the drugs from? He told me, with a straight face, that an old head from the neighborhood gave it to him to hold. I asked him, "What old head?" ready to kill every fucking living male in my neighborhood, as my son said, "I don't know his name" again with a straight face. I then asked my son, "How did the school know you had the drugs in your bag?" He said, "One of my friends told them."

The female detective in charge of the case then took me aside and said, "Mom, this is common in our neighborhoods. Older dudes will give young kids drugs to sell because if they get caught, they get into less trouble." She then went on to say, "It happened to me and my son, so I know what you're going through." I was grateful for her compassion, but I wanted to burn my entire neighborhood to the fucking ground. After all, I'm the Block Captain and I live in a house where my mother died. For those two reasons alone, my son should have been off limits by any "old head" in the neighborhood.

They kept my son for a few hours as his dad stayed with him, and I left to get my mind right. The detective told me they were sending the case over to the 19th district, and someone would be reaching out to me soon. They wanted my son to come in to look through a book to see if he recognized in the pictures the person who gave him the drugs. They also wanted him to ride around in an unmarked car through the neighborhood to see if he could point out the guy who gave him the drugs.

I knew the next several days were going to be unnerving. I didn't want my son going to a police station to pick anyone out. I knew what that experience was like and could not believe my child would have to go through that, nor did I want him to ride around with police officers to pick someone the fuck out. I also knew that I had to deal with the school issue, and I wasn't ready for any of that, all while working for a maniac, who was monitoring my every move including call-outs—which I rarely did.

The poet and I strategized how we would manage this mayhem. I told him that I could not be part of a ride along and it was agreed that I wouldn't, but I did go to the precinct with them. Luckily my girlfriend worked there and upon seeing us put the word out that my son was a good kid and there was no way he would have brought drugs into the school with the intent to sell them. I was thankful because at least I knew his reputation superseded him and us. But my biggest question during that time was, who the fuck gave my son drugs and why didn't the school notify me before the police officers.

I mean come on! I am a community member. I know what is in my community and I know my community has an element of crime in it. But I also know that my sons' school is in that community, and if the school is "about the community", then the school should know there is a thin line between the community and the school, figuratively and literally, and there is no space for Zero Tolerance with those variables coinciding with one another. As I mentioned earlier, I chose my son's school because of its principles to follow the Nguzo Saba. In those principles are values and conditions of Black life and it is to be upheld by every Black person who swears by it.

My son's school did not follow at least two of those principles, Umoja which is Unity and Ujima which is Collective Work and Responsibility when my son transgressed. Was my son wrong, of course, but as a community school, we were supposed to handle that situation together. Instead of getting to the root of the problem in the community that was/is bound to trickle into your school, even in the book-bag of one of your highest achievers, whose parent was one of the most active, and a firm believer of your tenets, you chose to hurl my son into a system of jail cells, trials, neighborhood beef, riding around in cop cars and a disruption in his academic process.

Fortified with anger, the poet and I were able to openly confront the school for their lack of empathy towards our son, his educational process, his community safety, and my devotion as a parent to the school. This was one of the times I relished in the power that two parents can have over one. The poet and I were a united front when it came to our boy during that difficult time in his and our life.

When we sat in the administrators' office and asked the necessary questions such as, "How did you know our son had the marijuana?" We were told that a student told their parents the night before and the father immediately called the administrator on his cell phone. The poet and I then asked the follow-up question, "Well if you had the information the night before, why didn't you call one of us?" Before he could respond I said, "You have my cell number and I just saw you at the Fatherhood Brunch Planning meeting?"

The administrator stumbled on his words saying, "I was waiting to see what happened." The poet and I both responded in unison, "So you were trying to entrap our child?" The administrator refuted that charge, but I couldn't let up. I repeated to him, "You had my phone number. I just sat in a meeting with you a week ago. If you knew my son was about to transgress why wouldn't you inform me so that I could have stopped it?" I continued with, "This school follows the principles of the Nguzo Saba, what part of the principles were you following by calling the cops on my son and having him ride handcuffed in a paddy wagon?" The administrator had no valid response other than, "Well we are offering him a voluntary transfer so that it won't affect him later!"

No longer did I have faith in the "new age" Black Educators who, I believed, should promise to not throw your Black son to the wolves but to take each transgression short of murder and turn it into a teachable experience. No longer was I a bragger about how infallible my child was. I was the parent of a human child and God had placed me in that position; therefore, it was my obligation to love and forgive that child for being so stupid, but also protect my child from the wolves in sheep clothing.

We got the voluntary transfer and my son endured his last semester of 7th grade in a public school that was more like a prison. But it wasn't a prison and he survived. He got advanced scores on his statewide PSSA's exams (as usual) and he passed with mostly A's, a few B's and one C. But that experience changed him, because he also got suspended for fighting, cut a class, and was late 15 times. No, it wasn't easy, but we made it to the other side of that and all I could do was praise God for his mercy and his grace.

Although my son never identified the "old head that gave him the drugs," word on the street became "the young bull ain't no snitch" and I became the "mom not to fuck with." Yes, it was important to follow protocol when dealing with the law on this issue, but there was a different set of protocol when dealing with the street. The poet made phone calls to flesh out the culprit and I conducted face-to-face interrogations of "old heads and young bulls" in the neighborhood. You see, I never knock a persons' hustle, but I needed to make it clear that my son was off limits, or it would be hard to hustle in my hood.

Ironically, the hypocritical school ended up in the news three weeks later for running a club in the cafeteria and almost lost their accreditation. But what was even worse was that the administrator, who called the police on our son, was later indicted on federal charges for stealing funds from the school. Talk about hypocrisy.

The only good thing about the 19 bags of weed experience was that it propelled me to get my shit entirely together. I took accountability for my son's behavior. I knew that had I not been laying around, smoking weed and complaining about bills and the lack of support I was receiving from the poet, my son may not have thought it was a good idea to take that marijuana risk.

I had to take a hard look at myself. I was letting him down and wasn't even realizing it. Sometimes as parents we can get so consumed with thinking our children are immune to our problems and how we cope, that we don't realize they are watching our every move. I knew my son wasn't used to seeing me not take care of things. He had to have been confused by my depressive behavior and as any son, especially a pubescent one, possibly thought he was helping me.

When I shared with the poet that I felt responsible for our sons' transgression, he told me I was tripping and that our son was smart enough to make his own decisions, and that he had simply made a poor one. I thought he was nuts and proceeded to sit my child down and apologize for neglecting him emotionally. To me, emotional neglect is just as harmful as physical neglect and I vowed to never leave him emotionally wanting again.

Violence Prevention

A few months later, the poet moved back to Philly and my son went to live with him. It was the plan. When we divorced, our son was two years old. We had both agreed that I would spearhead the primary years and the poet would close out puberty to 18.

As my son moved toward adolescence I in turn, resorted to praying, fasting and counting my blessings. I gave up weed AGAIN, stopped taking my anxiety meds because I felt like my mood had improved, dusted off my business plan and started asking God to remove me from the Bad Blood Center. I had had enough and wanted out!

In true God fashion, he used a woman to help me make my move. She was working with our center but going to Drexel to pursue her doctorate. She was a spunky sister and I liked talking to her. She and I both had endured a parents' addiction and although she used coursework to get her through, we both ended up in the same conference room one day sharing our goals and dreams.

Since she was so easy to talk to, I shared with her that HIV and doing administrative work was NOT my passion and that my passion was really violence prevention, the incarcerated community and starting my own prison van service. She wasted no time telling me that her preceptor at Drexel University was working on a violence prevention project in Southwest Philly and that I should send her my resume. I told her that I would, but that I was only interested in volunteering for now, because I needed to finish writing my business plan for my van service and time was of the essence. I was sick of working for other people and was ready to work for myself.

With the information of her preceptor in hand, I went back to my office and edited my resume and drafted a thoughtful cover letter, expressing my interest in volunteering on the project. About a week later, I received a call from her preceptor, Dr. Vaughn, and we hit it off almost immediately. She said she would forward my information onto the principal investigator at Children's Hospital of Philadelphia and have him follow-up with me. I was excited about the possibility of getting back involved in the community and that it would be in my childhood neighborhood. In the meantime, I was still navigating the highs and lows of HIV research and working with a narcissist.

Two weeks after speaking with Dr. Vaughn by phone, I found myself meeting with the principal investigator of the violence prevention project and ironically his office was in the same building as the Bad Blood Center, so sneaking out the office for the meeting was not an issue. I was grateful for the convenience and after meeting with him, I knew I had to be on that project.

He was a gentle man and he was white. It was while sitting in his office that I realized I had not worked under a white man since my technology days in Silicon Valley. Yes, the president of PPV was a white man, but I didn't work directly under him.

As I sat in Dr. Jeff's office, I found myself being able to articulate my needs to work with a research team that put the community first and actually listened to the needs of the community. He was receptive, and his face turned redder at the excitement that I knew research and understood community needs. What I didn't expect was for Dr. Jeff to tell me that he didn't want me to volunteer, but instead he wanted to hire me part time to serve as an outreach worker. He would pay me $16 an hour to go to community events in Southwest Philly and pass out literature about violence prevention.

I was ecstatic because volunteering is great but being paid is greater. He also told me that although I would attend weekly debriefing meetings with the team, and be hired by Children's Hospital, I'd report directly to Dr. Vaughn who was employed by Drexel University. Again, I was ecstatic because I had a good vibe with her.

The position proved fruitful in more ways than one. It was an outlet for me to serve my community, but also for me to release the headaches from working in that damn Bad Blood Center. I met community leaders that were holding Southwest Philly down. I met researchers who actually cared about what the community thought, felt and needed.

I also learned a new style of research called community based participatory research. It's the kind of research that allows the community to have a say in what data is collected, who's collecting the data, and how the data would be used. I was on fire working part time and although I had no love life, for once I didn't give a damn. I was too busy serving.

I was also writing. I had made a promise to myself to finish my business plan by the time I was 40 and it was fast approaching, so I knew I had to keep plugging away. I'll admit the business plan was extensive. I had everything in it from the target market, marketing analysis, and the perceived competition to who would carry out each task. The damn business plan was almost 30 pages and it was good.

Between writing and getting back into the community with the violence prevention work, I was allowed to see that even though I was no longer visiting a loved one in prison, there were many people who were impacted by incarceration and still needed the service and it was my responsibility to provide it. What was most ironic about me not visiting someone in a prison during this time, was that I found out that Faster had gotten himself re-arrested and sentenced to 8-20 years in prison. I was not surprised, nor did I have any empathy toward him.

However, his predicament made me think heavily about the mentality that goes into becoming an offender. I pondered over the conditions poverty and hopelessness can cause in one's life, especially given the crisis I had just narrowly escaped with my son. It also allowed me to think heavily on how my transportation service could mitigate some of these conditions in my own life and others.

I then tasked myself with choosing the right name for the transportation service. Which was an interesting process because

I had always likened incarceration to slavery. I would think about the impact incarceration was having on Black lives and Black families, and go into a tailspin of hyper-vigilant emotions. I'd think of Harriet Tubman and how she'd freed the slaves through the underground railroad, and knew that the van service was the "new underground."

One day, while having these thoughts repeating in my mind, I found myself sitting at a railroad crossing in Southwest Philly on 58th Street, just past Woodland Avenue as a train passing by had me at a standstill. As I watched the train, wondering how many cars were attached and what they were carrying, quite naturally I thought of Harriet Tubman and the underground railroad again as I often did at train crossings. But in that still moment, something deep in the core of me clicked.

I would use the railroad symbol as my logo. I kept looking at the double R's on the sign as I waited for that long ass train to pass and thought "R and R—rest and relaxation, R and R—ride and, R and R—ride and what else, R and R—ride and what am I trying to do here, R and R—ride and what, R and R—ride and rebuild, yes that's what I want to do, I want to rebuild families, R and R—Ride and Rebuild, Ride and Rebuild—Rebuilding Families One Visit at a Time!" After 8 years I had finally come up with a name that had more meaning to my spirit than I could have ever imagined.

After coming up with the name, I started putting the railroad symbol on everything associated with the business plan. That was, until my good lawyer friend Yumn told me that if I used the railroads' symbol it would be a copyright infringement. I don't know what I was thinking, but I enlisted the help of her husband to create a logo that would not send me into litigation with the railroad company. Admittedly, the logo he created was much more appealing than theirs and I couldn't wait to put it on my truck, website and anything else that required signage.

Once I had my business name squared away, I talked about it incessantly at the Bad Blood Center because I finally had hope that this idea was my way out. There was a Puerto Rican woman who also worked there and was extremely business savvy. She asked me to pitch my idea to her one day to see if it would be a good investment. Of course, I did, but I also made her sign a non-disclosure agreement first. Business is business.

After the pitch, she was extremely interested in funding it, but her financial resources were tied up with a house she was flipping, so she told me about an organization in North Philadelphia that provides seed money. Since I had met my deadline of completing the plan, I was interested in seeing if an outside funder thought it was a viable business opportunity, so I reached out to them.

The meeting went great and they did offer me financing but the interest rate was too high, and I wasn't interested in starting my business with that deficit. So, I hunkered down and strategized ways to get the funding I needed. I also had to figure out a way to get the hell out of that Bad Blood Center. I could not believe I was still even working there and was hating who I felt like I was becoming—an ungrateful complaining ass person.

One evening, after a long day at that dreadful Center, I was in my home laying on my back in the middle of my queen size bed, thinking in complaints. You know the kind of thinking that starts with, "I don't have this" and ends with "I don't have that." Well midway through my mental complaining I had a sudden consciousness shift.

As I laid upon a relatively expensive mattress, I started to counter my thinking with thoughts of gratitude. I said to myself "Crystal, how dare you lay on this comfortable ass mattress, in the same room that Ms. Yvonne took her last breath, and not feel abundantly blessed." I rolled over onto my stomach and looked at my bedroom door.

There on the inset of the door was chalkboard paint. I had painted the door with chalkboard paint so that I could write affirmations to myself to remind me of the blessings in my life, which clearly prior to that moment I had been forgetting to do. On the door were the words "Remember to Love." As I read the words, I thought "Yeah remembering to love is great, but what about thanking God for the seen and the unseen." I crawled out of the bed, walked into the bathroom, grabbed a paper towel, dampened the towel, walked back to the door and wiped those words away. In its place I wrote "Thank God!" After writing those words, I laid back onto my bed, stared at the door and counted my blessings.

The very next day, I started acting serious about getting out of the Bad Blood Center. I registered my business with the State and had a serious conversation with Dr. Vaughn about my intent to leave the Center, and desire to work on the violence prevention project more fully. I also started paying my bills on time, going to church regularly, tithing more, and managing my mental health. But more importantly, I disengaged in negative conversations at the workplace and focused on getting my shit together. When God said it was time for me to move, I'd be focused and ready.

What I've learned about God in the past is that He is definitely about his timing, and I did not have to wait long for his tap on my shoulder letting me know my run at the Center was over. On July 30, 2010, eight weeks after writing "Thank God" on my bedroom door, the Director called me into his office and told me he had a bit of bad news for me. He'd have to let me go and rightfully so. I had recently screwed up his travel accommodations that had somehow involved the female German colleague who was obsessed with him, which resulted in her calling me a bitch, and HR getting involved. I knew we would never recover from that and was glad to be let go.

So when he said those words, it took everything in my power to not jump across the table and hug the shit outta that poor excuse of a man. But instead, I took a deep breath and worked out the details of my departure. I would leave on that day but be paid for the next 5 weeks—regular pay every week. Yes! I would be allowed to claim unemployment if I did not find a job by the time I got off the payroll. Yes! I would be able to cash out my vacation time, since I was never able to take any, it amounted to approximately 160 hours at the end of my last pay. Yes! And yes, I could have the MacBook Pro "since it's old" to job hunt. He was so used to spoiling himself that he really thought a 1-year old laptop was old. Nevertheless, I was extremely satisfied with the blessing that God was bestowing upon me in that uncomfortable meeting.

After packing my few items, because I was told I could clean my office out whenever I wanted to, I left in time to catch the 1:30pm showing of the movie *Salt* starring Angelina Jolie at the Bridge theatre in University City. I was on my way to my new happy work life that included running my own business, and giving back to my community. And for that I was grateful, grateful! When I told folks I got fired their initial reaction was shock and sadness, but I'd quickly change their tune when I explained that being fired from that job was like being dumped by a nigga that treated you like shit. Ironically, they got it and wished me good luck in my future endeavors.

PART VI

TRIPPIN' THROUGH THE LAW OF ATTRACTION

-Road Trippin'-

Award Winning

Hands down, unemployment compensation, part time work, and freedom are the best threesome I've ever had. For the next 3 months I enjoyed the process of living. I went back to walking on Kelly Drive more and volunteering at violence prevention community events in Southwest Philly. I was spending my time between Kingsessing and Francis Myers recreation centers working directly with our community advisory board for the project. There were some amazing community leaders on that board, and I built relationships that would manifest themselves in future endeavors not yet revealed.

At Myers, where I once played daily as a child, I was able to run a version of a program I helped develop at the Black Cultural Center called Girl Talk. It was a program that allowed young girls to discuss everything from hygiene to relationships. The original program was conducted in an elementary and high school, but this program at the recreational center was conducted with adjudicated teenage girls. Those meetings were real work. At first some of the girls were reluctant to talk during our group meetings, but after attending a few times and realizing the topics were relevant to their everyday life and current predicament, they began to loosen up.

I really loved this group, and because of their adjudicated status, during activities and discussions I was able to use scenarios that were deemed inappropriate with the girls from the original program. For instance, we were able to talk about what would happen if a young lady was riding in a car with a young man and he had drugs or a gun on him. If pulled over by the police, how likely would he be to give her the case? We talked about physically fighting another girl for a young man's attention and the repercussions that might bring, like getting arrested. I even talked with the girls about the possibility of being accused of a crime that they did not commit. I shared my personal story, and many of the girls were shocked to learn that someone teaching them about relatable experiences had an experience of her own.

The violence prevention project allowed me to use so many past experiences and skill sets under one umbrella. I was responsible for creating a youth advisory board to help us move our research efforts along and to give youth an opportunity to use their voice in changing their community. We recruited youth from the Southwest Philadelphia neighborhood and created a curriculum that supported their development. We also created an opportunity for youth to work as youth reporters, with an internship at the Southwest Globe Times community newspaper. I simply could not get enough of giving back to my community and enjoyed being out in the field.

One day in the field, while attending a Block Captains event at the convention center located in downtown Philadelphia, the universe shifted for me. I was there fulfilling two roles, as a Block Captain and as a violence prevention volunteer. I was manning a table and distributing violence prevention information. I loved distributing these pamphlets because I thought the information was extremely vital to every community in the city. I could recite what was on the brochures without even looking at them. Some one-pagers told parents how to talk to their children if they were a victim of a crime. Others told children how to talk to their friends if their friends were a victim of a crime.

I was busy handing this much needed community information out when a woman approached my table. It was so strange because before she walked up, my table was busy, and as she stood there, it was only her and I. She asked what the information on my table was about, and as I looked into a face that resembled his, my words stumbled ever so slightly, "It's, it's um, it's violence prevention information" I told her. She said in a soft voice, "This is good. This is real good. I lost my son to violence." I could not pretend that I didn't know her. After all, she was wearing a t-shirt with her son's face on it. So, when she said that she'd lost her son to violence, I simply said "I knew your son." And then there were tears. Slow hot tears, streamed down my face. Sweets' mom said, unknowingly, "Oh no, don't cry." And all I could say was, "He was a really good guy."

I wanted to tell her how his life impacted mine and how his death propelled me to be sitting at that very table in front of her doing violence prevention work. But I couldn't, because I realized I still hadn't healed from the pain of losing him. So, I let her walk away and I silently re-committed myself to fully actualizing my purpose, to give back to my community and serve those impacted by violence.

A few months later, in October of 2010, I was ready to go back to work full-time and was offered a position at Drexel University School of Public Health, under the leadership of Dr. Vaughn. It was an exciting time to be at Drexel University. They were a fair university and paid me well. Neither they nor Dr. Vaughn questioned my choice not to have a degree, but instead honored my journey that combined my street smarts with research experience. For the first time in my career, I was valued for my community knowledge. Finally, I felt like my "lived experience" counted for an education at an anchor institution in Philadelphia.

Of course, I could have gotten a degree by then. But with all the contributions I had made to research, by supporting projects on various research levels, I could not see myself sitting in a classroom trying to get a Bachelors' degree with my personally crafted Masters' level experience.

It just didn't make sense to me, and since many universities and colleges are pushing their degree agenda, and not considering lived experience as an equation to degreed experience, I was thankful to finally work for one who didn't question whether or not I belonged there doing community work. After all, how can you conduct research in a community and not have someone from the community add validity to your research? At this point in my career, I never second guessed my validity nor my value. I owe a lot of that to the leadership of Dr. Vaughn, though. She valued me, and it showed.

Not only did Dr. Vaughn trust my community knowledge since she was not a native of Philadelphia, she trusted my research skills. We wrote grants together, met with funders together, and when it was time to implement research, she trusted me in the field alone to manage the project and the team. This woman literally changed my perspective on Black women in the workplace. I had had my run of the catty, non-supportive, crabs in a barrel, Black women in the workplace. But the team that Dr. Vaughn and I created in her lab was unlike those and integral to our collective success.

The team was gendered and ethnically diverse, came from various socio-economic backgrounds, and were brilliant. Until working directly under Dr. Vaughn, I had never seen a team support one another the way that our team did. We submitted our work to publications and conferences together and we traveled together. We also celebrated accomplishments and we grieved losses together. It was an incredibly supportive environment that encouraged me to keep striving toward my goal of starting my van service.

One day in late April, I received a call from the politically savvy former Penn student. He had heard about a business plan competition hosted by the Women's Opportunities Resource Center (WORC) in Philadelphia and thought I should enter it. The competition was *"for women owned businesses that had a strong social or community impact as part of their regular operations or culture of the business, a clearly defined concept and customer base, and a plan that could communicate how the business would work."* He said that the deadline to apply was in 2 weeks, but he thought it was worth me hunkering down and going for it.

After the call, I did my due diligence and found out the requirements for the award. It seemed simple enough. Submit your business plan and a PowerPoint presentation to present to the judges. There was a $2,500 award for first place (and free business services) and $1,500 for second place.

The deadline was May 2nd and we would know four days later if we had been chosen as a finalist. We wouldn't know if we had won until the night of the awards ceremony, which was scheduled to occur two weeks after that. I was hyped. It would be my second time presenting my business plan to someone with the hope that they'd see the need that I saw.

The application process was so easy that it didn't take me long to submit. Once submitted, I tucked the thought of winning away and carried on with life. A life that included a letter from Faster telling me about his newly incarcerated status for "being reckless."

Of course, I wasn't shocked that he was in jail; I already knew. I was just shocked that he had reached out to me. But I just couldn't bring myself to reach back out to him, because quite frankly, I was disappointed in him. How ironic that as I was gearing up to embark on fully realizing my dream to start the van service, Faster would be right back at the beginning of where we had started from. It was sickening.

Nevertheless, completely true to their word, I found out four days after submitting my business plan to the competition that I was a finalist. I was ecstatic. I'm not going to lie, deep down on the inside of me, I knew I had written a good plan. After all, I already experienced successful results in the past after writing my reparations plan. I knew my intentions were in the right place with wanting to create a business like this and I was simply happy that those judges thought so too. I'm convinced that mentioning Harriet Tubman during my presentation sealed the deal, but I still wasn't sure if I was one of the 2 winners.

The award ceremony was held at a fancy law firm, Montgomery McCracken Walker and Rhoads on Broad Street in downtown Philly. The ceremony was coupled with a silent auction and had a shitload of wine and hors d'oeuvres. I invited, of course, Dr. Vaughn who had been a source of encouragement since I first mentioned my dream to start a transportation service to her. I also invited a colleague from Children's Hospital and a few of my childhood friends. I felt so supported in that room that even if I wasn't a winner, I felt like one.

After a few glasses of wine, the ceremony started. I was thankful for the wine because my nerves were all over the place, and the wine helped me calm them. As the announcer spoke, I was tuned all the way in. She started by saying, "When we began this process, we only intended to give out two awards, but because this business plan was so inspiring, we had to create an award just for it..." I said to myself, "They are talking about me!" Almost immediately after that thought, the announcer said, "This award comes with a $350 gift for this woman to purchase the Philadelphia Business license needed to operate in the city and it goes to Ride and Rebuild, LLC!"

She then went on to share what Ride and Rebuild was all about and after her words, I was called up to the front of the room to accept the award. I walked up there with confidence, that was until my ankle slipped in my platform heels and I almost fell in mid strut. Nevertheless, I accepted my award, gave a quick thank you to the committee and judges and strolled back to my seat proud of how far I'd come with my vision.

That was an exciting night, however, I was not prepared for what followed. The next day, I received a call from a well-known reporter, Jeniece Armstrong from the Daily News, for an interview. The phone interview was enlightening. I had never given an interview for something I had created, nor had I been asked about the gritty details of my relationship with Faster. Telling that story to a complete stranger should have been weird but Ms. Armstrong had a way of eliciting information from me that I didn't know I wanted to even share.

The article was released the next day and my phone did not stop ringing. I was shocked at how many people still read the Daily News, considering more of us were reading our news online. Friends and family were so supportive of what they read that any jitters about exposing my truth to a news medium were eased away by the love I received. Finally, the day after the article was published, I was contacted by WORC because the winners were scheduled for an interview with Loraine Ballard Laurel from the local R&B radio station, WDAS 105.3 FM.

It was during that on-air radio interview that I realized I had to get my affairs in order and fast. I had no truck and no website, so when she asked, "How can listeners schedule a ride?" I was quick on my feet and said, "We'll be up and running by January, and all transportation information can then be found on our website at www.rideandrebuild.com." Needless to say, the next several months were a whirlwind of paperwork, truck hunting, website development, fundraising and believe it or not, religion changing.

New Thought

Religion has always been a part of my life. I have studied as a Jehovah's Witness and up until this point, I had practiced Christianity for most of my adult life. However, I often struggled with the concept of Jesus as God and would find myself in heated debates with other Christians as to where in the Bible did it say that Jesus was God.

I also struggled with the theory of the Trinity as God the Father, the Son and the Holy Spirit. I absolutely believed that Jesus existed, and was actually a fan of the greatest man on earth, but I could not pray to him after spending a significant amount of time learning the Witness faith. It was just hard for me to call God anything other than what I was led to believe was his first name, Jehovah.

I was comfortable speaking directly to Jehovah and didn't understand why I had to say "in Jesus' name" at the end of my prayers. I would find myself sitting in that big church on Lancaster Avenue poking holes in the pastors' entire sermon and feeling guilty for having done so after each service.

The Church and the fellowship were serving me, but the "word" was just not sticking. I would often stagger in there after a night of partying, feeling like what difference does it make that I did a whole host of "sinning shit" the night before if all I had to do was put my burdens on Jesus and he'd take care of the debt. I felt no accountability for anything in my spiritual life living with the concept that all I had to do was repent and my sins would be forgiven.

Don't get me wrong, I loved the "church" and most of the people that I attended with, but there was something off about the Bible and the Jesus dialogue that just didn't resonate with my spirit. I was often uncomfortable when the pastor would tell us that anyone who did not believe in Christianity was going to hell. I'd cringe at the thought of all my beloved Muslim friends and Jehovah Witness family members that would never make it to the promised land with me. Then I'd sit in the church and call the pastor all kinds of names in my head, and of course feel guilty afterward.

I was an active member of the church too. Often holding Bible study meetings at my home, attending women's retreats and leadership events. I felt part of the community, but again, my spirit was flipping like a fish out of water on the inside. I just couldn't get the concept of Christianity down to the science that other "good" Christians were able to, and I knew that something major was about to happen because of that. Remember, God always gives me what I want, good, bad or indifferent!

The changes started to occur slowly, and it involved my son. It was right after he had gotten in trouble with the law for the 19 bags of weed. I immersed him into the church and since he was born of free thinkers, me and a poet, he questioned everything in the Children's Church. When I would go to pick him up after service, I'd see him sitting either by himself or outside of the room with the look that said, "the group leader needed to speak with you AGAIN", all over his disobedient face.

I could not understand why my son had to question everything. Why couldn't he just let the leaders lead? But again, he is my child and I should not have expected anything other than him having questions; after all his first sentence as a baby was "what's that?" Not to mention if you recall, Ms. Yvonne herself had gotten kicked out of Bible study a time or two during her Christianity run for asking unanswerable questions.

Finally, after sitting my son down to get to the bottom of why he just couldn't "act right" in Children's Church, his question to me "Why would you go to a place that told you everything you did all week was wrong and then make you pay them for giving you that information?" made me decide to allow my 12-year-old son to figure out his own spiritual path. I did not "make" him go back to that church or any church ever again. But his words stuck, because every time I listened to the pastor tell me I had been a sinner all week and that the only time I thought of God was on Sunday, I felt compelled to keep my damn tithes in my pocket.

One day, at the end of a staff meeting, I was venting in the conference room to a colleague about my experience with the church. She allowed me to rant and rave about my dealings with Christianity. Finally, she said to me, "I think you'd like my place of worship…you should join me one Sunday."

I asked her, "Do ya'll believe that Jesus is God?" She smiled and said, "No, that's not our thing." I responded, "Well what do you all believe?" She replied, "we believe in New Thought." Of course, I asked the appropriate follow-up question, "What's New Thought?" She simply stated, "We believe all paths lead to God and that there is only one infinite God."

I was intrigued. She told me that if I wanted to join her that Sunday, I was more than welcome and that she would pick me up from my home. I was grateful and agreed to attend.

That Sunday she called when she was 5 minutes away. I told her that I would be standing on my porch. I was excited to attend a place of worship that did not believe that Jesus was God. I didn't know what to expect but as I eased into her passenger seat in my Sunday's finest and Bible in hand, I was ready for whatever.

The ride to Elkins Park was peaceful. I asked her many questions about the type of congregants that attended and when I learned that her "reverend" was a woman, I had to hold onto my seat. After all, I had just left a patriarchal religious construct that allowed women to be "first lady's, but not reverends or pastors." I was more than intrigued at this point.

As we made a right onto Beech Street off 19. and Cheltenham Avenue, I wondered how much longer the ride would be. Several hundred feet later, we made a left turn into a driveway. I was perplexed because I didn't see anything that resembled a church on the horizon.

The only signage on the premises was a sign for Temple's Tyler School of Art. I thought to myself, how ironic Temple is the home of a church that doesn't believe that Jesus is God. But later learned the "church" was not on Temple's property but beside it. Driving down the short driveway, we veered slightly to the right and I saw what appeared to be a cottage style building on the left. We parked and exited the vehicle.

It seemed that I saw and felt everything simultaneously. From the sight and smell of the bright green grass on the grounds, to the soft sound of birds chirping in the trees, the summer breeze wrapped itself around me and I felt a loving stillness. The entire scene was serene and overwhelmingly peaceful. Something in my spirit settled and a sense of calm washed over my entire body. As I followed my colleague to the wooden doors to gain access to the building, a smile pulled at the corners of my mouth and I allowed my face to release any tension that came with walking into the unknown.

Stepping in the building with my right foot leading the way I knew I had found my spiritual home. The entire space smelled of incense. There were congregants walking about greeting each other with love and hugs. As my colleague introduced me to everyone we encountered, I received a warm welcome and embrace.

I think what impressed me the most was that although the congregants were diverse in ethnicity, the majority were Black and had "natural" hairstyles. The women had dreads and sister locks, and some of the women had low haircuts like mine. The men and women wore afro-centric printed attire and although their clothing was not traditional church attire, it was all wonderfully made. I was impressed with all that I was taking in.

The service started promptly at 11am and many of us made our way toward the doors of the sanctuary. As we entered, we were greeted by a congregant with a hug and program detailing the service of the day. I took my 7. hug and program and sat down beside my colleague.

As I listened to the musical selection being played, I was surprised that it was not a gospel song, but a song by Earth Wind and Fire. I was on cloud 9, thinking to myself what kind of magical place is this? The reverend then entered the sanctuary along with congregants with purple stohls adorning their necks. She walked to the podium, not to be confused with a pulpit, because the podium was angled to the right of a three-step stage that led to an arched breezeway that showcased a stained-glass window with fresh flowers all around.

As the reverend greeted us with a smile, she told us that we would open the service with the ringing of the Chakra Bowl. The purpose of this practice was for us to release any energy that would not serve us during our time at the Center of Peace. We were invited to close our eyes as a "practitioner" stepped up to the large white glass bowl, took a small wooden rod, placed it on the rim of the bowl and moved the rod slowly, clockwise against the edge creating a hum that grew into a beautiful lovers' moan throughout the room.

Initially I watched the practitioner, but almost immediately I was overcome with the need to feel that vibration internally. So, I did as instructed, and closed my eyes. As the practitioner with the purple stohl rang the bowl, every bit of anxiety, uncertainty, and dis-ease, slowly left my body.

Soon thereafter, a small bell rang and as I slowly opened my eyes, I saw another practitioner walk up to the podium and open a book. I looked around and saw that everyone else still had their eyes closed, so I quickly closed mine, not wanting to disrupt the flow of whatever was to come next. Sitting with anticipated breath, the practitioner started to talk in a soft voice saying to-day's reading was from the book *The Science of Mind* by Ernest Holmes. She then began to give the reading and concluded by asking us to say in unison, "And so it is."

When I slowly opened my eyes, I felt high. Like a good-good weed high. I felt like I was in heaven on earth. I was excited to see what would come next. I did not have to wait long, the practitioner who was reading, took a seat, and a trio of women walked up to the right of the stage.

In that area was a keyboard and a gentleman sitting behind it. The women instructed him to play an instrumental track. Once the music started, the entire congregation started clapping in anticipation. Clearly this was their favorite song and I could only assume these women were going to give me a performance to remember.

I was not disappointed, one sounded like Rachelle Ferrell, the other Denise Williams and the third harmonized with the other two effortlessly. I was moved by their voices and the fact that they did not sing a gospel song. I was so intrigued by their performance that I did not realize congregants had gotten out of their seats and were dancing in the aisle.

Not the typical praise and worship, catching the holy ghost dance, but actually two-stepping, partnering up and "bopping" to the beat. I got out of my seat and just started clapping my hands and snapping my fingers because I felt no condemnation and only love in that peaceful place. If the music and dancing didn't seal the deal for me, it was the hugs after the song was complete. Members were walking over to one another and embracing each other with love and adoration.

As the hugs came to an end and the congregants went back to their seats and the Reverend approached the podium. She was a short, round, brown skinned woman with silver and black hair cut in a bob. She gave thanks for the person who rang the bowl, the person who gave the reading, the trio who sang and the gentleman who made sure the music worked. She thanked us for being there. She even gave thanks for the people who were not there, knowing that they were covered in love by the creator wherever they were. She gave thanks to the creator for allowing his words to flow through her in the message. She gave thanks to the creator for simply being the creator.

Once she was done giving thanks in her sermon, she began to tell me that I was perfect, whole and complete and that I am a direct illumination of God. She told me that my birth was not a mistake. I was not born of sin. In fact, she told me I was born out of love, because God does not make mistakes. She told me that since God does not make mistakes, there is no way that my life could not be the perfection that I had, in my mind, created it to be. How could my life be anything but perfect if I share the mind of God, after all God made his children in his image. I was hooked on this woman's words.

She continued to tell me that there is only one God and that Jesus was righteous in his love for God. She expressed that Jesus was the first to exhibit the law of attraction—what you think is what will be. This was music to my ears, because I often would tell anyone who'd listen that Jesus was the first "rider" for God. I passionately believed that his *belief* in the power of God was so strong, it allowed him to perform miracles.

I too often thought that my belief in God allowed me to perform miracles as well, like navigating the emotionally and mentally violent institutions of higher education. I mean damn! I thought I could do the work without a degree and I did. It was only by God's power that I was able to not buckle under the pressure of raising my son through the 19 bags of weed experience. I thought we would make it through that ordeal, and we did. And if those two experiences weren't perfect examples of my belief in the power of God, being able to move back to Philly after those horrific allegations involving Sweet and Haroon, and still being able to prosper and love, definitely solidified my faith in the one God and the idea that what you believe is what will be.

At the end of the sermon, she called the "prosperity team" to the front to receive the offering from the congregation. There was no long speech about giving because it's what God told us to do. There was only the request to give with the intention of love so that the funds could be used to further the mission of the center. I was so happy to give my money to this place.

I know this sounds crazy, but I felt like I had been treated to the greatest show on earth and making a financial contribution to their cause was the least I could do. Finally, I had found my spiritual tribe. When the offering basket was passed around the congregants sang acapella, *"I am so blessed, I am so blessed, I am so grateful for all that I have,"* and I felt every word of that song. After the collection was received, she offered a prayer to carry us from the sanctuary, to our homes and through the week, until we fellowshipped with one another again.

There was so much about that first day at the Center of Peace that changed the course of my life for the better. For starters, I activated my "thoughts become words, words become things" power. I was intentional about my thoughts, making sure I did not stay too long in ideals of lack and limitation. I tried my best to think in abundance as well as visioning for my life assets and opportunities not yet tangible. I was finally able to see that I was responsible for what occurred in my life, good, bad, and indifferent. All week there was an internal glow that I knew was coming from the depths of me. I couldn't wait to get back to that place and eat up more of that spiritual food.

The following Sunday, my colleague was unavailable to go but gave me explicit instructions on how to get there on public transportation, since I didn't have a car or my prison truck yet. I hate to admit that I did not follow her directions at all, and ended up having to walk over a mile in Birkenstocks, in the summer rain, to the Sanctuary. The Center is located on the Elkins Estate in Elkins Park, PA, literally across the street from Philadelphia if you cross Cheltenham Avenue.

But because I decided to take a train and not the bus like I was instructed, I ended up on the opposite side of the grounds. They were beautiful, to say the least. There was lush greenery everywhere, a pond and monuments placed throughout. I just couldn't figure out how the hell to get to the other side.

At one point, I heard some "kids" playing and decided to walk toward their sound, thinking they could direct me to the street to get off the grounds. As I got closer to the kids, I heard them yelling "heyyy…heyyy…heyyyy". I could not stop smiling, thinking my trek would soon be over, that was until about 50 feet away from the "kids" I looked up from under my umbrella and saw three baby goats, yelling "heyyyyy…heyyyy…heyyyy." I froze because I suddenly realized I had never seen baby goats all willy-nilly in the world. I looked at them, they looked at me, and I did an abrupt about face saying to myself the entire time, "Please don't chase me, please don't chase me."

They didn't, but by the time I made it to the Center I was wet, tired and discouraged. I kept saying, "The devil is trying to block my blessings." But as I settled into my seat in the sanctuary the message enveloped me in so much love, clarity and truth, that I knew me getting lost on my way to the Sanctuary had nothing to do with the devil. I had to take accountability for my part in that snafu. I simply had not followed explicit directions and because of that my trip had been uncomfortably altered. I did, however, say to myself, "I need to get my Ride and Rebuild truck, enough of this public transportation shit!" and set my intention on manifesting my truck.

Within two visits to the Center of Peace, I realized that manifesting is a real thing, because on Monday after getting lost on the Elkins Estate, my Uncle Vernon called to tell me that he had found a 15 passenger Chevy truck for Ride and Rebuild. I met him in Sharon Hill the next day to see and test drive it. The following day, I went back and purchased that truck, and that upcoming Sunday drove to the Center of Peace for more centering.

Dream Team

As always, my life operates in layers. On the top there's the dream I'm actively manifesting, in the middle there's the daily mundane tasks that need to occur in order for my dream to manifest, and on the bottom is all the dumb shit that just has to happen in order for me to count my blessings. Although I was more peacefully centered now in my life, trying to get Ride and Rebuild off the ground literally tried to tap me out, and I did not know if I was coming or going.

For starters, my son, my beautiful intelligent son, was trying to be in a rap group. But not just a regular old, he's the DJ and I'm the rapper kind, but the full on—DJ, rapper, blogger, product designer and photographer group, which consisted of himself and 5 of his friends. Now, you would think the poet would have taken the lead on this initiative, since he's the "artist" in the family and my son was currently under his care. But, he was too busy starting and stopping his own life to carve out any creative time for Empire Gang! Yes, that was their name. Every Mere Penny Is Real Everyday, Gang!

I didn't mind the weekly Sunday meetings in my spare room with the group of boys and one girl. It was enlightening to have access to 5 teens who had no issue with discussing everything but rap group shit. We talked about visions, ambitions and goals. We even talked about sex and drugs.

No, I did not have their parents' permission to meet with them, nor to discuss those topics. But I also did not have one parent come and check on their child while they were in my presence. It's funny how people really don't care what their children are doing when they're not at home.

I was glad that my son and his friends trusted me and my space to keep them safe and serve them through discussions that would aid them through life. Those conversations proved extremely fruitful as those 5 teenagers began to grow right before my eyes. I know some of the choices they inevitably made would not have been able to come into fruition had they not been meeting at my home on those Sunday nights. We would have weekly discussions and I'd learn more about their interests.

One of the boys wanted to be a chef, so I contacted the Walnut Hill Culinary School and set up a time for us to attend their open house. The only young lady in the group was interested in photography, so I reached out to Jeniece Armstrong at the Daily News and took her, my son, and the two student reporters working on our violence prevention program for a tour of the Philadelphia Inquirer. I was completely in my element working with those kids, and my proudest moment was when I decided to host a fundraiser for Ride and Rebuild and enlisted their help.

I was a few thousand dollars short from reaching my goal to get the business running, and I needed to think critically because although my license was secure, I had to go through the Pennsylvania Public Utility Commission to officially transport people across the state. The PUC had approved my application, but I needed to show that I had the proper insurance. The down payment for the insurance was hefty and hosting a fundraiser seemed logical.

I reached out to Lorene Cary at the Art Sanctuary to use her new space in South Philadelphia for the event. She was excited to help and waived the fee. I needed entertainment, so I asked the poet to perform for free, which he obliged. I had a few of my girlfriends support me in setting up, bartending, accepting funds, making food and conducting the raffle. The young people were there to help set up, clean up and take photos. The fundraiser was a success and I enjoyed every moment of the event. I always say, "If you're not having fun at an event you planned, then what was the point?"

Although the fundraiser was a success, with Yumn donating the most and former students from Penn being the number one financial online supporter, I still needed additional funds. It just so happened that the Puerto Rican woman and former colleague at the Bad Blood Center had reached out to me and invited me to a fight party at her house.

When I went to her fight party three weeks before I was about to miss the deadline to provide proof of insurance to the PUC, she asked me in her beautiful kitchen "Are you all set to start your business?" Maybe it was the tequila, but I didn't hesitate to say, "It's crazy. I know so many people that have or have had a loved one locked up, that I cannot believe I still don't have enough money to get this fucking insurance!" She promptly replied, "Well how much do you need?" I told her, "About two grand." She said, "Come back on Monday when we're not drinking and let's talk." That following Monday, I went to her house, we talked, and she wrote me a check for the balance of the insurance.

I was grateful for her support. But when I think back to that time, there were quite a few people that stepped up to help me during those months before I officially went on the road. One good brother, who I met at a cookout in Southwest Philly, was the first to step into the role of hands-on supporter.

I was standing on the corner, when my cousin who had just come home from jail after a 10-year bid, called me over to him. He said, "My man wants to meet you." I asked who his man was, and he pointed to a brown-skinned handsome brother sitting in a car. I said, "Well how is he going to meet me sitting in the car?" and started to walk across the street away from my cousin and Mr. Handsome.

My cousin must have immediately relayed the message, because Mr. Handsome put the car in park, turned it off, hopped out and walked toward me. He truly was a beautiful man. As he approached me, he held out his hand, and as I extended mine, he took it and kissed the back of it. I said, "Oh you wanted to meet me, meet me?"

Mr. Handsome and I talked a while and exchanged numbers. He told me he had always had a crush on me, which I thought was interesting because I don't recall ever seeing him a day in my life. Since he was fine, I allowed myself to be flattered. I asked him what exactly he wanted from me. He told me, "If nothing else, friendship."

Admittedly, I was attracted to Mr. Handsome, but I could manage a friendship much better than a fuckship. Especially since he also mentioned that he was taking a break from his relationship and didn't know where they were headed. I could use a friend, with no strings or benefits attached, because I had way too much going on in my life and fucking with someone who was halfway in a relationship already was not the move. However, as time went on the friendship with Mr. Handsome became paramount in getting my truck on the road and he, along with everyone else who had supported the development of Ride and Rebuild, became my dream team.

Mr. Handsome was especially helpful, giving me names of brothers at multiple institutions to reach out and send my business information to, in his name. He even purchased my GPS system for my truck. He was incredibly supportive and although I wanted to cross that line, I remained steadfast and kept Mr. Handsome as just a friend. Besides, my work with the youth was about to take an unexpected turn, and I needed all my wits to process the change.

One night as our weekly Sunday youth meeting wrapped up, I was ushering the young folks out of my house because I needed to get my son to his dad's house, where he still lived. The young men of the group decided to "play" fight with each other. The aggression that I saw being released was intriguing; it was as if they just had to get something off their chest and no amount of coaching from Ms. Crystal could diminish their need to be male. After about a good 6 minutes of the foolishness, I hollered "alright, cut it the fuck out!" and the action ceased. Afterward, my son and I hopped in the car and took the 20-minute trip home to his dad's in Germantown.

I loved those short rides with my son. We were able to reflect on the meeting we'd just had, the upcoming week, and anything else that was going on with him. It was important for me to talk to my son about the changes occurring in the neighborhood too because he was a teenager now, and the consequences were becoming dire as the Black males grew around us. I could always, for the most part, count on my son to follow my street advice, especially since I had shared with him the Haroon, Sweet, and me tale. He was always receptive to whatever science I dropped on him, especially with the increase of drug sales occurring in our neighborhood.

I dropped him off and headed back to Overbrook. The ride home was calming as City Avenue had minimal traffic on a Sunday night. I was in a good place, having done my weekly work with the teens. As I rounded the corner to my block, I saw the police tape. The police were out of their cars talking to one another. I rolled down my window and asked, "Officer, I'm the block captain, what happened?" The officer walked over to my car and said, "There was a homicide in the driveway. I'm going to need you to back out of the block." I did as I was told. Luckily for me my block has two entrances, and I was able to enter from the opposite end and park.

As I walked toward my house, I overheard my neighbors replaying what they heard and who had been shot. It was one of my son's childhood friends. Not one of the teens who had been frequenting my home on Sunday evenings, but another childhood friend that he had played Yugioh cards with on my porch on many summer days.

A friend who had two parents in the home. A friend who was well taken care of. But a friend, who had decided to entertain the street life. A friend who favored pills. A friend who I had just seen in the Bodega on the corner the day before and told him, "you take care of yourself." A friend who was gunned down in the driveway for the neighbors to hear his screams, and for the police to throw him in the back of a police car to rush him to the hospital, where he was pronounced dead upon arrival.

It was difficult breaking the news to my son. Up until that point, he had never experienced death by homicide. I allowed him to process it but would not allow him to purchase a t-shirt with a photo of his friend and the letters RIP on it.

I explained to him that because we did not know who murdered that young man, I did not want him being associated with whatever neighborhood beef was playing itself out at the time. In short, I didn't want my son to be a senseless target. I did, however, allow him to go to the funeral. Although I hadn't yet used my van for Ride and Rebuild, I used it to take the neighborhood youth to the funeral including the burial site.

My block was never really the same after that homicide, and the youth slowly stopped coming by on Sunday's for our weekly group meetings. It wasn't as if they stopped needing the support, but they had all been impacted by the trauma that community violence has on a young brain. Unfortunately, the group meetings weren't enough to block out the pain.

On the Road

Although the young people had stopped meeting weekly with me, I often saw each of them in the neighborhood. I would stop them to debrief on what they were up to and what, if any, steps they needed to take to move into or out of a predicament. These were good kids, so the predicaments were minimal, like what classes to take at school, what girlfriend they needed to get rid of, and whether or not they were still practicing their art and what advice I could give them to keep pursuing it.

I didn't want to stop meeting with the youth, but the timing of the group dissipating was beneficial to Ride and Rebuild. It was finally time to get this show on the road and I was so very ready. Although Haroon and even Faster were supportive regarding the idea of starting my van service, it was Mr. Handsome, who made sure I officially got on the road. He checked to see if the truck was properly maintained and if I had made the connections with his friends on the inside to build up my ridership. I assured him that I had done all the proper tasks, and even though I had, I still took my first trip with only three passengers.

The first riders of Ride and Rebuild, were two women and a baby. I didn't care! I was excited to just have people in the van. We were headed to Smithfield State Correctional Institution, located in Huntingdon, Pennsylvania. Although my van service was listed on the Department of Corrections website, I still had to do my very own due diligence and get the word out. So, I reached out to a childhood friend who was currently serving time at that prison to spread the word, and I wasn't disappointed that it had only netted three riders. In fact, I was grateful.

Having less people in the van on that first trip eased my fears, knowing that I had never traveled to that part of Pennsylvania before; even with a GPS system, the probability of getting lost was there. For me, getting lost with two women and one baby was less stressful than getting lost with 12 riders on the van.

Although I had designated pickup and drop off locations, since there were so few traveling, I picked them up at their homes. I know for a fact I would not normally do that, because learning from the pilot study I had conducted years' prior, waiting outside for women who may have overslept, couldn't find their identification, or had changed their mind, was not something I was interested in experiencing ever again, especially knowing that I then would have to drive three and a half hours back and forth across the state. But these first riders did not disappoint; they were on their steps when I turned onto their street and we were off and on our way to the prison.

That first ride was indicative of what each ride afterward would be like. The women were chatty until we hit the highway, and as soon as the road opened, and the music settled into their core, they were fast asleep. It was exactly what I believed would happen. It was also a testament to me that these women trusted my driving.

When we arrived at the prison, I parked, and we all proceeded to the entrance of the institution. As I mentioned, I had a childhood friend who was in that prison and he had added me to his visiting list so that I could visit him. I was excited because I was interested in learning what my riders would experience checking into the institution, and what better way than to have a visit myself.

The first thing I noticed was how helpful the guards were. I had only been to Rockview prison and I had heard that each prison was different and that the guards could be racist. These guards seemed opposite. We were asked if we had on underwire bras, and we all confirmed that we did not. We were then asked, one by one, to enter through a metal detector. We did. After the metal detector we were asked to go into a smaller separate room, where our hands were scanned for drug residue. Even though I had not smoked any weed the night before, I was still nervous about that part. But once I scanned clean, I was cool.

The next part was unusual. You see in Rockview, you weren't allowed to go into the visiting room until your loved one is meeting you on the opposite side of the door. But at Smithfield, you were allowed to go straight into the visiting room and wait for your loved one to come. Now, although I loved my childhood friend dearly, by the time he walked through the visiting room doors I was pissed!

He had taken a half an hour to get there. And in those 30 minutes, everything was starting to get on my nerves. The children were too loud. I swore I could smell the stench of the bathroom that was located 20 feet away from me. I felt like everyone was staring at me wondering if I was EVER going to get a visit. If that wasn't bad enough, by the time he brought his ass in the room, most of the good food was gone from the vending machine. It's funny how you could not have seen someone for almost 8 years and even though you should be focusing on the joy of seeing them again, I was too damn mad to engage with him for the first 10 minutes of our actual visit.

As I sat angrily for those first 10 minutes, I realized that I wasn't angry at how long he had me waiting; it was that I was physically and emotionally tapping out. I hadn't really taken into consideration that I'd been up since four in the morning preparing for that trip, had driven one hour through the city to pick up my three riders, drove another three and a half hours across Pennsylvania, and then was expecting myself to sit in a 5-hour visit, and complete a return trip with no rest. I had underestimated my capacity to sustain myself throughout the day, and the adrenaline that had propelled me at the beginning of my day was seeping away. When I finally was able to express this to him, he said he understood, but then proceeded to give me a list of things to do for him when I returned to Philadelphia, which pissed me off all over again.

Nevertheless, the return trip was pleasant. The women and baby fell into a deep sleep as we traveled toward Philadelphia. I knew it was the music because my iPod was loaded with soulful sounds that would make a person think of the one they love and then drift into a peaceful slumber. But also, seeing my riders sleep assured me that like when we started out, they felt comfortable with my driving and the validation of that first trip was all I needed to keep going, even though I was exhausted.

In the next couple weeks, I received riders from the department of corrections website, and word of mouth. I had a few friends with family members on the inside, and they were spreading the word as well. I reached out to a good brother in Rockview prison, and he added me to his list so that I could visit him when I brought riders up.

But I soon realized that I would need to cut back on my personal visits. It was hard to break the news to the two brothers I had been visiting because I knew that I was not only an administrative asset helping them to facilitate outside endeavors, but my visits were also a relief from the mundane of prison life. Nevertheless, I had to do my best to take care of myself. After all, I was still working full time at Drexel and on the road on the weekends, so there was never any down time for me and it was becoming physically challenging.

I was also connecting with the community more. My friend from SCI Graterford, informed me that there was a fatherhood program run out of the prison focused on bringing children to visit to keep fathers in their lives. He told me the program had an outside team and thought I should reach out and he would do what he could from the inside to get me on. I was ecstatic.

Since it had always been my passion to start this type of program, knowing that it already existed assured me that I didn't need to recreate the wheel. I could instead lend my expertise to an existing program. I was even more excited when I learned that one of the members from the external team was an elder who was on the community advisory board we created with the violence prevention program. I reached out to him and he said he'd put the word in that I wanted to join the team. I felt the alignment of all my ideas unfolding and it was a wonderful feeling.

But as I was starting to get my bearings in the van service world, my truck started to act funky. I knew I needed a tune-up and was referred to a mechanic by Mr. Handsome who was still very active in helping me with Ride and Rebuild. So, I trusted his referral. That was until the following Saturday, at mile-marker 276 on the Pennsylvania Turnpike, my truck, loaded with 10 women, stopped running. I was livid, but luckily I had the premier coverage on my Triple A plan, which meant they would either try to start it or tow it to my mechanic back in Philly.

I called Mr. Handsome and he immediately went into fix it mode, asking me if I was safe, how many women were with me, and that he would call the mechanic immediately. I felt secure knowing he was working it out on his end. But the problem exacerbated when Triple A arrived and told me the truck wasn't starting, they could get it back to Philly, but not all of the riders. I was sick!

I got back on the phone with Mr. Handsome, but this time I was not nice, because in my head it was his fault for referring me to the, now in my mind, "jackleg mechanic." But again, he went into fix-it mode. He told me that he could get to us but the car he had could only fit 6. I told him that was good enough and called my girlfriend Mecca, who has always been there for me in a crisis. She agreed to come to get the other four.

I thought they would have to meet me on the Turnpike. But the tow company agreed to take a few of the women and the

Turnpike Patrol agreed to take the rest of us to King of Prussia Mall. Mr. Handsome and Mecca were waiting for us when we arrived. I was more overwhelmed than I had ever been, but knowing that I had people willing to assist me in the toughest times meant the world to me. On top of that, the women were incredible, they never complained and some even said, "Things happen, it wasn't meant for us to go today, and that's ok." Of course, I organized a free trip for them after that fiasco.

When I arrived back at my truck in Philly, I had a few choice words for the mechanic as he assured me that he would get to the bottom of what went wrong. Apparently, there was something wrong with the distributor, which he fixed and before nightfall, my van was parked safely in front of my home. Mr. Handsome apologized profusely for all the hell I had endured. I knew it wasn't his fault, but it was thoughtful that he wanted to take responsibility for it.

A few nights later, as I was sitting in Outback Steakhouse with my girlfriend enjoying a great dinner, I received a text from Mecca asking me if I had seen the news. Heart dropping, I texted back "No, why?" She responded, "Mr. Handsome is wanted for murder!" I gasped and simultaneously Googled our local news station, and sure enough, Mr. Handsome's face was plastered in an article stating that he was wanted for murder. I cringed. Not because I had never received horrific news about a friend, but because I just could not see this friend making this kind of move. Especially since I had just seen him and the compassion he exhibited to me and my riders just did not match up to the crime that he was wanted for.

I left the restaurant in a daze and the next few days were spent trying to wrap my mind around the absence of Mr. Handsome. Unfortunately, he'd decided to "go on the run." Word on the street was that he wasn't going "in" without a fight! I kept wondering if he would reach out to me and if he did, what would he even say?

One night, about a week later, I had a dream that he and I were standing in the middle of a wide road, with the sun rising behind him. He said to me "They are going to think you know!" I said, "Who will think I know, and know what?" As he turned to leave, he said "them" and pointed to something behind me. When I turned to see what Mr. Handsome was pointing to, I woke up.

Two nights later, I was putting the final touches on letters to inmates that Mr. Handsome referred me to, as well as the cousin of Mecca who I didn't know was serving a life sentence at State Correctional Institution Somerset. I addressed the envelopes, sealed, stamped and placed them neatly in my inbox on my desk so I could easily grab them in the morning when I left for work. I cut the light off in my home office, which was actually my other bedroom, and went to bed.

I slept fitfully, with thoughts of the past week on my mind. Still dark outside, at 5:45 am, I heard rustling outside my bedroom window that overlooked my street. Being a light sleeper, I immediately woke up and listened. I heard the rustling again and some voices. I thought to myself, "Somebody is trying to steal my damn truck and at 5:45am!"

I crept out the bed to look out the window, and instead of a thief, I saw six US Marshals in full riot gear. Two were standing across my small street, under the light. Two were walking away from them toward my house, and the other two were walking up my steps. It took everything in my power, to not faint but to run to my bedroom closet to grab a sweater, because I was literally in panties only. I knew that if I had tried to put clothes on, my front door would have been knocked down.

Grabbing a cardigan, I ran down my stairs to the living room door, just as they were about to use the battering ram to enter my home all while yelling "open up, US Marshals!" I snatched the curtain on the door to the side, so that they could see that I could see them and unlocked the door. As I opened, they asked,

"Are you here alone?" In a startled and pissed voice, I said, "Yes, now come in before you wake up my neighbors…I'm the block captain!"

Five of them entered, with AK47's drawn, three ran up my interior steps to the second floor and one even dropped his helmet. The other two Marshals stayed on the first floor with me. One told me to sit on the couch, passing me a warrant to search my property, and the other headed toward the kitchen.

As I sat, the lead Marshal, who had handed me the warrant, asked if I knew why they were there. Calmly, I said, "I guess it's because someone I know has been on the news all week!" The Marshal responded, "Well more than that, we were told that you were hiding him here." I said, "Well, as you can see, there's no one here but me." He then replied, "Well you can tell us what you know about him here, or you can come downtown with us to answer questions." I responded, "Well you need to ask all the questions you have here, because I'm not leaving my house."

He then proceeded to show me a picture of Mr. Handsome asking if I knew him and for the second time in my life, I was confronted with telling law enforcement what I knew or didn't know about an alleged criminal. With a deep sigh, I told him I did know the person in the photo. The Marshal then shared that Mr. Handsome was wanted for murder. I responded, "So I heard."

Before he could ask another question, the other Marshal, coming from the kitchen asked me if anyone was in the basement and I told him, just my cat so be careful when you go down there not to upset him. He opened my basement door and went down. The lead Marshal then began to ask me when was the last time I had talked to or seen Mr. Handsome. I was honest because if they had tracked his phone calls like I know they had, I was sure the Marshal knew the last time I had talked to him. I told him, not since the day I was stranded on the turnpike.

I could feel that the lead Marshal wanted to be "Marshaly" and mean, but the energy in my home just wouldn't allow for it and I slowly started to see his demeanor turn from rogue cop to civil servant. He then tried to convince me that Mr. Handsome was the most violent offender walking the face of the earth. I told him, "Well the person who's been on the news and who you are describing, is not the person that I know."

Just then the three Marshals who were upstairs started to walk down the steps looking defeated. One came over to the couch and before he could ask me a question, I asked him "Can you open that closet door and get me a coat because I'm sick of sitting here in my panties." He obliged and got me a coat.

When the Marshal handed me my coat, he asked if I was a government worker. I told him, I wasn't and asked why. He said, "Well you have a calendar in that second room with prison names on it." I chuckled (yes you can chuckle when you know for a fact you are not hiding an alleged fugitive in your home) and said, "No, I have a transportation service to the prison, that's my schedule." He said, "Wow, what made you get into that?" I gave him a side eye and stated, "That's a conversation for a different time" and turned my attention back to the lead Marshal. I asked him, "Are we done here?" He said, "For now, but I do think he's going to reach out to you and when he does, we need you to call us." He then gave me his card and he and the other Marshals' left my home.

As I locked up my house and put my coat back in the closet, I dreaded going upstairs because I just knew they had ransacked my home. But to my complete surprise, there were no over-turned beds or anything out of place, aside from the closet doors opened, and the shower curtain pushed back. I later learned that a search is less invasive when officers are looking for a person as opposed to evidence.

After closing the closet doors and adjusting the shower curtain, I went into my bedside table drawer and grabbed the sage and my lighter. I stood in my bedroom, panties and cardigan on, and started the slow process of burning sage throughout my home to get their human and automatic rifle energy out of my house. I started in my bedroom, chanting the words "you are perfect, whole and complete" while burning sage under the bed, in the closets, in the shower, and did not stop until I was standing in my basement with my bewildered cat watching me burn the last bit. As the smoke settled I thought about how intuitive my dream had been, and after that, I let the tears drop.

As you can imagine, I was completely shaken by the energy the Marshals brought into my home. I mean, it was the place where Ms. Yvonne died. It was the place that I was co-raising my son in. It was the place that I served youth in. It was the place I had loved men in. It was the place that I had created my van service in. It was a safe space. It was my sanctuary and it had been violated. But having been heavily practicing the Science of Mind theology, I also knew that our thoughts and behaviors attract our experiences. Although I did not wish to manifest that nightmare, somehow my affiliation with Mr. Handsome led to the disruption of my peace.

Unfortunately, I could not truly process the trauma that experience had had on me, because the very next day I received a call from my friend at Graterford telling me that I had been invited to join the Fatherhood Program's external team. He informed me that a meeting was coming up the following week and I was expected to attend. I used that 15-minute phone call to thank him for putting me on, and then gave him a coded version of the travesty that occurred in my home the night before. He told me to come up there so we could talk face-to-face, and as I dropped the marketing letters to the inmates at the various prisons in the mailbox, I assured him that I would make my way there soon.

Pushing Through

Instead of seeking therapy immediately after the incident at my home, I pushed myself deeper into my work at Drexel, community activism, and the van service. Monday through Friday I was conducting research in Southwest Philly, simultaneously attending meetings with the Fatherhood program, and on the weekends trekking up the turnpike. All while Mr. Handsome was still on the run!

I'd be lying if I said I did not miss his presence in my life. He was a good friend and someone I could count on for my van service. After that incident with the van breaking down on the turnpike, I started experiencing a bit of anxiety every time I approached mile-marker 276, as if my truck would break down again in that exact location. As the anxiety would start to consume me, it would become exacerbated with the thought that Mr. Handsome would not be there to get me off the road. It would take me utilizing breathing techniques or mantras I had learned from the Center of Peace, like "I am perfect, whole and complete" to bring my anxiety down.

Since this wasn't my first time dealing with anxiety, I knew exactly what to do. I went to my primary care doctor, shared my current trauma, and asked for a refill of my Ativan, which she immediately did. I was only prescribed .5mg and I took it every time I went on the road after that. It didn't necessarily take the thoughts away, but the feeling of cortisol being dumped into my bloodstream eased a bit.

After the Marshal incident and the subsequent anxiety on the road, I also made a conscious decision to completely stop visiting anyone in prison. It was taking too much of a toll on me physically and since I was working with the Lifers on the Fatherhood program, I had access to the inside of a prison, and psychologically that was wearing me out. Partly because up until that point in my life, I had never been beyond the visiting room of a prison. Working with the Lifers, I was allowed to go deep within the halls of an over 80-year old penitentiary and it was disheartening. Despite the upbeat nature of the brothers, seeing so many in burgundy apparel with DOC labeled in cream bold letters on their back almost always made me think of slavery and that I was on a heinous plantation.

Our meetings were held in the auditorium and to reach the auditorium from the main entrance, you had to walk what felt like four city blocks. I know the brothers couldn't help it, but as I passed by, I could feel their stares on the front and definitely on the back of me. I was mindful of what I wore inside the prison, but it still didn't stop the stares. Nor did it stop me from hugging brothers I hadn't seen in years, when I did get a chance to run into them on that long walk to the meeting space. Hugging was not allowed, but I couldn't seem to follow that rule, even if I wanted to.

The meetings were a bit overwhelming because it seemed to always involve at least 20 brothers from the inside, plus our five to ten from the external team, and of those individuals there were only about 4 women, including me. It was simply too much testosterone in one confined space for me. However, it seemed that whenever we met inside the prison, we got more accomplished than in our external team meetings. I had to admit, the brothers on the inside had their shit together and knew exactly what outcomes they desired; they just needed us to have our shit together for it to come into fruition. But again, it rarely happened once we left from inside those walls, and because of that I wanted to limit the amount of time I spent inside prisons from that point forward.

So, on my Ride and Rebuild trips, instead of visiting the brothers in Smithfield and Rockview, I started exploring the counties that those prisons were located in. The first county I explored was Huntingdon, Pennsylvania. It was an idyllic town, nestled in the Tuscarora mountains. It was famous for having more churches than any other Pennsylvania town.

As the season changed from early spring to early summer, I started to walk the streets of Huntingdon, discovering a park that had a canal turned creek streaming alongside it. I would drop my riders off and go to that park. I'd walk around the park, as it had a paved path for walkers, to get my blood circulating after the long drive up. Then depending on my mood, I'd either walk through the downtown which consisted of two blocks and eat with the natives, or sleep in the van for a few hours and eat afterward.

When summer approached, I had to get more creative with where I spent my time, because the van had become too hot to sleep in. I signed up for a library card and would go there, open a book on my lap, and sleep for hours. I knew that no one bothered someone who slept while reading. This technique proved beneficial to my overall feeling of safety in those all white spaces. The folks in the library were always kind and never looked at me as if I didn't belong. I felt such good energy in that library, that I made sure I got a library card in the other Pennsylvania counties with prisons I visited so that I had a place to rest when I was in their town.

There were other activities I did while on the road. I found movie theaters and would always check out the latest blockbuster. I even visited a cave once and learned about the "white nose" epidemic that was killing off thousands of bats, almost making them extinct in the region. I had favorite restaurants I visited and allowed the locals to get to know me and debated in conversations about "prison life" with white elders who didn't know any better.

I'd explain to them that in a town like Philadelphia, crack occurred, and we lost a lot of good minds and good men to that struggle, which then allowed for their county to have a prison and create jobs for their families. Those conversations weren't easy, but they were necessary to change the narrative of "us vs them." As I think back on those times, I know it was because we had a Black president, that those natives were willing to hear and even consider my rationale.

In the early days of Ride and Rebuild I was learning more than I ever thought was possible about the rest of Pennsylvania. I had heard that unlike Philadelphia, the rest of the state was conservative and in those early days, I saw it subtly. There was always this sense of superior Christianity in those towns and when my women, who were largely of the Islamic faith, would enter the stores in those towns, the stares were uncomfortable.

The libraries were also very conservative with large quantities of religious books on display. There were even WIFI parameters that asked you to not visit certain websites—so in those early days I had no access to Facebook while on the road. But I loved exploring those towns and having all that free time to myself. With so much on my plate back in Philadelphia, I looked forward to my weekend getaways.

As time moved away from the Marshal incident, and with the help of my anxiety medication, I was able to think a bit clearer and developed a true friendship with one of my connections from the prisons. He was one of the responders from my inmate marketing campaign and he was Mecca's cousin. I found him easy to write to and when I would receive his responses, I felt cared for and safe. Perhaps it was because he was extremely articulate and compassionate with his words, and because I remembered the terror he had been on the streets before his bid, I was impressed with his growth.

It seemed like he had all the right words to say to me, and his letters would come just when I needed them. We agreed that we should meet face-to-face, which he kept calling a sit-down. But for a few months I had issues getting on the visiting list. First the paperwork never arrived, then my birth date was entered in the DOC's system incorrectly. It eventually worked itself out and after about four months of writing, I found myself back inside visiting a brother in prison. But this time at State Correctional Institution, Somerset, four hours from Philadelphia.

I was extremely nervous about this visit. It was like I had been preparing for a blind date. And although we had been writing to one another, I had never heard his voice over the phone. I knew what he looked like because he had sent me an updated picture in one of his letters, but I still wasn't prepared for that fine specimen of a man that entered the visiting room. As he walked toward me, I told myself, "I'm going to marry him."

That first visit was everything my spirit needed to push through the trauma of that incident with Mr. Handsome. I was finally able to sit with this brother and tell him word for word what happened before, during and after those Marshals came to my house. I had written to him about some of it, but I would never put half of what I was able to share with him in person, in a letter for correctional officers to read prior to giving to him.

He listened intently, never passing judgement on Mr. Handsome for putting me in such a vulnerable predicament, and when I finished, he looked me in my eyes and said, "Well I'm thankful to Allah that you made it through all of that." It was in those words that I knew not only would he be a good friend, but he would also go to his Lord on behalf of me in prayer. And I needed all the prayers.

When I left the visit, it was nothing but adrenaline that got me down that highway. After all, Somerset is 4 hours away from Philadelphia and if you count that one hour pick up and drop off time, I was looking at a 10-hour day pushing a truck around Pennsylvania. The whole ride home I wrote a letter to him in my head and the next day I penned my words:

June 25, 2012

Dearest Khalil,

Well it's the day after our visit. I hope you know that I made it home safely and in good spirits, I must admit. I really and truly enjoyed our visit, Khalil. As I was rounding the corner to park on my street, I checked my phone and saw that I had a missed call from Mecca. Immediately I dialed her back and she expressed that you had called her and asked if I had returned safely. I was pleasantly surprised. I love a man of his word, because as promised, you called to check on me.

So, the visit was great. It was more than I expected but everything I had hoped for. This morning when I awoke I did something strange. I re-read all the letters I had written to you. I wanted to see if there was anything that I had written to you to make me feel the way I felt when I left Somerset—starting from my initial correspondence. Strangely enough there wasn't. I wanted to see if my intentions in my correspondence (or your response to my correspondence) could have prepared me for what I felt after leaving Somerset or even waking up this morning.

Let me explain. When I left Somerset after our meeting I was in a somewhat tranquil state. I talked a bit with my passengers, but consistently found myself in a contemplative internal dialogue. I kept shaking my head from side to side because the thoughts that kept popping up were a bit confusing to me...almost laughable.

First I kept thinking to myself "Buck is still handsome!" Then I'd shake that thought and laugh to myself and think... "Well what did you expect?" Then I'd think to myself "Buck sure has beautiful teeth"

*and then again, I would think to myself and laugh...
"Well what did you expect?" But as I rode on down the
turnpike I started to have more serious thoughts...like
"I wish he wasn't so far away...I wish I could sit with
him more often...I wish I had more time to spend with
him...I wish I could remember everything he said...I
wish we had discussed religion...I wish...I wish...I
wish..."*

*Finally, I had to say to myself, "Stop wishing and stop
thinking Crystal. Don't trouble yourself with all that.
You are going to find yourself wishing for more than
you bargained for." So, I kept putting thoughts of you
in the corner of my mind. But I will admit it helped
me get home safely and in good spirits. However, as I
mentioned above, as soon as I was about to park on
my block I spoke to Mecca and she informed me that
you had called and asked about me. So of course, I'm
thinking, how sweet, he's a man of his word, but then I
also thought...I wonder if he had been thinking of me
from the moment I walked out of that visiting room?
So, Mecca is blabbing away about your call and I'm zon-
ing out...she then comes over and mentions that you
said I had "great energy". Thank you!*

*But as Mecca was sharing this information with me,
my mind was swirling. I understood what you meant
by great energy, but of course I was thinking...what
part of our visit made him say that? So then as she
was sitting in my "business lounge" and I'm rummag-
ing through paperwork trying not to make eye contact
with her in fear of disclosing my inner wishes, I kept
replaying our visit through my mind. As I stated, I truly
truly truly enjoyed my time with you.*

*I was happy when she left, because I had only about
15 minutes alone with myself from the time I dropped
my happy passengers off until the time she arrived. I*

needed to process the visit a bit further. However, when she left I found myself making me a tuna fish sandwich and sitting on the couch and telling myself, "Don't think about Khalil right now. You' re exhausted, hungry and the energy you felt was intense. Sleep on it and see how you feel in the morning." So, I watched a bit of TV and then crawled in the bed.

I slept well, but when I awoke this morning, you were the first thing on my mind. I thought about your smile, your fingernails, your beard, your glasses, your kufi, your smile again, your honesty, your words of encouragement, your laughter, your thoughtfulness, did I mention smile, and your hug. I also thought about my ride home and how the experience of just being with you put my journey in a groovy mood. I had Erykah Badu playing and while the women were sleeping, I held my miniature ceramic turtle in my hand while simultaneously gripping the steering wheel thinking of you as our song 'Time's a Waistin' guided me down the road.

Khalil, I promise you, you made my day yesterday. I am so thankful to God for allowing that visit to be more than I could have hoped for. Thanks for telling me I wasn't too fat, thanks for sharing that you thought my eyes were beautiful and thanks for stating that "I got past you" when we were younger, and you regret it. Lol. You are truly an ego booster! I felt like a woman when I left you yesterday. Like a real grown ass woman. Only a real man could ever have the power to make me "feel" like a woman.

Before I forget…thank you for pointing out that visiting room window and showing me where you rest your head. Now I have a visual of where you are probably reading this letter (and if you aren't in your cell, go there now to finish this letter). I'm thinking about the speaker over your window and the light fixed above the cell on the exterior. I'm thinking about the desk in front of the window. I'm thinking of you peering over the desk to look out the window towards the visiting room to remember where we sat. I'm thinking of your bunk bed and you laying your head on your pillow. I'm thinking of those 2 ridiculous 19" TV's in your cell, one with cable and one without. I'm thinking about you Khalil, and I'm liking it.

Truly,

Crystal

A couple weeks after I sent that letter to Khalil, Mr. Handsome turned himself into authorities and began the battle for his freedom. I in turn, felt a sense of relief, because one thing the Marshals made sure to mention to me was that they knew about the word on the street that he wasn't going in without a fight. So, while he was on the run, I kept dreading the idea of him being hunted and gunned down like an animal who had escaped the wild.

I also felt like I was being watched while he was on the run. Although I checked under my vehicle for tracking devices and I never found one, I still had the uneasy feeling that my every move was being surveillanced, especially with me traveling upstate as frequently as I did. But, with him being in custody I could finally grieve the loss of him and be comfortable with my anger at his stupidity.

I'll admit, there were times when Mr. Handsome and I interacted, and I'd drop science on him about perception. My theory was, that if someone thinks you're getting more than them, then you will be a target. He knew what the streets were about, but he also had no qualms about playing in those streets. I wasn't judging Mr. Handsome for how he moved, I was just saddened that I couldn't help him move in a better direction.

Unfortunately, two weeks after his capture, the stress of life, coupled with poor eating habits, and lack of proper exercise resulted in me learning that I had "attracted" Type II Diabetes. I was devastated. Not because I was the first to get the disease in my family, my Uncle Vernon had warned me years ago to watch my diet because he had also attracted it, but because I thought I knew better and should have done better. Ironically, my Drexel team and I were working on a Diabetes prevention intervention with community members and knowing that I had gotten this disease made me feel like a fucking hypocrite in the field. So, I made a vow to conquer this illness immediately.

PART VII

TRIPPIN' THROUGH RESILIENCE

-Visit Day with a Real One!-

In Perspective

Learning that I had developed Type II Diabetes, although devastating, was not shocking. I mean if I really wanted to be honest with myself, I was doing everything in my power to manifest that chronic disease into my life. I ate poorly, I worked too many hours, was still consuming a tad bit too much alcohol in my "free" time, and the stress of driving long distances on the road all led to it. I also had a new understanding of the term "it runs in the family," because even after evaluating the lifestyles of my uncle and especially my mother, the same behaviors of over-indulgence, high stress, and lack of self-care rang true in all of us. I just knew that I had to do everything in my power to get rid of it.

When I shared the news with Khalil that Diabetes was the reason why my leg was tingling and I was unable to shake the fatigue after long hours of work, he was distressed. His reaction was completely unexpected too. I didn't realize that when someone is incarcerated and they hear that a loved one on the outside is sick, and there is really nothing they can do about it, it becomes their emotional burden. I assured him that I would be fine.

Besides, I was working on a Diabetes prevention program and I had all the tools I needed to beat this thing. He told me to be careful and that he would send me some literature on the disease. There was no point in reiterating to him that I had all the literature at my fingertips thanks to my job and Google, so I just agreed to receive it, read it, and apply the knowledge.

Although I absolutely did not want to have to deal with a chronic illness, it was a relief to be able to explain why my body wasn't feeling well since starting the van service. There were physical struggles with operating the service from the onset. I had never pushed a 1-ton vehicle before, nor had I pushed it with almost 1-ton of passenger weight, so the wear and tear on my short legs were unforgiven.

Early on, I had found myself at the doctors getting cortisone shots in my knees because they were over extended. For a short period of time, I had to wear a knee brace. There also were circulation issues with sitting for those long hours. One doctor suggested yoga, and upon arrival to my prison destination, elevating my legs in the truck.

That worked for about a month, but once I started taking the Diabetes medication, I definitely felt much better. I did, however, continue to elevate my legs or would walk through the towns to get the blood flowing again. I also changed my diet drastically. I stopped eating fatty foods, and cut out drinking all together.

I still smoked weed during the weekdays when I wasn't driving because it helped ease my tensions. I exercised more and found myself becoming more centered and balanced, thanks to attending the Center of Peace whenever I had a free Sunday, which unfortunately wasn't often. I lost weight too, enough weight to make me feel like I was getting my life on track.

I was so grateful for the support of Khalil. True to his word he sent me literature from the prison, with sections highlighted by a yellow neon marker that he wanted me to pay close attention too. He would call and check on me daily to see if I had taken my medication, had eaten a proper diet, and gotten enough rest. This guy was creating a sweet spot in my heart that could only be reserved for the kind of love that would place no demands on me. Because I absolutely needed to be loved in an undemanding way.

I looked forward to our nightly calls and I loved receiving his weekly letters. He was such a caring soul and he never asked for anything in return. He never asked me for money, and when he knew that I needed to rest after those long drives he told me that if I couldn't make it in to see him when I arrived at Somerset, it was okay with him. He just wanted me to be healthy and well and admittedly, I was falling deeper and deeper into that love.

I would share with Khalil that I'd never had a man not need something from me. I told him that in all my relationships I was the sole giver of time, talent, and treasure, and to have someone who I had never been intimate with show me so much compassion was at times incomprehensible. Being the modest man that he was, would respond, "you deserve it."

I had never been cared for in that way and would find myself fantasizing about being his wife within the predicament of incarceration. After all, I had loved several men who had found themselves in the predicament of incarceration, but never someone who was serving life and that I would even consider going the long haul with. But since I often viewed myself as someone that has miracles performed by God for them, I was sure I could be the wife of a man doing life without the possibility of parole. So, I kept fantasizing.

In the 17. year of his conviction I found Khalil's life sentence interesting to observe. He had been in Somerset since the judge ordered him to spend his life behind bars. He was a spiritual man, a devout Muslim, and highly respected in the facility. He was extremely knowledgeable about the law and worked in the law library. Although he was a serious man, when he would relax his mind and allow a bit of humor to seep in, he could be funny. What I found most intriguing about Khalil was that he never masturbated. I kept asking in various ways, how in the world could he manage that time without rubbing one out? He would chuckle and simply say, "Discipline."

Although Khalil told me I didn't have to come in and visit him because of my illness, I could not keep myself from inside that prison. I loved sitting in his presence. I loved the way he smelled, smiled and felt when we would share a hug. I would even ask him to recite the Islamic prayer Al-Fatiha for me, even though I had no idea what it meant.

Khalil was eloquent and never uttered a curse word to express himself. I on the other hand, still cursed in our conversations and he never ever once asked me not too. He was a breath of fresh air. I had men who were not nearly as articulate as he tell me I shouldn't curse, it wasn't lady-like, which I thought was ridiculous because they were still trying to fuck regardless of my vernacular.

One of the many benefits of having Khalil in my life, showering me with compassion, was that I realized I didn't need the company of other men. After the fiasco with Mr. Handsome, I was literally off men. I couldn't trust them. I could work with them, but not allow them into my personal space. Having Khalil check on me was strong enough to keep my personal space male free. It was a relief to not have to entertain men during that time in my life. I had learned that men had been my biggest distraction throughout the years, and not having one physically up my ass was a relief.

Khalil's support helped me put many areas of my life in perspective during that time, and that also included my community work. I had been working with the Fatherhood Program, going in and out of the prison, attending meetings at the state representatives office, and it was exhausting me. Don't get me wrong, I loved the mission, but in working on the external team I learned when you have more people wanting recognition for doing work and not enough people actually doing the work, you have to figure out an exit plan.

I had been trying my best to assist with their program planning while running my business and working full-time at Drexel, but there were just too many ego hurdles to jump over and I had to step down from serving. At first, I felt guilty because I had met some great people on the team. I loved the brothers on the inside, some having been part of the violent organization that introduced crack to my beloved Southwest Philadelphia neighborhood but had completely turned their spirits around, and I didn't want to quit on them. But Khalil assured me that the work I had done for them had not been ineffectual, and that my health was paramount. He said, "Don't beat yourself up. You did more than you realized and when you're up to it, you can always go back and help out later."

So, I sent a letter to the Lifer leaders of the initiative explaining why I was stepping down, but giving them a lessons-learned and next steps memorandum that would sustain them in continuing their mission. There was no love lost and the state representative, who received a copy of the memo as well, kept saying, "I really hate to see you leave Crystal, I could see you running this." I was flattered, because despite what the media would later depict of him, out of all the external team leaders, I knew that his heart was really into the movement. But my chapter had ended with them, and I was back out riding and rebuilding families in Philadelphia and falling deeper in love with Khalil for encouraging me to put my health first.

Falling in Love

Loving Khalil was extremely easy. In fact, it was the easiest love I'd ever experienced. Unlike Faster, he didn't lie to me, kept his promises and I knew where he was at all times. And for a woman who's ever loved a "thug," knowing where he was meant a good night's sleep.

With Khalil's love, I was able to rest in it and for the first time in my life, I allowed myself to be vulnerable with a man. Loving Khalil was more than enough to keep the memories of Faster and Haroon dormant. It's as if his love gave me the safety I needed to set their trauma-bond free from me.

After a while I could no longer contain the feeling of falling in love with him and had to express it every chance I got. I would tell Khalil that we should get married, and he would always respond with, "you think you could handle that?" There was no doubt in my mind that I couldn't handle being his wife. He didn't require much, just visits and phone calls, and maybe a few trips to the Criminal Justice Center or online searches to help him gather information for his appeal. Although he was serving a life sentence, he'd vehemently expressed that he was not spending his last days in prison, and an appeal or new trial was always in the forefront of every move he made.

I loved assisting him with his research efforts. It was interesting to read through his trial transcripts or go to the scene of the alleged crime and take photos for him to add to his Post-Conviction Relief Act packet. He was always grateful for my foot work, and I was happy that I was able to bring him some solace in such a tiring fight. Being his assistant was gratifying and because he made sure to thank me for my efforts, I was always willing to do more, even though he rarely asked much of me. I did assure him though, that it didn't matter what I had on my plate, I would help him to get free.

When I first started visiting Khalil at Somerset, he'd often express the desire to transfer from his current location to Graterford which was closer to home. His parents were aging and he knew it would be a matter of time before they'd no longer be able to make the four-hour trek to see him. I gave him my honest opinion about Graterford.

I told him the prison is old, there is no air conditioning and everything on the inside is rusted out. I also shared that there are too many temptations in Graterford for a brother like you who has street credibility and a clean record. I knew that if he were to transfer to that prison and get around brothers from the old neighborhood, anything was liable to happen to change his course.

I also informed him that I was on someone's visiting list down there already and was not interested in being removed from it, because you could not be on two lists at the same institution. Finally, I shared that I may want to become involved with the Fatherhood program again and me loving him may jeopardize my ability to conduct business there. After all my "I don't think it's such a good place for you" talks, he decided to put in a transfer to an institution that was closer to Philadelphia, but not Graterford.

I was so excited that he was going to transfer because I was convinced I'd visit him more if he was closer. We did not know when the transfer would go into effect because the DOC never tells when a move was happening until the night before, so we just had to play it by ear. I still had to Ride and Rebuild, and that's what I consumed myself with.

One of the things I loved most about operating the van service was listening to the needs of the women. They would often say, when a visit was over, that they wished they could have stayed longer or gotten locked in there with their loved one. We'd often laugh, but one day I asked the Somerset ladies if they'd be interested in an overnight trip. They did not hesitate to respond in unison with a resounding "YES!" I told them I'd figure out the logistics, and plan an overnight trip in the upcoming month.

I was excited to share with Khalil that I was planning this trip because it would also give me an opportunity to see him for two days in a row. By this time, Khalil knew that I was madly in love with him and wanted him to be my husband, because at every opportunity—through phone calls, visits and letters—I told him. He was just as excited as I was for the two-day visit.

I informed the women that for a nominal fee, the trip would include transportation, two visits, and a shared hotel room. There were 5 women who agreed to the terms and one week before Thanksgiving, my birthday weekend, we stayed overnight in Somerset. Unfortunately for me, Khalil had gotten transferred that Tuesday so I was unable to visit him, and instead did what

I would have normally done in an upstate town in Pennsylvania; I explored.

Khalil was transferred to State Correctional Institution Mahanoy, located an hour and forty-five minutes from Philadelphia, and 6 miles from Pottsville, PA, where Yumn grew up. Since Mahanoy was already on my schedule for visits, I knew that I would be seeing him within the two weeks post the overnight trip. That would give him enough time to get acclimated with his new environment, which was similar to Somerset because it was built in the same year, was newer, and had better creature comforts for inmates, like air conditioning.

It was actually one of the institutions that I recommended Khalil petition to be sent to because I knew it matched his current quality of life. I know folks would probably think that an inmate would not have a certain quality of life, but having been in several prisons you easily realize that depending on the year a prison was built the conditions could vary from prehistoric to modern. Besides, I knew that Khalil didn't need to be focusing on things like air quality when he was falling in love with me and trying to become my husband.

Visiting Khalil at the new facility was easy. The guards were extremely nice, almost too nice. The lobby was large, and the visiting room was well maintained and had more than enough seating. They even had an outside area, which was nice because Khalil and I would sometimes sit outside on our visits at Somerset, and I definitely didn't want to give up those moments of catching a breeze with that fine man.

On our first visit I asked him the customary questions: how are you holding up, what's it like here, and are they treating you well? He told me he was doing fine, the institution is pretty much the same as Somerset, and he's had no issues. He shared that there were a couple brothers who had been up Somerset with him that were there, and it was good seeing them again after all this time.

As we were sitting in the visiting room, I looked around and saw two older inmates with dreadlocks. They were on separate visits. One of the elder men was playing chess with an elder visitor and the other dreadlocked inmate was engaging with a white couple. They looked familiar so I asked Khalil if he knew who they were, and he responded nonchalantly, "Oh the one playing chess is Eddie Africa from MOVE and the other guy with the white visitors is Mumia Abu Jamal."

I was immediately star struck. To Khalil they were just comrades in the struggle, but to me they were icons. It was like watching a version of "Where are they now?" play itself out before my very eyes, and I proceeded to tell Khalil my 56 Street story. He was intrigued but never shared any information about the two icons other than, "they're good dudes." Over time, I learned to stop gazing at Mumia and Eddie when I'd see them in the visiting room, which was often, and would just sit back and enjoy my visits with Khalil.

I loved Khalil being so close to Philadelphia. On days that I didn't have a trip I would just drive up there to see him. Those moments were the best, when I didn't have to worry about passengers and whether or not one of them was able to visit, or got kicked out early for touching their loved one inappropriately. On those solo visiting days, I could ride up the highway, blasting my music deep in thought, arrive at the prison, take my time going in and take my time coming out. Those visits were the ones where I would repeatedly ask Khalil when we were going to get married. He'd just smile and say, in due time.

I could not understand why he just didn't want to get it done already. I had already met his daughter, his mother and father. I was best friends with his cousin so there shouldn't have been any hold ups. But for some reason he kept delaying it. I did everything to show that man that I was in it for the long haul. For instance, I knew Khalil did not celebrate birthdays, but I loved celebrating birthdays and his was coming up in April. He was turning 41 and since I could not send a gift, I sent him 41 cards. Not one of them said "happy birthday," but I made sure I wrote a love note in each of them letting him know that I was glad he had been born. I guess the cards worked because, finally, on a solo visit in May of 2013, he asked me to marry him and I said absolutely.

Now here's where it got a bit tricky. I had no real clue on how to get married inside of a prison. I just knew that I wanted him to be my husband and he wanted me to be his wife. But because Khalil was so resourceful, he attacked the issue from the inside. The first thing he did was reach out to his counselor to see if marriage within the prison walls were permissible, and it was. He was told that I would need to contact the courts of the county his prison was in to find out the cost and protocol.

I wasted no time getting the information. I learned that to get a marriage license we would need to have a teleconference provided by the court, where Khalil would be at the institution and I at the courthouse reviewing and faxing the information to be signed. Managing the appointment was a bit of a headache because it would require me traveling there on a day that I did not have a trip, but also when the teleconferencing equipment was available at the institution.

Before we could do any of that, however, Khalil and I were instructed to meet with his counselor for her approval of the marriage. I was taken aback by that, but as we met with her and she explained why, it made sense. The counselor's job was not to discourage us from getting married, but to make sure I was not being forced into the decision. I found that a bit ridiculous, especially since I felt like I had been the one pressuring Khalil to marry me.

She asked if I was aware of his sentence length, because apparently men were lying to women about their sentences to get wives. I assured her that I was. She then asked if I had any concerns about Khalil's sexuality, because men were having sex with men inside the prison walls and lying to women about it. I assured her that I was confident that Khalil was not having sex with men. She then asked me, what I had planned to do about a relationship without sex. I told her that I'd had enough sex to last me a lifetime and that I would be just fine. As our meeting concluded she stated that she saw no reason for us not to proceed with the marriage, and informed Khalil that she would note the recommendation and put it in his file. I was elated!

I then set out to find an Imam to marry us. Since I was quite comfortable with my New Thought spiritual practice it didn't matter who married us, and I wanted to honor Khalil's Islamic practice by having an Imam conduct our ceremony. I reached out to Yumn to see if her mother knew of an Imam who would be willing to marry us. She immediately relayed the information to her mother, who then relayed my contact information to the Imam she knew, who happened to be the Imam for the prison. I was so excited when I told Khalil, as I could not believe how things were falling into place.

A few days later I received the Imam's call while working at one of our sites for our Diabetes Prevention program, which happened to be in one of the major mega churches in Philadelphia. I hurried to find an empty meeting room in the church to give him my undivided attention. As I spoke to him, I could not help but notice how melodic his voice was, and how he kept referring to me as "sister." I felt extremely comfortable speaking with him. From the onset, I knew that he had spoken to Khalil because he kept referring to him as "the good brother."

After our introductory chatting, he immediately explained that he would not be able to perform the ceremony because he was an employee of the Department of Corrections, and it would be a conflict of interest. I was discouraged but completely understood the policy. I expected for us to end the call after that disclaimer, but he kept talking.

He asked me if I had children and I told him that I had a son, who had just recently decided to practice Islam. He then asked about my faith and I explained my version of New Thought, but told him explicitly that I believed in one God. He then asked me, "Sister, if your son is Muslim, and your fiancé is Muslim, then why haven't you converted?"

I told the Imam, "Well, I never thought about it. I'm comfortable with what I know and what my spiritual practice is doing in my life." The Imam, gentle in his approach, said, "That's great, do you believe in Angels?" I said, "Of course I believe in Angels." The Imam said, "Well you believe in one God and the Angels, what about the story of the Prophet Muhammad?" I told the Imam, "Oh I love the story of the Prophet Muhammad, he makes me think of Jesus in the way he loved and honored God."

The Imam said, "Well sister, if you believe in one God, the Angels and you are aware of the Prophets work, then what's stopping you from taking your Shahada?" I assure you, the way the Imam said Shahada made my heart flutter in peace. I told him, "Well nothing's really stopping me from doing it, I just never really thought about it." He replied, "Well, I could give you your Shahada now, over the phone if you'd like?" And in the basement of a megachurch, I took my Shahada and became a Muslim.

When I hung up the phone, I sat for a few minutes and said to myself, "What in the world just happened?" About 30 minutes later, Khalil called from the prison and I told him what I'd done and all he said was "Alhumdullilah, how do you feel?" I told him, "Honestly, I don't know how I feel, I don't even know what to do next. I do know that we still need to find someone to marry us!"

A few weeks later, the local courthouse referred me to a commissioner who would marry us for a small donation to a community organization. The process was easy enough. He would meet us at the prison and conduct the ceremony in the visiting room, prior to visiting hours.

I, a new Shahadah, had an over-garment made for the occasion and my son who was already a practicing Muslim, wore a thobe of a complimentary color. We were married in the presence of his daughter, my son, and Mecca during Ramadan. No one ate except me, because Islam allows Muslims who have chronic diseases to fast in other ways. It was a beautifully uncomfortable experience, to say the least.

Prison Wife Life

One of the things I noticed first about being married to Khalil was that nothing had physically changed in my life. I still slept alone, ate alone and conducted business alone. The only major change was trying to navigate Islam on my own. Khalil was extremely considerate with me and my learning curve.

He sent me literature and told me the first thing to do was learn the Al-fatiha, because without it, my prayers would go unheard to God. The literature was interesting, but learning Arabic was difficult and from the onset; I questioned why I had to pray in another language. Khalil did his best to explain the practices of Islam to me and even though all my close girlfriends, Mecca, Kaiah, Pocah and Leslie, were Muslim, I just couldn't wrap my head around all the protocols needed to access God. It was the most spiritually confusing time of my life, and unfortunately, practicing Islam only lasted about six months for me.

I felt so uncertain about my life during that time and not being able to pray in the way that I was used to, like in the bathroom on the toilet, or in public without washing up first was just too much for me. I understood why Muslims practiced Islam in that way, but I just couldn't do it. Khalil was gentle when I explained to him that I had to walk away from the teaching because the disconnect I felt from God was more damaging to my psyche than I needed it to be. He assured me I wasn't going to hell for making the decision that was best for me, even though I knew his religion said otherwise. Nevertheless, I left the religion and re-engaged with my practice of New Thought.

I was grateful for reconnecting with the Center of Peace because I was experiencing transitions in my life that I wasn't quite prepared for being the wife of an inmate. The transitions started slowly and would have easily gone unnoticeable if it didn't accompany strong negative feelings. For example, being married to a man that I could not fuck was absolutely painful.

I would go on those visits, sit in his essence and get all hot and bothered because since we were now married, kissing was permissible. I loved his kisses, but I hated leaving the prison knowing those kisses wouldn't be accompanying me or greeting me at my front door when I arrived home. When I would share that longing with Khalil, he would manage my mood and then say, "In due time. I won't be here forever."

He never discounted my feelings and as I shared more and more with him that my sexual desires were starting to resurface, he would, again, help manage my mood by addressing what I was feeling. I'd share that those kisses were awakening something deep in me and I needed to do something with the energy; after all, it had been almost two years since I had been with a man. Khalil made many suggestions, like exercise more, focus on your community endeavors more, he even suggested that I masturbate. I did as he suggested but none of that replaced the feeling of wanting to be touched by him and I was becoming undone.

I kept telling myself, "I can do this!" It wasn't really about wanting to have sex; it was about being married to the perfect man who could not honor the tenets of his religion in our marriage. As a Muslim, men are supposed to be able to physically protect you, financially support you and, intimately satisfy you.

None of that was occurring in our marriage, aside from some financial support, because Khalil never hesitated to send me funds when the van service wasn't bringing in enough—

which also at this time was something that I was starting to realize was a problem. But regarding physical protection, it was
almost non-existent. Yes, Khalil was still connected to brothers
in the street and if a crisis were to truly ever unfold, I know that
he would be able to make moves for me. But, in the instance that
crisis was unfolding when you truly needed your mate, he would
be unavailable, and we both knew it.

Being married under those conditions was stressful. I don't
know why it never felt like that during our courtship, but it
showed up for me once we took our vows. I was also becoming
burned out with working full-time and driving those long hours.
I had adjusted my van service schedule to accommodate Mahanoy more, because Khalil was a mover and he ensured that my
van remained filled. But as the burnout set in and the desire to
be taken care of in a traditional wife way increased, I started to
hate going in on visits.

I hated getting searched before a visit. I hated when the picture machine was down. I hated waiting in line for the vending
machines once inside the visit. I hated the kids running around
hollering. I hated seeing people sneak and fuck on visits, knowing that I could never take that risk. I hated the chatter. I even
hated looking at the guards, even though they were always very
nice to me. But most of all, I hated leaving that institution without my man.

Khalil could see that the prison wife's life was getting the
best of me and he did everything in his incarcerated power to
ease my burden. He would allow me to just come in there and
rest my head on his shoulder without talking for the first 30 minutes of our visits, because it seemed that I just couldn't physically adjust to going in that prison anymore. Eventually, he would
tell me that it was okay if I didn't have the energy to visit, just
make sure I was available for our nightly calls. But at that point,
I couldn't even muster up the strength to tell him that I hated
waiting for those calls. I knew I was unconsciously resenting him

for being incarcerated without the possibility of parole, and it wasn't fair.

On top of struggling with being his wife, I was getting tired of driving up and down the turnpike. It seemed that the stories of the women that once inspired me about "riding for a loved one" were making me depressed, because I knew that I was not doing well with my "ride." I would also start to get angry when women would complain about a sentence length that paled in comparison to Khalil's life sentence. I was becoming overwhelmed by the entire journey, and the only thing that kept me sane was visiting the Center of Peace.

It was in the Sanctuary that I would allow myself the freedom to be honest with myself that "riding for a brother" was hard work. This bid was unlike Faster's because Khalil was, in the words of Lauryn Hill, *"the sweetest thing I've ever known"* and I didn't want to let him down. But I was suffering. I was also suffering with the knowledge that so many women were holding brothers down and not catching a break in the process.

On the van, women would share that their loved one was up for parole and then a few weeks later, learn that he was denied. Women, especially mothers, were sharing that they weren't getting any support from the "friends" of their loved one, so the financial burden was becoming too much to bear. There was also, very often, a deep correlation between supporting an incarcerated loved one and still repeatedly being exposed to violence in their own communities. Mothers would travel to see their son's father to deliver the horrific news that their child had been murdered. Many of my riders were catching hell from all sides.

The trauma stories on the van were palpable. Women were also sharing how they had been taken advantage of by lawyers during the trial and were unable to afford lawyers during the appeal process. To make matters even more unbearable, there were women who's loved one had been released and not even three months later were back in custody because of a parole violation and they were calling my phone to report the bad news.

The most difficult moment of operating Ride and Rebuild was when a wife who had faithfully traveled with me for almost two years, called to tell me her husband had unexpectedly died due to complications with Diabetes. I was devastated, because I was the second person she had thought to call in the middle of her grief. Each time I would travel to that institution, I would replay her cries in my ears, over the phone that day and my heart would ache for her.

One day, in the middle of processing how difficult this journey had been since my truck had broken down on the highway, I received an email from a woman I'd met on the Fatherhood program team. She was the director of the Restorative Justice program at the Philadelphia Mural Arts program. The email was short and succinct. She asked if I was interested in being interviewed for a project spearheaded by them to explore mass incarceration. I replied immediately, "Of course, sign me up." I just needed to get this journey out of my head and into the ears of someone else who wasn't directly impacted.

She forwarded my information to an artist, Eric Okdeh, who contacted me for an interview. Four weeks later, we met at a coffee shop on Fairmount Avenue directly across the street from the country's first penitentiary, Eastern State, famous for revolutionizing the prison system from punishment to reform. It's safe to say Philadelphia is not only the birthplace of America but the criminal justice reform movement as well. Admittedly, when I parked my truck on the side of that antiquated building, I thought of all the women who must have walked through those doors to visit a loved one. I even thought of my grandmother Ms. Marie, my fathers' mother, who had to have visited my grandfather, who was once housed on the other side of that wall, and it exhausted me even further.

When I reached the coffee shop, the artist had not yet arrived, so I ordered a drink and found a seat. Ten minutes later I received a call from the artist, expressing that he was running a bit behind because he was stuck in traffic leaving Graterford prison. I told him to take his time.

While I waited, I stared out the window and let my mind drift up and over that prison wall with thoughts of "quitting the van service business." I was still working full time, so I knew my bills would be paid. I just couldn't shake the exhaustion from serving, and my Diabetes was not being managed properly because of it. No matter how hard Khalil tried to love me through the ups and downs of my moods and business challenges—including underpricing my services, I was still struggling.

Deep in thought, I didn't see the artist come in until he was standing at my table. He knew it was me because I was the only Black person in the entire coffee shop. He had paint all over him and was sweating. I laughingly asked, "Did you run in here?" He said breathlessly, "No, I just hate being late" and began to apologize profusely. I told him he was fine and asked if we could move our meeting to the seating outside.

As we sat outside across from one another with the penitentiary looming over my left shoulder, he told me that he worked with the Lifers at Graterford through the Mural Arts Program, teaching them how to create murals. He had been commissioned to create this mini-mural project to shed light on the criminal justice system, and he was interviewing folks across the spectrum. He told me he was intrigued by my business because he always wondered how people visited prisons. So, for the next hour, I shared my journey with him.

I told him about why I wanted to start Ride and Rebuild, and how it was done. I shared that I had also "drank the Kool-Aid" and married a lifer. He asked how that was going and I was honest when I said, "It's hard as fuck." We talked a bit about my love for Khalil, and my hate for the criminal justice system that takes a person away from his family and community without the possibility of allowing them to return, even though all signs point to that person being reformed. He nodded his head in agreement, and I then told him about the women.

It wasn't difficult to talk about the women to the artist, and I was surprised that the words sprang forth with no effort. I shared that these women weren't just wives, but mothers, sisters, aunts, nieces, daughters and even grandmothers. I told him that they were funding the criminal justice system and some of them weren't even aware of it.

They were paying for lawyers, commissary and even visits, not to mention the amount of money it cost to feed these brothers on the visit. I told him about the health conditions of these women, including myself, and that the stress of loving an incarcerated person can wear you down and cause chronic disease, including anxiety and depression. I told him that when I first started Ride and Rebuild, it was to rebuild families, but now I'm realizing I need to keep women grounded on this journey because they are the forgotten soldiers in the war on mass incarceration. With complete sincerity, he said, "I couldn't agree more."

When the interview was complete, I thanked him for allowing me to vent my frustrations and that I was glad to have been asked to share my journey because for some reason, talking about it was therapeutic. He asked if he could take my picture at the van, I said of course, and we walked across the street. As I stood in front of my van with my Dashiki on, and Eastern State Penitentiary in the background, I knew that I could not let the women down and I had to keep riding and rebuilding for them.

About a month later, the artist sent me an electronic draft of the 3'x 5' mural he was creating to be exhibited with approximately 40 other mini murals. I was so excited to see what he had created. As I opened the email and clicked on the file with the image attached, I was not disappointed. He had managed to capture my face as it so closely resembled Ms. Yvonne's as she had aged, my truck, and me standing in front of it. I loved everything about it, except the words he had chosen to use from the interview.

As I stared at words that focused more on the men during incarceration, which I had shared in our conversation, it didn't capture the essence of what I was feeling during our talk, and the feeling I had when I walked away—that women are the ones who need to be acknowledged in this incarceration journey. For about 20 minutes I stared at the electronic mural and contemplated emailing him to change the words. I asked a couple of my colleagues for their thoughts and although we agreed the mural was beautiful, if I wasn't comfortable with the words on it, then it would have been futile to sit with him in the first place.

When they left my office, I immediately emailed him and told him the words that should go on the mural. As an artist I thought he would be pissed, but he was the exact opposite. He told me that if I wasn't happy with how I was being portrayed, then he would do whatever it took to portray me in the light that I desired. I was grateful and four months later, the mural along with 10 others were exhibited at the Philadelphia Arts Alliance. Friends, family and even my former colleague Diane came all the way from D.C. to support me at the unveiling.

At the exhibit Eric shared how the murals came to be. He conducted the interviews, designed the murals, and the inmates at Graterford prison painted them. He pulled me aside and told me the inmate who painted mine, Charles—who I did not know, was insistent on getting every detail correct. I was so inspired that my prison journey had such a full-circle experience, that it renewed my energy about love and my purpose.

Although going inside the prison was still a bit draining, I knew I needed to be close to Khalil, so I started visiting regularly again. However, I also knew that I could no longer be married under the predicament of incarceration. It took sitting with that muralist to readjust my thinking to align with what I honestly believed; women are bearing the burden of the business of prison and needed relief. But before I could advocate for them, I needed to start with myself!

Thankfully, Yumn invited me to join her in Basel, Switzerland and Istanbul, Turkey for a winter vacation. I'd been given an opportunity to step away from my day-to-day and process my relationship. I had never taken an international flight before, and was quite impressed with all the free stuff they gave me. I had ear plugs, earphones, a toothbrush and toothpaste, and even slippers. On that eight-hour flight, I slept, watched movies, and intermittently thought long and hard about how I would break the news to Khalil that I no-longer wanted to be a prison wife.

Although this thought lingered in the back of my mind, it did not dampen the excitement of being out of America. I arrived in Basel just in time for their annual Fire Festival. Of course, I had no idea what that meant, but after taking a short nap from my flight, I was out along the River Rhine celebrating in the dark. The festival is held annually in the evening with all the lights in the city darkened and the only light visible is from fire or the lighted floats.

This cultural event was unlike anything I had ever experienced. At the fire portion of the festival, Yumn said to me "When I tell you to get low, get low." I had no idea what she meant until I almost passed out from smoke inhalation and heat. I remember turning to her and yelling over the crowd, "I can't breathe!" She immediately yelled back to me "GET LOW!" I dropped in a squat position and was immediately greeted with cool fresh air. Aside from that death-defying moment, the Fire Festival was one for the books. I stayed in Switzerland for another 3 days and then we, including her husband and son, took a flight to Istanbul for another 3 days. Yumn told me that I would receive stares in Turkey. When I asked why, she said "Because there aren't many Black people there." I was fascinated.

Istanbul was beautiful. Upon our arrival, as we traveled through the city en route to our AirBnB off the famous Istiklal Street, the Islamic Isha prayer was coming in. Now living in Philadelphia with the largest Muslim population in America, I had never heard the Adhan called in the city. In Istanbul, it is called throughout the city on loudspeakers and although traffic did not stop, many drivers were pulling over to pray. It was a sight to behold.

The city of Istanbul had a lot to offer to my senses. It was aesthetically pleasing, and the food was delicious. I toured all the historical sites, including the Blue Mosque where Malcolm X once prayed, the Basilica Cistern, and Topkapi Palace. It was in Topkapi Palace that I felt the spirits of the great men of religion.

There are many chambers in the Palace and in one there is Abrahams pot, Joseph's turban, Moses's staff, David's sword, and the Prophet Muhammad's footprints on display. The Audience Chamber has many items belonging to the Prophet Muhammad, including his sword. The Qur'an is also recited continuously in this chamber. I literally thought it was a record being played until I walked by the man sitting behind a microphone reciting it.

This experience was another one for the books, and although I later learned that my family were in fear for my life because of ISIS, I didn't have a care in the world. That was until my final night, when Yumn's cousin met us for dinner. Like me, she was returning to the states in the morning and since Yumn was in town, wanted to see her before she departed. However, unlike me visiting the region for vacation, her cousin was working in Syria providing aid on behalf of the U.S.

It was at that dinner I realized a couple things: 1) ISIS was real and after experiencing 9/11 I was not interested in any trauma orchestrated by "terrorists", and 2) I had been gallivanting on beautifully historical land that was extremely close to a conflict region. After dinner, Istanbul seemed a bit more unsettling. But then I had to remember that I was a Black woman and that I too had come from a conflict region growing up in Southwest Philadelphia, and I'd be just fine.

Although I didn't get the stares on the streets of Istanbul that Yumn thought I would, I definitely received them at the airport the next morning. My driver arrived about 4am and as I hugged a sleepy Yumn farewell, I quietly prayed that I'd make it back to the states in one piece. When we arrived at Ataturk airport, I immediately noticed that you not only check your bags at the door, you cannot enter without going through a full body scan. It was after the body scan that the airport personnel found favor with my braids.

Before I could say anything, they were asking me questions in Arabic while simultaneously feeling my hair. I knew they meant no harm, because they were smiling the entire time, but as anyone with any sense knows, you do not touch a Black woman's hair. But instead of getting offended, I just smiled and moved my happy to be headed back home ass quickly through two more checkpoints and onto my plane. As I sat on the plane heading back to America, I solemnly thought of Khalil, and although that beautiful Islamic city made me think of him daily, I knew that our marriage was over. Turkey made me realize that once again, I operate best when I am free.

I was gentle with Khalil when I shared that I wanted a divorce. I admitted to him that my desire to be touched had become overwhelming and that I knew he would never be the kind of husband who would allow me to "just do me," and I would never be the kind of wife to fuck around on my husband without permission. I also shared with him that fully realizing I was alone on the outside world had become unbearable and little things, like getting a home repair done or even having a platonic male friend visit me, seemed problematic for me and our union.

Khalil agreed that he would never give me permission to take a lover and that he was grateful that I had even considered him in not taking one, knowing he could do nothing about it. I assured Khalil that he was my friend and I would never misuse his trust for me. I also told him that I would forever be grateful to him for how he helped heal my soul after the incident involving Mr. Handsome and the U.S. Marshals. I was honest when I shared that he had restored my faith in men, and would always be the lover I never physically had but who healed the deepest parts of me that no dick could ever reach. Khalil agreed to the divorce and two years after our wedding day, like a lightning bug held in a jar, he set me free.

Real Resilience

Once I was no longer under the contract of marriage, I started to look at my other "contracts" that I no longer wanted to be under, and working full time was one of them. I was exhausted and knew that if I wanted to give Ride and Rebuild a true chance, I'd have to focus all my attention on it. I knew leaving Drexel would be a financial challenge, but the university had changed over the years since I'd been there, hiring new leaders who were more focused on numbers and not community impact, and it was time to transition.

My colleagues were very aware that I was the owner of a prison transportation service, especially after the Mural showed up for an exhibit in the building I was working at. The School of Public Health had begun to recognize that incarceration was a public health crisis and was fascinated that one of their employees was celebrated by the Philadelphia Mural Arts Program for their contribution to alleviating the burden. There was a large reception where I spoke about my experience and subsequently, the mural was on display for a full month. Every day I walked into my building I saw my mothers' face in myself on that wall. It was weird and gratifying all at the same damn time.

Having that mural catapulted me into organizational spheres that I didn't even know existed. For example, there was a doctor who worked in my department. She was degreed in medicine and philosophy, and was instrumental in increasing the awareness of trauma, vicarious and secondary to the world through her collaborative creation called the Sanctuary Model®.

We had worked together on a project that Dr. Vaughn, a community leader, and I had created to build resilience in other community leaders in Southwest Philly using her model. I loved working with Dr. Bloom for many reasons: 1) she was a practicing Buddhist and always on a thousand chills, and 2) she knew her shit. I also like that although she's highly paid to train in her practice, she gifted us her expertise and gave the community leaders a 2-hour dose of her model for free.

Working with Dr. Bloom on that project opened my eyes to the long-lasting effect of being exposed to trauma, something I had never quite understood. I was unaware that the brain did not reach full development until the age of 25, which meant that most of the choices made prior to that could be considered juvenile. I thought of Khalil serving a life sentence for a crime committed at 22 and knew the legislation to release juvenile offenders across the country would have to be expanded from 18 to the age of 25 if it were to really hold any weight.

But I learned more than what trauma does to the brain, I learned what it can do to the body as well, over a lifetime. One day while waiting to go into a meeting to discuss our resilience program for community leaders, I was reading through Dr. Blooms' book *Creating Sanctuary* where she kept mentioning the Adverse Childhood Experiences Study, ACES for short. The study was conducted in California by an insurance company to determine if negative childhood experiences impacted a persons' health over the long haul.

I was intrigued by this book and what I was learning. I took a brief break from reading to Google all that I could find out about ACES, and it was a lot. The results from the 14,000 predominantly white participants, who were now baby boomers, concluded that if as a child/adolescent you were impacted by at least four out of ten of the trauma-related incidents listed in the survey then you'd most likely develop poor health behaviors and experience poor health outcomes.

I was captivated by the notion that your childhood could literally fuck you up for life. I couldn't wait any longer, I had to know my ACES score. It took a millisecond to find the survey online, one second to print it, two minutes to take it, and 15 minutes for my colleagues to talk me off the ledge after I got my results.

Out of a score of 10, I had an ACES score of 8 and I was horrified. I was so grateful for Dr. Vaughn and the community leader, who happened to be a Doctor of Ministry, for counseling me through that experience of finding out my results. They kept saying, "Crystal, yes you may have had many adverse experiences growing up, but you should really focus on how resilient you've been through it all, and remember that trauma isn't what's wrong with you, it's what's happened to you!"

I knew they were right, but everything bad that had happened to me kept flashing through my mind. I thought about growing up in Delran under the trauma of a lesbian mother, who had a penchant toward fighting her lovers. I even thought of a time before that when I was touched inappropriately by a family friend.

I remembered my uncle's indictment and how unstable it made our household, resulting in an eviction. My thoughts continued to race toward my mothers' crack addiction and how I suffered watching her break under its pressure. Finally, I thought of Sweet's death and how it nearly caused mine. I was literally rocked to my core at the realization that my poor health behaviors like not eating properly, lack of consistent exercise, consuming too much alcohol, mismanaging my weed intake, and bearing the burden of stress that resulted in me attracting the poor health outcome of Diabetes, were all a result of the shit I had experienced growing up.

Although that information was hard to digest, something about knowing it and having the language to call a thing a thing, empowered me and I started to activate. I would share ACES information with the women on the van and I would start to see them as I was, a Trauma Survivor. Recognizing my own trauma story and my diligence in spreading the message, life started to shift quickly, and I got more involved with Dr. Bloom's work.

She invited me to Washington DC to become a founding member of the Campaign for Trauma-Informed Policy and Practice (CTIPP). She even paid, out of her Drexel budget, for me to take the 5-day Sanctuary Training in Yonkers, NY to become certified in the model. We then worked together on a video series titled Working Toward a Trauma Informed Philadelphia and I, subsequently, joined the Philadelphia ACE Task Force to help get the message out about ACE's in the city and later became a member of the steering committee. Although I was still employed at Drexel doing this work, when I showed up at these meetings, Dr. Bloom made sure to let folks know that I was there representing Ride and Rebuild and the women who support an incarcerated loved one. It felt good to be recognized for my work in that way.

A few months later, I resigned from Drexel University to become a full-time transportation provider. I also found myself wanting to do more with the women as it related to trauma and the impact of incarceration. Especially, since I had now been introduced to the story of Khalif Browder, a young man who had been arrested and housed in Rikers Island as a teenager for a crime he did not commit.

I was devastated by the outcome of that young man's life as he had committed suicide two years after his release. But more importantly, I was heartbroken by the impact this trauma had on his mother, Venida Browder. She was his number one supporter and had succumbed to illness caused by unresolved trauma— showing up as a heart condition—and died just as a documentary about her son's life would be released.

Learning of their story, it wasn't enough to just talk about trauma. I wanted to make women aware that incarceration is the trauma and supporting a loved one through it has as many psychological and physiological negative effects on her as being incarcerated herself. But I also wanted them to know that with trauma comes resilience and to me, what they were doing was "Real Resilience!" Although "bidding" with an incarcerated loved one is frowned upon, they needed to be honored for being the silent soldiers in the war on mass incarceration.

As the universe has always conspired to catapult my intentions with my mission, shortly after my trauma-informed declaration, I received an email from one of the CTIPP board members informing the group of a grant opportunity. Now, most grants are funded to non-profit organizations and clearly Ride and Rebuild was not that, but Spirit told me to go for it. It didn't hurt that the CTIPP board member could steer me in the right direction to ask the right questions to get the right answers about submitting my proposal. The question I had was simple: would this funder, fund a for-profit business? The answer was yes, if I had a fiscal sponsor who would manage the funds for me.

Ironically, I was volunteering at theVillage in Southwest Philly, a residential and outpatient treatment organization that served youth in foster care, among other things. I was in a community meeting at their site one day when we were discussing the wellness of youth in Southwest Philly. I shared my history of growing up in the neighborhood, making sure not to leave out the part about the level of violence and heartache I'd experienced as well as my mother's crack addiction, and that it was my personal mandate to give back to the community whenever I could. After the meeting, the President approached me with tears in her eyes stating that she'd never heard anyone share such personal information in one of her meetings before. I told her, "It's my life, I am who I am."

She then asked me to help facilitate a session at an upcoming conference. I agreed and subsequently became a member of their Southwest Childrens' Wellness Collaborative steering committee, organizing to raise awareness about the impact of trauma on children and creating opportunities to mitigate them. She also later asked me to be part of their organizations' 26-member board.

So, when I learned that I needed a fiscal sponsor, I did not hesitate to contact the president of that 100-year-old, multi-million-dollar organization and ask for them to take on that responsibility. I had never received a faster yes in my life. The meeting literally took 10 minutes.

Armed with a fiscal sponsor and an opportunity to apply to acquire funds to support women set me on fire. It finally occurred to me that all the stress leading to the creation of Ride and Rebuild, from experiences including my journey with Faster, the death of my mother, the challenges of working for narcissistic bosses, the 19 bags of weed, the trauma of Mr. Handsome, the subsequent burnout, while trying to keep my promise to Sweet, were not in vain. There would be an opportunity for me to use the research experience, grant writing, and program planning skills that I had developed in my work journey through PPV and higher education to acquire funds for something that I would be responsible for and that I wholeheartedly believed in. Besides, I knew what these women needed, because I had listened to them on those long trips. Also, I too was part of the demographic, and aside from a conjugal visit (which is non-existent in Pennsylvania), I definitely knew the support I had needed loving someone who was incarcerated.

I wasted no time crafting the most detailed proposal. I knew I wanted to offer four workshops for the women that had a trauma-informed approach. The program would also have a peer-to-peer model, so I asked women who I trusted, that had supported an incarcerated loved one, and had traveled with me before or had knowledge of the four areas—trauma, diet and exercise, money management and the relationship with self—to be my facilitators. I would give incentives to participate, like free childcare for participants while they participated, a free ride to an institution of their choice, and a $25 gift card that they could use toward mental health services or self-care management after they completed the four-week program.

Eight weeks after submission, I learned that I had gotten the Real Resilience grant. I was not surprised that the program was funded. Besides, I now knew the power of the law of attraction and manifestation, good or bad, and I had activated that power to secure that grant bag! I was also grateful that I had chosen a fiscal sponsor that would allow me to use their space to conduct my weekly program and in the neighborhood that I had experienced so much growth in, Southwest Philly.

Our target number of women to enroll was 32. We were able to get the 32 women, some who traveled from as far as North Philly to attend. However, because of life's ups and downs, only 28 women completed the program. I was still completely satisfied with that number, because that meant we served 94% of our target, and in research that's a major win.

Running the program was exciting because the women showed up faithfully, engaged in the activities, were comfortable sharing their journey in a safe space, and loved the food that one of the participants was hired to provide. I'm not sure who got more out of the program, the participants, the facilitators or myself, but what I am sure of, is that it was therapeutic. To culminate the experience, we celebrated with a certificate ceremony and released a video of the Real Resilience program.I experienced a lot of personal growth during that time. I was thankful to have been able to serve women in that capacity and was proud of myself for creating it and seeing it to fruition. However, I could not deny that I was exhausted and burned out by all things prison life. I thought leaving Drexel would free up my time to dedicate more of my resources to the van service, but what I hadn't quite calculated was that the van service never really made money and that my Drexel paycheck was actually funding it.

But that burnout was a force to reckon with. It didn't matter how many yoga classes, massages or salt-water float and cryo-sauna sessions I paid for to reduce the inflammation in my body caused by countless hours driving, I was tired of the anxiety of the road and tired of not having my financial needs met. I was even tired of picking up folks, tired of driving, tired of going onto prison grounds, and tired of being stared at like an outsider in towns that I was once welcomed, pre-Trump.

Traveling in upstate Pennsylvania after the 2016 presidential election became a burden I had not quite prepared for and it was adding to my already taxed mind, body, and spirit. During Obama's administration, I was confident being the only Black person in an all-white space. However, slowly the fear of anything "other" in those small towns became depressing, and at times extremely uncomfortable. There were more Confederate flags being flown on pickup trucks, in front of homes, and plastered on bumper stickers. Even my Muslim riders received more fearful stares and I was often looked at disdainfully. Upstate Pennsylvania had become unbearable and unfortunately Philadelphia had decided to show its ass too.

Philadelphia's criminal justice system had incarcerated the city's favorite young rapper on a probation violation charge. His judge had given him a two-year hit, and the city was in an uproar. There were protests occurring at the Criminal Justice Center and intense news coverage all over the world. I am well aware of the unfair treatment brothers and sisters receive in our court system and although the level of attention this case received embarrassed me to be called a Philadelphian, I was so grateful for the unrest. Finally, the world had to look at its criminal justice system and consciously do something about it.

Like many Philadelphians and the country, I followed this saga as it played out. Fortunately, the rapper was able to galvanize moguls in the entertainment and sports industry to support his plight. As a result of it, they were able to get that young brother free and created an alliance to add to the many other organizations working toward reforming the criminal justice system. However, as I watched and waited for the outcome, I kept thinking about the women in his family, in particular his mother.

I could not help but wonder what her state of mind was like during that unsettling time. I thought of Venida Browder, Khalif Browder's mother too. In fact, I thought about Faster's mother, Khalil's mother, and all the other mothers who were riding on my van to visit their sons in jail. I knew she had to have been experiencing a tiredness that only comes through the trauma of incarceration by affiliation.

Admittedly, watching the world tune in to understand the impact of prison on Black life was liberating. I wanted to join the latest movement created by those interested in criminal justice reform. But as I watched it all slowly come together I knew, like the rest of the world, they didn't fully understand the other part of the struggle. Women were funding the backend of the criminal justice system, and there would be no true reform until those of us who are impacted the most are at the table informing programming and policy change.

I knew that if I wasn't going to have a seat at that table, then I needed to create my own because I was tired of doing everything by myself. Yes, I had hired a couple women to drive over the course of the seven years, but the bulk of the driving and running the Real Resilience program was on me and because of that, burnout had seeped in for real. I also realized that I had created a business that was a novelty and not many people had done it at the scale in which I had, which meant there was no model. I was the model and I had to learn as I went along, and I made mistakes.

The major mistake I made that could have alleviated most of my stress, was not turning Ride and Rebuild into a non-profit early on in its development. My accountant told me in year two, that it should be a non-profit, but I was so busy working and just trying to serve that it never occurred to me that I'd been in the non-profit business for over 25 years and yes, I should have converted the business. For all intents and purposes, this was a social impact business and in my opinion, social impact projects should be funded by philanthropists.

With this new thought of utilizing philanthropy to fund this work, one day an email was forwarded to me of another funding opportunity that I just couldn't pass up. It was a monetary social impact innovation award being offered by a local foundation that I was familiar with and had heard positive reports on. The award would allow recipients to further their work in the community and I decided to apply for it.

After all, creating a table would require seed money and the $25,000 award would definitely help. That money would also help me to finally convert Ride and Rebuild into the non-profit it needed to be. The application entailed submitting a written proposal, a 1-minute video about why I should win the award, and it included a voting process. Once you submitted your application and video, the voting committee would decide who would be eligible to receive votes to win the award.

The entire process was as easy as writing the grant for the initial Real Resilience program, and fourteen days after submission, I learned that out of 88 applicants I was one of the 5 finalists. I also learned that winners would be announced at the National Council Conference for Behavioral Health in Washington D.C., which was essentially the Oscars of behavioral health.

The foundation paid for my travel and accommodations. The venue was located at the National Harbor Convention Center and I stayed in a beautiful boutique hotel. Once I had checked in, I changed my clothes and headed over to the venue to participate in a panel discussion about the importance of honoring women who support an incarcerated loved one. It was exciting to share with the large group of conference attendees that these women existed, and my program was making sure the stigma of supporting someone in prison was being reduced by providing opportunities for women to heal the trauma caused by the impact of incarceration. The Q&A at the end of the panel assured me that the attendees were intrigued by the program and if nothing else, I was satisfied with that.

After the panel, I met up with Yumn and her husband, who now lived in DC, for dinner and drinks to catch up and unwind. I was grateful for the sweet distraction from the conference. The voting process had concluded that evening and winners would be announced the next day at an evening ceremony. I was a bit nervous, wondering if my program would be selected as the winner of the award.

I knew the money would help support more women than the original grant did. Because on the prison van, program participants would gingerly express how much they learned about themselves during the four-week program and upon leaving the van, other women who weren't able to participate would quietly ask when another cohort was starting. I didn't have the answer then but was hoping I would when I got back to Philadelphia after the conference.

The next evening in my hotel room, as I was preparing to attend the ceremony where the financial fate of Ride and Rebuild and Real Resilience would be decided, I stood looking at myself in the mirror. I could not deny that my journey through creating my prison van service was worth every win and loss that I had experienced in life. In that hotel bathroom, I finally felt myself standing in gratitude and love for the road I had traveled.

As I peered into my reflection, I knew that every ride I had taken, every person I had transported, every family I helped rebuild, every prison I'd visited, every meeting I had attended dis-

cussing incarceration and every community event I had participated in, my promise to myself and Sweet to give back to women
impacted by violence had been fulfilled. I didn't know it would
be through prison transportation but even with the exhaustion
and burnout I was feeling at that very moment, I was honored
to have taken that route. And as my weary image stared back
at me, I could honestly say that this life, my life, was resilience
personified.

-The Mural-

EPILOGUE

I did not win the award because I did not get enough votes. In full transparency, I was grateful. I was exhausted and had gone through so many variations of growth that led to creating my transportation service that if I didn't take the time to write it all down after not winning that financial prize, I would never see the joy in the overall prison van service experience. For many reasons, being prompted by my ancestors to tell my truth has been therapeutic.

For one, the text here described a lot of my struggles, and although there were many good days on the journey, the crux of my life and the Ride and Rebuild movement had been shaped by trauma. I knew what trauma felt like, but I didn't know the true language of it. Learning the language of adverse childhood experiences and trauma through my work with Dr. Bloom is what I leaned on and continue to lean on to heal. I am grateful to have learned the difference between acute, chronic, and complex trauma and when I experience any of the three, which steps I need to take to save my soul-self. I now know to pause, step away from situations, assess the feelings in my body and make the necessary adjustments to protect myself in a loving and healthy way; and yes, marijuana is still a part of that, but medicinally!

For two, compassion fatigue is a real thing. As a community activist, small or large, and an empath relating to the struggle of others, you can burn yourself out quickly. There were many times throughout my life that I experienced compassion fatigue, but again, didn't have the language to put a term on the feeling. I now know that compassion fatigue showed up when I needed to leave PPV and those universities, because I was constantly giving to situations that weren't changing fast or supporting me enough for my spirit. I was tired of caring for a "thing" that didn't care for me. I also now know that compassion fatigue had shown up when I was contemplating shutting the van service down right before I met with the muralist. I had been exhausted by all the traumatic stories of incarceration on those van rides and needed relief. I also know compassion fatigue had set in when I needed to divorce Khalil. I was exhausted by loving a man who loved me, but couldn't express it in a natural way and I was tired of feeling sorry for us.

Thirdly, there were times when I was writing this book that I was grateful for choosing the spiritual practice of New Thought. I am a firm believer in the law of attraction which is why I never question why something happens to me. Many of us call it, Karma, but I now prefer to call it the Law. I know that I am constantly manifesting, good, bad, or indifferent experiences in my life and those experiences are only showing up because I am attracting them through thought.

So, when I was writing the part about Mr. Handsome, I wasn't surprised that after 7 years I received a call from him asking me to visit. I also was not surprised at my "yes" response. I needed closure and as the Law would have it, I received it. I was finally able to look that brother in the face and share my pain of that experience with him and his absence in my life, and because he was the truth that I knew he would be, he apologized for putting me in a position where Marshals would show up to my home, and for abandoning me when I needed the friend in him the most. That apology set everything right between us, because what more could he do under the predicament of incarceration.

Interestingly enough, I also attracted Faster while writing this book. He showed up after completing 9 years of his new lengthy sentence. Admittedly, I had visited him once when he was on his way out of the penitentiary and was housed at Dallas State Correctional Institution—yes that's seven prisons that I have been inside in Pennsylvania, actually eight if you count SCI Chester for a meeting with the Lifers spearheaded by the state representative. Nevertheless, when Faster was released, we "connected" and there was regret all up and through that experience. I finally realized that Faster was never supposed to finish this trip with me, but was absolutely the catalyst in my life to lead me on the path to creating Ride and Rebuild.

As for Haroon, yup, you guessed it, I attracted him as well in this writing process. Our paths happened to cross one day in the visiting room while I was on a visit with Khalil. It was extremely awkward for me, especially since he sat directly behind us. To this day he denies seeing me sitting in that damn seat, but he absolutely knew I was in the visiting room because we greeted each other in the lobby. Nevertheless, Haroon has always been a staple in my life—like bread! In fact, I had consulted with Haroon for many years' prior to writing our story because we both knew that our Sweets' experience would be shared here, and I wanted his consent. Admittedly, had Haroon not been an advocate for this book, this version would not have happened.

Fourth, I also attracted an unexpected friend during this writing experience, and she was my biggest competitor in the van service journey. I happened to see her in our local breakfast spot, which I found ironic that we lived in the same neighborhood. I approached her table and asked if she was okay because I had heard her van had been in an accident the previous weekend. I could tell she was shocked that I approached her, but I'm assuming my vibe was right because once we started talking, she invited me to join her, and I did.

From that day we realized that we were soldiers in the same war and needed to be allies. We both had the same anxieties that came from owning a prison transportation service including driving on the road and actively loving someone who was incarcerated. Since that day in the diner, we check on each other once a week and brainstorm business strategies so that we can both figure out a way to win in business without killing ourselves in the process. Undoubtedly, her youthful energy is what pushed me to get this book out when I didn't feel like thinking one more remembered thought.

Finally, what surprised me the most while in this process was that while going through a few of my mothers' belongings, I found a letter written from my grandmother Mildred to her husband whom she was madly in love with. It was a short one-page letter. In it, she described her current predicament of managing life with four kids, and that she was sorry she couldn't visit him over the weekend because her "machine" was broken. I'm assuming her machine was her car, as she also wrote that she didn't want to get wet in the rain trying to find another way to visit. I intuitively knew the letter was written to him while he was incarcerated. After all, I had written many letters similar to the one I was reading. A few weeks later I visited my Uncle Vernon, who is still guiding me on my life journey, where he confirmed that his father had been an inmate at Moyamensing Prison, previously located in Philadelphia at 10th and Reed, at the current site of a supermarket.

After that confirmation, it finally occurred to me that I had never been doing this prison work for the sake of Faster and our relationship. I had been doing it because the ancestral strength of my grandmothers were guiding me to fulfill this part of my soul contract for them. I had done what spirit had instructed me to do—serve women where incarceration was a barrier to love. So, with over 300,000 miles and 11,000 hours driven, and more than 1300 families served repeatedly on 1100 trips for 364 weekends, while watching the seasons change 28 times, I knew I needed to redefine my own trauma narrative by closing Ride and Rebuild. So, I did.

Although shutting the service down was emotionally difficult, I felt freer to heal once it was officially done. But I also knew my work with the women was not over, because I'm affirmed in the belief that it's my responsibility to include women in the conversation of criminal justice reform. I don't have the capacity to drive anymore, but I have the capacity to talk! And since I've finally finished this book, I will share the journey of women who are funding the backend of the criminal justice system through my podcast—Real Resilience P.W.L. We will be heard and honored for our resilience even if we have to honor ourselves!

Tune in!

-Podcasting, Real Resilience: Prison Wife Life-

IN GRATITUDE:
People, Places and Things

People

Giving thanks to my foundation, Ms. Yvonne and Bobby, my future, Mar-Mar, and my elder Uncle Vernon for allowing me to share parts of their truth with you. I'd like to thank my homegirls, M.D, Y.A., L.F. S.W., D.T., K.C. and P.W. for riding many of these storms with me. You helped keep me grounded and honest and for that I am grateful. Also, to L.F., when I didn't know how I would formulate these words, thank you for sitting on my porch and saying to me, "Crystal, just write!" Here we go, homie! For the homegirls who proofread this book or listened to parts of it and encouraged me to keep writing, E.B., M.B., N.J., and K.B., thank you for your time and thoughtful feedback. For the brothers, A.P., T.R., L.M., M.S., C.D., K.H. and C.W. what a ride! I am who I am because of the experiences we shared, and I thank you! To my siblings, thank you for loving this Philly wild child unconditionally. Special love to my sister J.G. for supporting every endeavor I have ever had. U.W. and W.K., from thought, to creation, implementation and closure, your unwavering support of me, Ride and Rebuild and Real Resilience was unparalleled, and I thank you. To the Lifers at SCI Phoenix (formerly SCI Graterford) thank you for allowing me to serve you through Ride and Rebuild. To my mentors, intentional and unintentional, D.W., L.C., N.V., and S.B., thank you for teaching me how to maneuver in spaces that tried to dishonor me. To the students who still rock with me after all this time, especially D.S. and J.W., what a trip! Also, to my BOK alumni, our trade school experience and diploma did many of us well, and I thank you for still being a part of my life. To the sisters that helped me push those trucks up the PA Turnpike, K.W., A.R. B.R and L.R, you are appreciated. Finally, to the women of Ride and Rebuild and the Real Resilience program, thank you for trusting me to support you in love. Your courage is what kept me going at times when I didn't have the strength to.

Places

California, your sunshine, experiences, lessons and peace are what I will always gravitate toward. I am so thankful that you are a resource for me. To Southwest Philly, thank you for allowing me to experience you as the backdrop of my life. I am resilient because of the lessons learned on your streets. To the free libraries of Philadelphia, Huntingdon, Somerset, Phoenixville, Frackville, the Barnes and Nobles' of Camphill and Bellefonte, the Midtown Scholar Bookstore in Harrisburg and Uncle Bobbie's Coffee Shop in Philadelphia, thank you for providing me a safe space to rest and write. Most of these words were remembered in you. To the cemeteries of my ancestors final resting place, Mt. Lawn, Eden, and Fernwood, thank you for providing me peace on my visits in a city filled with chaos. Finally, to Kelly Drive, you are still my go-to place for mental clarity and I appreciate the groundskeepers of that space for continuing to make it beautifully available to me.

Things

Therapy, medicinal marijuana and music, you are the threesome that keeps my mental health vibrating at its optimal frequency, thank you for existing. To my Chevy trucks that transported families across the state of Pennsylvania, thank you for your service soldiers. With all those miles and all those hours, we didn't have one accident and I'm grateful. Finally, to volunteerism, thank you for allowing me to authentically serve as well as opening doors that would have been normally closed to a *sista* like me.

Made in the USA
Columbia, SC
24 August 2020